T0355636

INCITEMENT

INCITEMENT

ANWAR AL-AWLAKI'S WESTERN JIHAD

Alexander Meleagrou-Hitchens

Harvard University Press

Cambridge, Massachusetts
London, England
2020

First printing

Library of Congress Cataloging-in-Publication Data
Names: Meleagrou-Hitchens, Alexander, 1984– author.
Title: Incitement : Anwar al-Awlaki's western jihad / Alexander Meleagrou-Hitchens.
Description: Cambridge, Massachusetts : Harvard University Press, 2020. |
Includes bibliographical references and index.
Identifiers: LCCN 2019040018 | ISBN 9780674979505 (cloth)
Subjects: LCSH: Al-Awlaki, Anwar. | Terrorists—Biography. | Qaida (Organization) |
Jihad. | Terrorists—Recruiting. | Salafīyah.
Classification: LCC HV6430.A5 M45 2020 | DDC 363.325092 [B]—dc23
LC record available at https://lccn.loc.gov/2019040018

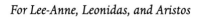

For Lee-Anne, Leonidas, and Aristos

Contents

Note on Transliteration and Quotations

Arabic words and names are presented in this book in italics in their anglicized form and without diacritics. An exception is made when citing other works, in which case the use of diacritics is preserved where appropriate. In cases where Arabic words have come into common English usage, they are not italicized (for example, jihad). Additionally, the plural forms of some Arabic terms have been rendered into English plurals (for example, *fatwas* instead of *fatawa*).

All quotations, including online writings, are presented in the original, including any grammatical or syntactic errors.

INCITEMENT

Introduction

A YOUNG WESTERN-EDUCATED Nigerian Muslim attempts to use a
bomb hidden in his underwear to bring down a U.S.-bound jet from
Amsterdam; a British-Bangladeshi woman attacks and repeatedly
stabs her local Member of Parliament in London; a U.S. Army Major
carries out a mass shooting at his base in Fort Hood, Texas, killing
thirteen; the offices of the *Charlie Hebdo* magazine in Paris are attacked
and its staff massacred; two Kyrgyzstani-American brothers set off
deadly explosions at the Boston Marathon. All of these cases of jihadist
terrorism in the West, and many more besides, appear disconnected
in any formal organizational sense. However, they are linked through
a set of ideas introduced to them by a man whose name continues to
resurface in connection with jihadist violence in the West: the al-Qaeda
ideologue and strategist Anwar al-Awlaki.

Born in Las Cruces, New Mexico, to Yemeni parents in 1971, Awlaki
began his career as an Islamic preacher in Colorado in the early 1990s.
Unlike other Western jihadist figureheads, Awlaki was initially a revered mainstream Islamic preacher in America who was considered
to be a legitimate authority on the religion by a large swathe of Western
Muslims. Before moving to Yemen in 2004 and eventually joining

al-Qaeda, he held a number of senior positions at American Islamic institutions and produced many hours of lectures about various facets of Islam and its relevance to Western Muslims. The status he earned during the early stages of his career gave him a profile and reach far in excess of other Western jihadist preachers who were able to draw in only a limited number of hard-core followers. He was a star of YouTube, the emblem of a millennial spirit that many in the West never stumbled upon—until his name began to emerge in connection with a string of terrorist plots. The threat Awlaki would eventually come to pose to the United States was considered so severe that, following the killing of Osama bin Laden in May 2011, he became the number one target of President Barack Obama's expansive drone program. Just four months after the Bin Laden operation in Abbottabad, Pakistan, Awlaki was killed by remote control while being driven through the deserts of northern Yemen.

How to measure the influence of a man who might well be considered the Pied Piper of Western jihad? There are various quantitative studies related to Awlaki's influence on jihadist terrorism in the West. My own research finds that, between 2009 and 2016, of the 212 total cases of individuals charged in America for jihadist-related offenses, sixty-six were in some way inspired by or linked to Awlaki.[1] The New America Foundation, a think tank based in Washington, D.C., similarly found that, between January 2007 and January 2015, Awlaki influenced, and in some cases was in direct contact with, sixty-three out of a total of 259 individuals who were either convicted of terrorism-related offenses in U.S. courts or died in the process of their attacks.[2] A more recent study, based on the court filings for 101 Americans indicted for Islamic State–related offenses, links Awlaki and his outreach efforts to twenty-four different cases. This makes him only marginally less referenced as an inspiration than the former head of the Islamic State (IS), Abu Bakr al-Baghdadi, and significantly more so than Osama bin Laden.[3] In the United Kingdom, a study of thirteen terrorism cases between

2004 and 2017 involving forty-eight individuals who were convicted for terrorism offenses or died carrying out attacks found that Awlaki's work represented six out of the twelve most popular media found in their possession by investigators.[4]

Number-crunching studies of this kind can tell us only so much. That numerous Western jihadists are found in possession of Awlaki's materials neither proves nor explains how he was a key inspiration in each case where his name appears. What it does demonstrate, however, is that Awlaki's works are, and have been for some time, on the essential reading (or viewing and listening) list for Western Salafi-jihadists. It is hard to exaggerate his influence. Awlaki offered the most comprehensive presentation of Salafi-jihadist ideology in English, and in a Western context. His lectures and sermons have helped to embed this ideology in the West, in large part because of his success in making it resonate with the experiences of Western Muslims. He played a central role in ensuring that Salafi-jihadism was no longer seen as a set of foreign ideas, related solely to overseas conflicts and the sectarian convulsions of the Arab world. It has now become its own counterculture *within* the West, one of the most violent and rapidly evolving of its kind.

Without Awlaki, it is unlikely that Salafi-jihadism would have gained this sort of traction in the West. First and foremost, he helped to convey a stark sense of Muslim victimhood—a notion from which the ideology draws much of its succor—among Western, English-speaking Muslims. He presented them with an image of a "war on Islam" in terms that made it more relevant to their lives, framing disparate events involving Muslims as part of a wider conspiracy. No longer would this Western, secular "plot" to destroy Islam and oppress Muslims be presented only in terms of foreign wars and occupations in distant lands. It was, according to Awlaki, a much more immediate threat, taking place right under their noses. If they did not act soon, he warned his followers, they too would eventually fall victim. Awlaki's intimate knowledge of the interests, fears, and concerns of Western Muslims ensured that he was able to bring this conspiracy to life in a way that none of his predecessors were able to do. This trope of a "war on Islam" acted as the centrifugal force that drove and legitimized the vast majority of his messages. Without it, the doctrines he preached would have been rendered almost meaningless.

Awlaki did not, however, operate solely in the realm of ideas. He was also integral to the transition from Salafi-jihadist theory to praxis in the West. Through his presentation of Islam as a violent, revolutionary ideology, he was able to convince significant numbers of Western Muslims that jihad was the pinnacle of Islamic worship. After joining al-Qaeda in the Arabian Peninsula (AQAP) in 2009, Awlaki (with the assistance of his Saudi-American expert propagandist sidekick Samir Khan) helped to develop and codify jihadist lone-actor terrorism, or what al-Qaeda termed "open source Jihad," and IS has since labeled "just terror."[5] This call encouraged Muslims in the West to carry out armed actions without relying upon any direct communication with al-Qaeda or any of its affiliates. Influenced by terrorist strategies of the past that were based on the theory of the "propaganda of the deed," this approach emphasized the violent act itself as a messaging vehicle and motivation for others to become involved in the movement.

Although he was dead by the time IS was founded and reached prominence, Awlaki's ideological and strategic legacy endures. In terms of popularity in the West, his contribution helps to explain the continuity between support for Osama bin Laden's al-Qaeda and IS among jihadists. A striking number of Westerners who have either joined IS as foreign fighters or acted on its behalf as lone-actor terrorists in their home countries began their induction into the global jihad movement by consuming Awlaki's output. His posthumous popularity is perhaps best underscored by the fact that one of the first English-language propaganda videos produced by *al-Hayat,* the official IS media center, was a lecture Awlaki gave in 2008 praising the establishment of the precursor to IS, the Islamic State of Iraq (ISI).[6]

Awlaki and "Radicalization"

Since the terrorist attacks of 9/11 there has been a slew of writing, discussion, and debate about the phenomenon of "radicalization." As shocking and epoch-defining as it was, in one way at least, 9/11 itself seemed a familiar form of terrorist attack—one that was planned in a war-torn country and masterminded by men with a grudge against the United States. In the years that followed, however, as Western governments threw increasing amounts of resources at counterterrorism, a new problem took center stage—that of radicalization, in particular "homegrown" radicalization, a term used to describe the process of adopting the ideas of and in some cases joining jihadist terrorist groups by people raised in the West. Academic departments and government programs sprang up to explore this phenomenon, and today it has become a household term. If radicalization matters, then the story of Awlaki and his followers must be center stage. For that reason, it is important to briefly discuss how this phenomenon has been understood and explained by scholars.

The definition of radicalization varies depending on the views of its user, and a main point of contention turns on the issue of how, if at all, ideas are linked to violence. Some choose to focus on the adoption of extreme beliefs, or what Neumann refers to as "cognitive radicalization," while others argue that the focus must solely be on violent behavior.[7] Here, I will rely on the definition provided by McCauley and Moskalenko, which effectively accommodates both positions. They refer to "political radicalisation" as constituting "changes in beliefs, feelings and behaviour in the direction of increased support for a political conflict." They also note that radicalization can "involve the movement of individuals and groups to legal and nonviolent political action (activism) or to illegal and violent political action (radicalism)." Finally, they define terrorism as simply the most extreme version of radicalization, "in which a non-state group targets not only government forces but civilian citizens supporting the government."[8]

Over the last decade and a half, numerous theories and models have emerged that attempt to explain this phenomenon. Many of these are divided in their approach between a focus on either top-down or bottom-up processes. The former tend to emphasize propaganda or external radicalizers. Conversely, bottom-up theories argue that an individual's radicalization is a grassroots process that comes about because of one's interaction in tight-knit groups with links to wider social networks. This book leans toward the former approach, focusing on the efforts made by Awlaki to attract new recruits. At the same time, it recognizes that why and how those individuals were receptive to such outreach in the first place is related to bottom-up dynamics such as the influence of their preexisting friendship or kinship group and other socio-psychological factors.

The most comprehensive radicalization theories draw from a range of disciplines, including social science, sociology, psychology, and history. These usefully identify a range of factors that influence involvement in terrorism, and the insights they provide shed light on Awlaki's impact. For instance, many theories acknowledge the importance of charismatic leadership figures who exploit and exacerbate a number of other factors that contribute to the radicalization process.[9] One of these is situational push factors often related to grievances based on negative social or political experiences that create a turning point in an individual's life, leading to a "cognitive opening." This makes them receptive to new ideas and worldviews; they become, in effect, a "seeker" who, in their search for meaning, is taken in by an ideology that makes sense of the world around them and offers an explanation for their problems and the blueprint for the realization of a (frequently utopian) new world.[10]

Studies also place some importance on identity. It is widely understood that extremist groups exploit an identity crisis that their target audience may be experiencing after reaching a turning point in their lives.[11] By defining and creating an "in-group" for a recruit to join, they also identify the "out-group" that is the cause of their problems and that must be fought and resisted.[12] Haroro Ingram explains how leadership figures like Awlaki can be understood as "architects of identity" who are able to construct both in-groups and out-groups in order to "shape their followers' cognitive perceptions and mobilize them towards collective action."[13] At his most effective, Awlaki was able to *create* meaning for his followers by identifying new grievances (or exploiting preexisting ones), constructing a new collective identity, and creating frames through which they could comprehend the world around them. This skill alone, however, was not enough. Just as important as Awlaki's framing efforts were his credibility and sacred authority. His reputation established him as a legitimate authority on Islam and gave him a large base of would-be disciples who were only too willing to uncritically adopt the frames he created.

Theoretical Parameters: From Radicalization to Social Movements

Some have criticized the radicalization literature both for its attempts to force individual cases, idiosyncrasies and all, into theoretical models and for its treatment of Salafi-jihadist violence as an isolated and novel phenomenon.[14] Detractors argue that, as a result, many scholars have ignored past research into recruitment and mobilization that can contribute to our understanding of the current wave of religious violence. A corrective to this tendency has come in the form of the application of social movement theory (SMT). Diani defines a social movement as: "a network of informal interactions between a plurality of individuals, groups and/or organizations, engaged in a political or cultural conflict, on the basis of a shared collective identity."[15] SMT refers to a set of theories that attempt to explain how and why people and groups become involved in various forms of collective action, or what is often termed as contentious politics.[16] This describes collective efforts to bring about political or social change to the status quo, often through the use of activism to pressure governments or other institutions.

It has been suggested that Salafi-jihadist groups are best understood as part of a wider social movement and that terrorism should be regarded as simply a form of contentious politics.[17] As such, Salafi-jihadist activism is said to share many of the dynamics of non-Islamic social movements.[18] Wiktorowicz therefore argues that studying jihadi activism by drawing on frameworks used to analyze a range of social movements helps to "provide a more comprehensive understanding of Islamic activism by exploring understudied mechanisms of contention."[19] This approach goes beyond the specificity of any single movement and allows for "greater theoretical leverage and comparative evidence for elucidating the dynamics of Islamist contention."[20] Similarly, Gunning claims that approaching the study of militant organizations and movements using SMT helps to provide the kind of historical context that scholars such as Silke, della Porta, and Ranstorp have often found wanting in terrorism research.[21] This also serves to "de-exceptionalise" the phenomena of terrorism and radicalization by analyzing them "as part of a wider, evolving spectrum of movement tactics."[22]

The social movement perspective offers useful tools for understanding how Awlaki fulfilled his role as a movement leadership figure. Despite his eventual affiliation with AQAP, Awlaki's work was conspicuous by its lack of sustained reference to al-Qaeda or any other specific jihadist group. This is because he recognized the power of social movements over formal organizations: while the latter are subject to collapse after the death of leadership figures or military defeat, social movements are more agile and resilient. Awlaki therefore emphasized the creation of a Western iteration of the global jihad movement, which he hoped would survive and grow based on the power and relevance of its ideas. This book presents Awlaki as what social movement scholars refer to as a "movement entrepreneur" for the global jihad movement in the West. Such figures, according to Tarrow, use "contention to exploit political opportunities, create collective identities," and mobilize individuals "against more powerful opponents."[23]

There are two specific components of the social movement theory approach that provide insight into Awlaki's efforts: framing theory and collective identity construction. Framing theory is premised upon the claim that individuals act within a movement because they have adopted a version of reality that has been constructed by its leadership figures.[24] It is concerned with how ideas and events are strategically presented in order to encourage recruitment and mobilization. Movements, according to this theory, establish what are referred to as "collective action frames" through which they ask their audiences to view and respond to the world around them.[25]

There are three core types of frame that are central to this study: diagnostic, prognostic, and motivational. Diagnostic frames identify the problem faced by a movement's target audience and apportion blame for the situation they are in.[26] Prognostic frames identify a range of solutions to the problem, including offering new strategies, tactics, and targets to be pursued by the movement.[27] While the first two framing tasks are geared toward creating a new perception of the world, the third, motivational framing, addresses the question of taking action. Snow and Byrd describe this using the metaphor of moving people "from the balcony to the barricade"—once they have accepted the diagnostic and prognostic frames, they still require the motivation to personally take part in the mission of the social movement.[28] Motivational frames are therefore a "call to arms," providing the impetus to take part in action.

In order for frames to be effective, they must resonate with the beliefs and experiences of the target audience. This process of "frame alignment" involves a strategic effort by social movements to attach their frames to the immediate interests and concerns of a given population.[29] Part of understanding Awlaki's impact will therefore include an appreciation for how he used his knowledge of the interests, fears, and concerns of Muslims in the West to ensure that the frames he constructed resonated with his target audience. Relatedly, the effectiveness of frames in helping encourage action also depends upon the credibility and perceived authority of the individual who is articulating them.[30] By the time Awlaki began calling his followers to take part in jihad, he was already considered a reputable Islamic scholar among many Western Muslims. Not only did he hold senior positions within mainstream Islamic institutions in America but his lectures also came to be seen as some of the most reliable and popular works on Islam in the English language.

Framing is also an integral part of the second element of SMT that this book will rely on: collective identity construction. The eventual goal of this process is for the target audience to conclude that there are no other options available to them but to become involved in collective action, both for their own protection and that of the group with which they have come to identify. Part of the framing task is therefore the definition of boundaries that delineate who is the in-group and who is the out-group. This in turn helps to develop a feeling of common purpose and values, allowing activists to see themselves as deeply linked to one another on the basis of a shared desire to pursue broader collective mobilization.[31] Strong, coherent identities influence how people view the world, apportion meaning to events, and rationalize the courses of action they take in response.

An appreciation for the importance of collective identity goes far beyond the work of social movement scholars, however. In his discourse on the nature and appeal of what he refers to as "mass movements," Eric Hoffer presents an appreciation of how they rely on the cultivation of collective identity while relegating self-interest and individual identity to "something tainted and evil; something unclean and unlucky."[32] For those who see their lives as "irremediably spoiled" and have given up on the self, mass movements offer an alternative view of their place in the world. Adherents are able to fulfill themselves through rebirth to a new life in the "close-knit, collective body" of the mass movement, which offers "a chance to acquire new elements of pride, confidence, hope, a sense of purpose and worth by identification with a holy cause." These, in Hoffer's view, are benefits that movement adherents have concluded they "cannot evoke out of their individual resources."[33] Collective action is therefore reliant upon the creation, as Snow describes it, of "a shared sense of 'oneness' or 'we-ness' anchored in real or imagined shared attributes and experiences" that contrast sharply with the identified out-group.[34] In defining this "we," it is therefore also important for a movement to define, as it were, "what we are not."[35]

Awlaki knew the power of collective identity. His responsibilities as a movement entrepreneur included the construction of a worldview in which his audience of Western Muslims came to regard their situation as irredeemable and their individual aspirations as not only out of reach but the product of a selfish desire to place individual worldly gain over the plight of the *ummah,* the global community of Muslims considered as a whole. Through the deployment of rhetorical and ideological devices, in particular the doctrine of *al-wala wal-bara,* Awlaki defined both the in-group that followers were to identify with and the out-group to which they were opposed. This helped to create a sense of separateness among Awlaki's followers and underlined the imperative to act on behalf of the group, rather than simply feeling part of it.

One of the critiques of the social movement theory approach is its often heavy reliance on rational choice and a logical consistency in the process of deciding to take part in collective action.[36] As a result, some argue that it needs to be augmented by a recognition of less tangible, yet equally important, cultural factors.[37] Of particular interest is the emotional power of storytelling and narrative creation.[38] This, argues Ganz, is "central to social movements" because it contributes to their core aims of creating agency, shaping identity, and motivating action.[39] Identity is often rooted in a shared historical narrative, and Polletta and

Chen also suggest that stories can assist in making frames more effective, acting as "a backdrop of understanding against which logical arguments have meaning."[40]

Awlaki also understood the importance of using culture to appeal to emotion. Writing about the underappreciated influence of Islamic poetic hymns called *anashid,* he advised his followers that "Muslims need to be inspired to practice Jihad. In the time of Rasulullah [the Prophet Muhammad] . . . he had poets who would use their poetry to inspire the Muslims and demoralize the disbelievers. Today nasheed [the plural form of *anashid*] can play that role. A good nasheed can spread so widely it can reach to an audience that you could not reach through a lecture or a book. . . . Nasheeds are an important element in creating a 'Jihad culture.'"[41]

Although he did not compose *anashid* himself, Awlaki helped to provide another pillar of culture through storytelling. His skill as a storyteller is one of the main reasons for the popularity of his early lectures, which were almost entirely based either on narrative histories of Muhammad (called *sira*) or historical accounts of the exploits of his closest followers (known as the *Sahaba*) who succeeded him as Caliph. This approach does not require listeners to possess any significant prior knowledge of Islam or its tenets, making his work more accessible than other, more scholarly efforts. Alongside analyzing Awlaki's frame articulation, it is therefore also important to show how he used stories to strengthen the emotional power of his frames and define a jihadist collective identity, casting his audience as leading protagonists in a narrative that stretched from the foundational years of Islam to the present day.

Drawing on the foregoing theoretical parameters, this book analyzes Awlaki's promotion of the global jihad movement in the West and considers too how his efforts impacted his audience.[42] It will examine Awlaki's contribution to the radicalization of Muslims living in the West and contributes to our understanding of how jihadist radicalization and mobilization has evolved, often without the direct involvement of formal hierarchical organizations.

Definitions

A number of political-religious identifiers will be used throughout this book that require some brief definition before proceeding: Salafi, Salafi-jihadist, and Islamist. The Salafi movement is generally understood to be a puritanical movement within Sunni Islam that calls for the return of Islamic belief and practice back to the time of Muhammad and the first three generations of Muslims known as *al-salaf al-salih*. This is made up of Muhammad's companions (*Sahaba*) and the two genera-tions that succeeded them (the *Tabiun* and the *Taba Tabiun*). Salafis therefore shun the majority of Islamic sources that go beyond this pe-riod and reject later Islamic practices as sinful innovations (*bida*). Ac-cording to this approach, the only legitimate sources in Islam are the Koran, the sayings of the prophet (the *hadith*), and the consensus of the *Salaf*.[43] While most Salafis share a similar creed (*aqidah*), different strands of the movement diverge significantly on the methods (*manhaj*) they employ to achieve change. Salafi-jihadist refers to the category of Salafis for whom jihad is the most important and legitimate method, the ideology of which undergirds the global jihad movement. The two other macro categories of Salafism are the quietists, who largely shun involvement in political activism and discourse, and the activists (also known as *haraki* Salafis), who involve themselves in various forms of political engagement.

Islamism, meanwhile, must not be conflated with Salafism, and rep-resents a distinct ideology that has at times been fused with Salafi theology. Not only do these have different historical roots, but they also diverge in their approaches to studying and interpreting Islam. While Salafis have a theological and scholarly focus, Islamists are more concerned with the establishment of political activist organizations, the best known of which is the Egyptian Muslim Brotherhood, founded by Hasan al-Banna in 1928.

Islamists regard Islam as a political system that, through its primary texts, provides the blueprint for the creation of a state and constitution, ideally in the form of the Caliphate.[44] In a similar fashion to the Salafi approach, many Islamist movements call for a return to the scriptural foundations of Islam, but they diverge from most Salafis in that they reinterpret these and apply them to modern social and political issues.[45] These primary texts of Islam are seen by Islamists as sources of divine guidance on worship and human behavior but also as an antidote to the cultural dominance of the morally corrupt West and its allies within the *ummah*.[46] Islamist groups and movements pursue a variety of methods, from political and democratic engagement to militancy.[47]

Purpose and Structure of the Book

Despite being the subject of intense interest, there are few rigorous studies devoted to understanding Awlaki's impact.[48] In an attempt to address this deficit, this book sets out to answer three interrelated questions: What factors influenced Awlaki's transformation into a jihadist and recruiter for the global jihad movement? What methods did he use to make the movement appeal to his audience? And finally, what features of Awlaki's messaging are apparent in cases of Western Muslims who were inspired by his work to take part in violence in the name of global jihad? The structure of the book is largely dictated by these questions.

The first chapter provides a brief biographical overview of Awlaki's time in America, the United Kingdom, and Yemen. While not delving into any great detail, much of which has been covered by other researchers, it allows us to understand the milieus and organizations he was involved with, offering some context to his output during different periods of his career. The discursive analysis of Awlaki's output begins in Chapter 2, which looks at his earliest works that are popularly considered to be representative of mainstream Islamic thought. Chapter 3 focuses on the Salafi-jihadist phase of Awlaki's career. It demonstrates how, by drawing on stories from Islamic history and Salafi-jihadist ideology, Awlaki's messaging efforts are best understood in the context of how social movement leaders inspire action. Chapter 4 assesses Awlaki's strategic contribution to the global jihad movement by showing how, through an adaptation of the propaganda of the deed concept, he recognized the communicative and didactic power of violence.

These opening four chapters of the book are, in part, concerned with where Awlaki fits within the spectrum and confluence of Salafism and Islamism. In doing so, I hope to categorize and offer a new analysis of Awlaki's ideological influences. This, in turn, will also provide insight into why and how he gravitated toward Salafi-jihadism later on in his career. Awlaki's turn to violence and the influence he has on Western jihadists are vital components of the story of the global jihad movement in the West. An analysis of both his ideological evolution—from activist Salafism to Salafi-jihadism—and the impact of his messaging will contribute to our knowledge on the movement's establishment in the English-speaking world.

Chapters 5, 6, and 7 are based around case studies of three Muslims in the West—Umar Farouk Abdulmutallab, Nidal Hasan, and Zachary Chesser—who, at least in part, were influenced by Awlaki to become involved in the global jihad movement. These cases were chosen because each represented one of a number of the more popular forms of jihadist mobilization in the West. Abdulmutallab, following a more "traditional" terrorist pathway, traveled to AQAP territory in Yemen, received training, and tried to return to the West and commit an attack. Hasan, however, was a lone actor. He chose to remain in his home country, had no face-to-face interactions with any terrorist groups, and planned and carried out a mass shooting in the name of the global jihad movement entirely on his own. Finally, Chesser began his jihadi career as a propagandist in America, creating English-language jihadi media that encouraged others to take a more active part in the movement. His involvement in this relatively low-risk form of activism eventually encouraged him to take more direct action, and he was planning to leave the United States and join the al-Qaeda-aligned Somali militia al-Shabaab before being arrested.

The focus in each of these case studies is mostly on the observable impact that Awlaki's messaging had on these individuals at certain key moments of vulnerability in their lives, rather than on the preexisting factors that drew them to search out and become receptive to extremist messaging. The book ends with a discussion of Awlaki's enduring legacy since his death. In particular, it demonstrates how his work directly influenced both IS English-language messaging and Westerners who joined the group or acted on its behalf.

This book is not a biography of Awlaki.[49] Rather, it is an effort to contribute to the discussion of Salafi-jihadism in the West and Awlaki's involvement in its establishment and expansion by providing an intellectual history of one of the most influential American Salafi-jihadists. It also places him within a historical context of the ideas a string of Salafi and Islamist thinkers formulated and the strategies they developed to implement them. The story of how Awlaki came to become the face of Western jihad is as remarkable as it is unique. Due to a confluence of factors including the timing of major global events and Awlaki's early career choices, it is unlikely that any other Western Salafi-jihadist preacher will ever replicate the success and influence he achieved. Awlaki helped Americans and other English-speaking Westerners better understand both the theory and praxis of the global jihad movement to a larger degree than any of his contemporaries. As we shall see, his legacy lives on today.

PART ONE

THE MAKING OF A GLOBAL JIHADIST LEADER

1

From America to Yemen

Anwar al-Awlaki's ideology was, in part, shaped by his own personal experiences and the relationships he forged with influential individuals and institutions during his time in the United States, Britain, and Yemen. Before analyzing his beliefs and teachings, it is important to first briefly map out his personal development and career path. This will help to place Awlaki against the backdrop of other Islamic intellectual discursive trends in the West and broader political developments as they relate to Muslims, Western security, foreign policy, and the concept of the *ummah*.

Awlaki in the United States

Anwar al-Awlaki began his career in the United States, where, among other postings, he was the imam of the Dar al-Hijrah Mosque in Falls Church, Virginia, and the Muslim chaplain of George Washington University between 2001 and 2002. His first appointment as an imam was in 1994 at a local Islamic center, where he would give occasional lectures while pursuing a degree in civil engineering at Colorado State

University (CSU). While Awlaki was at CSU, he was involved with the Muslim Students Association (MSA) and even served as the president of the CSU chapter of the group. His association with this organization gives us an early clue about Awlaki's initial ideological influences. The MSA represents one of the first efforts by the Saudi Education Ministry and its Muslim Brotherhood allies in the Kingdom to influence Islam in the United States.[1] It was set up in 1963 with Saudi funds by Iraqi-born Muslim Brotherhood members Ahmad Sakr, Ahmed Totonji, and Jamal Barzinji.[2] The organization was not an effort to establish Salafi-jihadism in the United States and had no interest in direct violence against the country. It did, however, begin a mission to spread the teachings of Islamist ideologues such as Sayyid Qutb among U.S. Muslims as part of a desire to steer the future direction of the religion in the United States.[3] Awlaki's early involvement with groups that had such ideological leanings is unsurprising given that they also reflected his own early influences, which will be discussed in more detail in the following chapters.

In 1993, while living in Colorado, Awlaki also traveled to Afghanistan in the hope of assisting the *mujahidin* who were fighting the Soviet occupation of the country between 1979 and 1989. After growing up hearing stories about the glorious fight against the Russians from Yemeni veterans and watching countless propaganda videos, he was inspired to go see for himself what they had achieved. However, the war was over by this point, and he gained little of note from the trip apart from perhaps a firmer sense of his burgeoning new identity as a pious, activist Muslim living in the West. As well as sporting an Afghan-style hat around the Colorado State campus following his return, he took to quoting Abdullah Azzam, a leader of the Afghan resistance and one of the intellectual forefathers of the Salafi-jihadist movement.[4]

Even from the start of his career as a preacher, Awlaki demonstrated that rare ability to influence and captivate young Muslims in the West, and he used this skill to motivate them to fight for Islam. After gradu-

ating from Colorado State University, he moved to Denver in 1995 and
soon became a part-time imam at the Denver Islamic Society, based in
the city's al-Noor Mosque.[5] During his time there, he encouraged a
Saudi student to travel to Chechnya to take part in the jihad against
the Russians.[6] "He had a beautiful tongue," according to a senior
member of a local Denver mosque who saw Awlaki in action, and he
would use it to recruit for jihad as soon as he was able. This was a skill
he refined in later years to devastating effect. The same elder later confronted Awlaki about his efforts to popularize jihad and his recruitment of the young Saudi, telling him, "Don't talk to my people about
jihad." It is also telling how the elder chose to characterize the difference between his approach to Islam and Awlaki's: "My way was *dawah*
[proselytizing]. . . . His way was *jihadi.*"[7]

As his reputation began to grow, Awlaki caught the attention of a
young Colorado-based Saudi Arabian businessman and entrepreneur
named Homaidan al-Turki. He soon recognized the potential of the
young preacher. After hearing him in person, al-Turki approached
Awlaki with an offer to record, produce, and distribute his lectures
as CD box sets under the imprint of his Colorado-based company al-
Basheer Publications.[8] The marketing campaign that al-Turki cultivated
around Awlaki is one of the main reasons for Awlaki's early popularity.
Up until this point, much of the Islamic media produced in the United
States was crude and amateurish, often found on homemade audio
tapes. Awlaki published five of his most popular lecture series with al-
Basheer, and the covers and CD of the box sets were professionally
designed.[9] As a result of this palpable difference with the rest of the
field, Awlaki's lectures stood out.

Along with the design of the CDs, al-Turki also introduced innovations in the content of Awlaki's lectures, splicing the voices of popular
koranic reciters into the lectures; when Awlaki cited Koranic verses
during a lecture, a melodic rendition would follow. Al-Turki also ensured that the CD box sets were widely distributed, hiring eager young

American Muslims to set up stalls at every major Islamic conference in the country. One of his employees was Tariq Nelson, a young American convert to Salafism who would eventually undergo his own radicalization before turning his back on extremism. According to him, at the conferences where he sold the CDs, the al-Basheer stall was the by far the most expensively adorned and popular: "He invested so much into it at a time when this business [selling Islamic lectures in English] was still in its infancy. Al-Turki used Awlaki to take it to the next level."[10]

In 1996, not long after Awlaki's confrontation with the local elder, he moved to San Diego, California, where he became the imam at the Arribat al-Islami mosque. It was during this time that he first attracted interest from the authorities; over the next four years, he would become the subject of two FBI investigations. The first, a short-lived inquiry in June 1999, looked into Awlaki's connections with a man named Ziyad Khalil, who at the time was thought to be a "procurement agent" for Osama bin Laden, though the investigation came to nothing.[11] The second investigation, in 2000, was launched in order to clarify his relationship with the "blind sheikh" Omar Abdel Rahman, who was involved in the plotting of the 1993 World Trade Center bombing. Again, the investigation led nowhere, and Awlaki fell off the radar.[12] Despite his ongoing connections to both individuals and organizations under suspicion by investigators, in 2000 the FBI closed its file on Awlaki.

One of the "suspect organizations" Awlaki was linked to was the Charitable Society for Social Welfare (CSSW), which tax records show Awlaki was vice president of in 1998 and 1999.[13] The CSSW was the American wing of al-Islah, an Islamist Yemeni political party headed by Sheikh Abdul Majid al-Zindani.[14] A few years later, in February 2004, Zindani was designated by the U.S. Treasury Department as a "Specially Designated Global Terrorist" and the CSSW as a front for al-Qaeda.[15] The FBI's interest in Awlaki would be reignited after 9/11 when it emerged during investigations into the planning of the attacks that Awlaki had developed a relationship with 9/11 hijackers Nawaf al-Hazmi, Khalid al-Mihdhar, and Hani Hanjour.[16] The 9/11 Commission Report claims that the men greatly respected Awlaki as a religious figure and that al-Hazmi and al-Mihdhar developed a close relationship with him after they moved to San Diego in early 2000 and began attending his lectures at the Arribat al-Islami mosque.[17] It is also believed that he was their spiritual advisor while they were living in the city and that he held a number of closed-door meetings with both of the men.[18]

During his time in San Diego, Awlaki's family persuaded him to apply for appropriate doctoral programs so that he could continue his studies following his graduation from CSU in 1994. Ceding to the pressure, he applied and was accepted at George Washington University in Washington, D.C. As part of an agreement to waive his tuition fees, Awlaki also became Muslim chaplain of the university.[19] While still in Colorado, he sought to better understand how people become effective leaders and influence people, reading books related to the topic including Stephen R. Covey's *The Seven Habits of Highly Effective People*. Awlaki pursued this interest more seriously at George Washington, and his official academic transcript issued by the university's Graduate School of Education and Development includes some interesting details. His major was Human Resource Development, and he took courses titled "Group Dynamics in Organization" and "Leadership in Organizations," receiving an overall grade point average of 3.75.[20] From the start of his career, Awlaki saw himself as a leadership figure, and many who knew and worked with him also saw his potential and the charisma and intelligence he had at his disposal to become a highly influential person.

In January 2001, Awlaki was offered the post of imam at the Dar al-Hijrah mosque in Falls Church, Virginia, one of the biggest and most influential mosques in the area. Similar to the MSA, it too was the result of a growing Saudi-backed Islamist influence in the United States and was founded in the early 1990s through the joint efforts of the Saudi

Embassy's Religious Affairs Office and the Muslim American Society (MAS), another Muslim Brotherhood–influenced organization.[21]

One of the future 9/11 hijackers Awlaki first met in San Diego—Nawaf al-Hazmi—also soon moved to northern Virginia and began attending the Dar al-Hijrah mosque, where he was joined by another member of the cell, Hani Hanjour. It was also at the mosque where they met Eyad al-Rababah, a Jordanian who helped them find an apartment. Rababah would later tell investigators that a chance meeting with al-Hazmi at the mosque led to him helping the young Saudis find somewhere to live. The 9/11 Commission Report is skeptical about this, stating that "some investigators suspect that Aulaqi may have tasked Rababah to help al-Hazmi and Hanjour. We share that suspicion, given the remarkable coincidence of Aulaqi's prior relationship with Alhazmi."[22]

After 9/11, Awlaki's connections with three of the hijackers made him an obvious suspect. In subsequent interviews with the FBI, he recognized a photo of al-Hazmi but denied any knowledge of what the al-Qaeda member was involved in. Despite a number of interviews and investigations, the FBI was unable to obtain enough evidence to charge Awlaki with any terrorist activity. In 2003, investigators working for the 9/11 Commission attempted to approach Awlaki in order discuss these connections further, but by this time he had already left the country. The report nonetheless strikes a suspicious tone about Awlaki's involvement, suggesting that al-Hazmi's arrival at Dar al-Hijrah shortly after Awlaki's appointment as its imam "may not have been coincidental."[23]

Awlaki's involvement with Hanjour, al-Hazmi, and al-Mihdhar remains one of the unsolved mysteries of his time in the United States. How much, if anything, he knew about the coming attacks and the involvement of these three men may never be fully uncovered. That Awlaki, even after openly associating with al-Qaeda for around eight years after 9/11, never made any claims about this suggests that he had no direct knowledge or involvement. Otherwise it would be hard to believe that, during a phase when he was attempting to build up his jihadist credentials, he would not have taken credit for the biggest success the global jihad movement has ever achieved against its archenemy.

Either way, the 9/11 attacks and their immediate aftermath mark an early major watershed in Awlaki's career, and it is at this stage that he emerged as a popular figure and began to cultivate a public profile outside of Western Muslim circles. He soon gained a reputation as the Muslim-American voice against al-Qaeda and Osama bin Laden. During that early scramble by the U.S. media to find answers about Islam and a friendly face to provide them, Awlaki became a favored source of quotes and soundbites. Along with his usual congregation, one of his first sermons after 9/11 was also attended by a gaggle of reporters. Awlaki would be followed around and interviewed for months.

There is no doubting that Awlaki provided just the message that was needed at the time. In sermons that were recorded by major media outlets, he spoke favorably about the "freedom" and "opportunity" that Muslims were able to enjoy in the United States. In a private email to his brother about 9/11, Awlaki declared how upset he was at the "horrible" attacks while also seemingly reveling in the spotlight which he found himself in: "the media are all over us . . . ABC, NBC, CBS, and the Washington Post." He hoped that he would be able to use this attention "for the good" of all U.S. Muslims.[24] One of his first public comments on the topic came in October 2001, when he spoke to the *New York Times* about the threat emanating from al-Qaeda: "In the past we were oblivious. We didn't really care much because we never expected things to happen. Now I think things are different. . . . There were some statements that were inflammatory, and were considered just talk, but now we realize that talk can be taken seriously and acted upon in a violent radical way."[25]

From this early stage, Awlaki's use of terms such as *violent* and *radical* demonstrates his acute awareness of Western discourse about terrorism and radicalization, while also acknowledging the link between ideas and action. His finger was on the pulse not only of Western Muslim thought but also of the wider Western political discourse of the moment. In the same month, for example, he told the *Washington Times* that "Muslims still see [Bin Laden] as a person with extremely radical ideas. But he has been able to take advantage of the sentiment that is out there regarding U.S. foreign policy. . . . We're totally against what the terrorists had done. We want to bring those who had done this to justice. But we're also against the killing of civilians in Afghanistan."[26]

Despite claiming to be against the violence of al-Qaeda, Awlaki drew a moral equivalence between the 9/11 attacks and the U.S. military response in Afghanistan. Though this is a common theme within Islamist discourse, it would also be familiar to any person following Western political and polemical discussions on the subject at the time. Filmed in October 2001 during a program about him for the television channel PBS, Awlaki again drew comparisons between U.S. foreign policy and the attacks, appealing to a certain segment of popular political thought that was emerging in response to 9/11. He suggested that although al-Qaeda acted erroneously, it was a response to U.S. aggression against Muslims around the world: "The fact that the U.S. has administered the death and homicide of over 1 million civilians in Iraq [due to U.S.-backed UN sanctions]; the fact that the U.S. is supporting the deaths and killing of thousands of Palestinians does not justify the killing of one U.S. civilian in New York City and Washington, D.C."[27]

At this early stage in his career, one can already sense his invocation of the war on Islam as the main diagnostic frame through which he wanted his audience to view global and local events. In the same interview, Awlaki suggested that, due to its alliances with Arab dictators, it was the United States that was chiefly to blame for the problems

Muslims face in the Middle East. The current Arab governments, he elaborated, "are dictatorships, tyrannical, totalitarian regimes—and if it was not for the U.S. backing them, they would crumble one after another."[28] Awlaki's comments here about the United States propping up oppressive regimes in the Arab world were in line with bin Laden's reasons for planning 9 / 11: the necessity of destroying the "far enemy," represented by the United States, so that secular Arab regimes would be powerless to stop the establishment of Islamic law.[29]

Awlaki seemed to agree with al-Qaeda's analysis and diagnosis of the problems with the current world order as it related to Muslims. He did not at this point publicly share its prognosis, namely a call for violence and the targeting of civilians and other American interests in order to alter the global balance of power. Rather, he said that America had to do more to "support freedom and human rights in the Muslim world" if it was to ensure against future attacks.[30] It should be noted, however, that this is not a view held only by al-Qaeda. Taken together with his comments about violent radicalism and the invasion of Afghanistan, it is clear that Awlaki was adept at finding a wider resonance for his messages by drawing on mainstream political arguments and ideas familiar to many Westerners.

This desire to appeal to as wide an audience as possible may also explain why, in a 17 September 2001 interview with *Islam Online*—at the time one of the most popular Islamic online portals run the by spiritual head of the Muslim Brotherhood, Yusuf al-Qaradawi—Awlaki strongly suggested that the Israeli intelligence agency Mossad was involved in planning the attacks in Washington, D.C., and New York. By this point, less than a week after 9 / 11, conspiracy theories had already started to take hold—especially in the virtual realm—in which, along with the U.S. president, Israel became a prime suspect. Asked about the true perpetrators, Awlaki responded by pointing out that "as far as I am concerned, we, the American public have NOT been presented with any solid evidence of who did it."[31] Later in the interview, he took this even further when asked if he thought Mossad was involved: "Israel was going through a serious PR crisis . . . there were lawsuits filed against the war criminal [then Israeli Prime Minister] Ariel Sharon in Belgium. That was a serious blow to Israel to have its highest official in such a position." He ended with that favorite refrain of the conspiracy theorist, asking if the timing of the attacks "raise a question mark???"[32] This type of discourse, although popular with many Islamists and Salafis, is certainly not exclusive to them. Taken on their own, Awlaki's arguments here could be easily attributed to certain sections of the conspiratorial and populist far left or far right.

None of the above, it must be said, provides any evidence that Awlaki began his career as a covert al-Qaeda supporter. But, the mixed messages do suggest that he was willing to say what he assessed his audience at a given time wanted to hear. When speaking to the American media, he provided condemnations of mass murder, rejected al-Qaeda, and praised American values. When answering questions during a more private online conversation, he dabbled in conspiracy theories that he would not have dared bring up in a more public setting.

Despite his apparent mistrust of the official government line on the perpetrators of the 9/11 attacks, Awlaki remained in demand in both media and official circles. Five months after his *Islam Online* interview, in February 2002, he was invited to speak at a luncheon at the Pentagon titled "Islam and Middle Eastern Politics and Culture." At the event, he apparently impressed attending staff at the Department of Defense. In an email sent to the lunch invitees, a Defense Department lawyer remarked how much she enjoyed his contribution: "I had the privilege of hearing one of Mr. Awlaki's presentations in November and was impressed both by the extent of his knowledge and by how he communicated that information and handled a hostile element in the audience. I particularly liked how he addressed how the average Middle Eastern person perceives the United States and his views on the international media."[33]

Adding to the inconsistent nature of Awlaki's messaging, within a month of meeting U.S. government officials, he took to the podium at Dar al-Hijrah and delivered a Friday sermon in which he laid out what he saw as a wide-ranging conspiracy to attack and destroy Islam under the guise of the George W. Bush administration's newly launched "War on Terror." This theme would dominate much of his framing from this point on, and his views on how Muslims should react to this threat would be subject to drastic shifts over the coming years.

Awlaki left the United States soon after this to live briefly in London. While he returned on a number of occasions, he was never again to reside in the United States.[34] The reasons why Awlaki decided to leave remain unclear, although they were not unrelated to the increased scrutiny he found himself under following the revelations about his links to three of the 9/11 hijackers. Years later, Awlaki would claim that he left after deciding that the persecution of Muslims in the United States by the U.S. government had reached unbearable levels, putting him and his fellow Muslims in grave danger.[35]

A senior imam at Dar al-Hijrah and friend of Awlaki's named Johari Abdul Malik tried to convince the preacher to stay but was unable to sway him. Sitting in his former colleague's old office at the mosque, Abdul Malik recounted how, during a meeting between the two, Awlaki "told me he wanted to leave because he was under a tremendous amount of pressure from the FBI and that he wanted to teach in an overseas university or perhaps go into politics in Yemen." However, Awlaki apparently omitted one crucial detail: "He knew that he had been arrested for the solicitation of prostitutes and that any revelation of this by U.S. authorities would have ruined him."[36] This is in reference to Awlaki's two arrests in San Diego in 1996 and 1997 and one in the Washington, D.C., area. He pleaded guilty to the 1997 charge of soliciting a prostitute and was sentenced to three years' probation and a fine.[37]

In addition, the FBI continued to amass details of his association with prostitutes after these convictions with the likely intention of using this information either to coerce Awlaki into becoming an informant or to discredit him in the eyes of his followers. Awlaki would later be informed of the FBI's interest in his sexual exploits by a member of his favored escort agency, who in early March 2002 tipped him off that an agent had been asking her questions about him.[38] In retrospect, Abdul Malik speculates that "while Awlaki was selling us this jive about politics and university lecturing in the U.K., maybe there was another motivation: to get out of there before they publicly uncovered his dirt."[39]

Awlaki was terrified that this would destroy his carefully cultivated image as a pious, conservative Muslim preacher, and it has since been suggested that this circumstance pushed him to become an extremist. His contemporary in the American Salafi scene, the popular American Islamic scholar Yasir Qadhi, believes that the threat of this revelation "left Awlaki with few options, and he had nowhere else to turn" other than al-Qaeda.[40] Similarly, in his study on how and why Muslim clerics adopt jihad, Richard Nielsen argues that Awlaki's transition was the result of "blocked ambition" and "his turn to full-blown jihadism seems to have been precipitated by the imminent derailment of his career as a cleric in the United States, in 2002."[41] This claim, however, is unconvincing. While the threat of having his reputation ruined might explain why Awlaki left his promising career behind and moved to the United Kingdom, it does not begin to account for why he embraced Salafi-jihadism and joined al-Qaeda over the numerous other options available to him. Put simply, being caught with prostitutes is not a sufficient explanation for his radicalization. It is also interesting that in the years since Awlaki's involvement with prostitutes was made public in 2013, there is little evidence to suggest that this had any impact on his followers, who were instead able to dismiss the claims as part of the wider war-on-Islam conspiracy.[42]

Awlaki in the United Kingdom

Across the Atlantic, Awlaki had by the early 2000s become something of a celebrity for British Muslims and spent time in the United Kingdom before moving there. According to Abu Muntasir, a founding member of what was then a politically activist Salafi organization in Britain called JIMAS, between the mid-1990s and the early 2000s Awlaki had become an established member of a milieu of English-speaking Salafi ideologues based in the United States and the United Kingdom.[43] JIMAS regularly hosted many members of this milieu to lead prayers and give lectures to British Muslims, including Awlaki. "I was very impressed with him," recalled Abu Muntasir, "he filled a gap for Western Muslims who were seeking expressions of their religion that differed from the Islam of their parents' generation, which they found it difficult to relate to." Even before 9/11, Awlaki was "one of the most popular speakers we [JIMAS] ever had. He had a gift for speaking that few could rival."[44]

JIMAS represented a strand of Salafism which was sympathetic to the classical jihad approach but did not endorse the global terrorism project being developed by al-Qaeda at the time. According to Abu Muntasir, terrorism against civilians in the West was "not even on the table" for him or his group. While some in the JIMAS milieu went on to become supporters of al-Qaeda's global jihad, others, such as Abu Muntasir himself, reformed and moderated their outlook, rejecting jihadism and a good deal of the Salafi approach altogether.[45] He is not surprised to see that Awlaki went in the direction of the former: "His outlook, his ideological worldview, is essentially the same as it was then, but his answers to our problems have changed."[46] Abu Muntasir even recalled how Awlaki would speak to him about a number of sheikhs in Yemen who "were waiting for the right time" and questioned if Awlaki was already in with al-Qaeda.[47]

When Awlaki moved to London in 2002, he found himself in an environment that was far more permissive to even the most strident forms Islamism and Salafism than what he experienced in the United States.[48] In London he was allowed, if not encouraged, to begin publicly experimenting with taking his views to their most extreme conclusions. Abu Muntasir claims that, soon after his move, Awlaki "began to hold closed study groups in London specifically to teach jihad, *qital* [fighting], and the permissibility of suicide bombing." By this time, Abu Muntasir had reformed his beliefs and was already very weary of Awlaki. He soon began to warn his followers and other friends that the preacher was "corrupting the young minds before they had learned Islam properly."[49]

As he did in the United States, Awlaki immersed himself in the politicized Islamist milieu that was emerging in the West. His main patrons during this period were leading Islamist-influenced organizations such as the Muslim Association of Britain (MAB)[50] and the Federation of Student Islamic Societies (FOSIS).[51] One of his first advertised appearances was in late 2002 at a winter camp organized by the MAB.[52] In the organization's magazine, named *Inspire*, the MAB advertised the event using language that was open to interpretation: "Once again, when it appeared that the flame of Islam would be extinguished for good, the process of revival is underway. Already thousands have joined this struggle in the lands under oppression and tyranny. You have now a choice to become part of this struggle. The train has stopped at your station and soon it will depart. . . . If you decide to join the train, the ride will be tough and demanding, but more exhilarating and rewarding than anything else life."[53]

Throughout June 2003, the MAB toured Awlaki around the country to give lectures to Muslims on subjects ranging from the war on Islam to the role of Muslims in the local community. On 18 June in London, he spoke at an event hosted by the MAB and the Islamic societies of four of the city's main universities, a further reflection of his popularity among young British Muslims.[54] At the University of Aston in Birmingham four days later, his talk was in praise of a number of leading Islamist ideologues, including Muslim Brotherhood founder Hasan al-Banna and "Umm Jihad" (mother of jihad) Zaynab al-Ghazali, who were both described in the advertisement flyers as "saviours of the Islamic spirit."[55]

On a number of occasions during his time in the United Kingdom, Awlaki also spoke at the East London Mosque (ELM), one of the leading mosques in the city, which is influenced by the teachings of the Pakistani Islamist movement Jamaat-e-Islami (JI) and its founder Abul A'la Maududi.[56] Here he delivered his popular lecture series based on the life of Umar bin-Khattab, the successor to Muhammad as Caliph. At the same mosque, he would later also give an inflammatory Friday sermon about the increasing threat British Muslims faced from both their own government and the wider global war on Islam.[57]

Rashad Ali, who at the time was a senior ideologue in the British wing of Hizb ut-Tahrir (HT), a revolutionary Islamist political party that calls for the reestablishment of the Caliphate but does not directly practice jihad in the West, recalls attending one of Awlaki's appearances at the ELM. HT members, who vehemently rejected any form of involvement in democracy, would regularly clash with the JI-influenced leaders at the mosque, who embraced democracy as a pragmatic measure. Ali explains how, on one occasion in 2003, Awlaki was brought in by the mosque to discuss democracy and its utility as a tool to gain influence. They hoped to use his popularity as a weapon against their rivals for the minds of Britain's Muslim youth. However, the event did not go as planned. Awlaki rejected any Muslim involvement in democracy, much to the frustration of the mosque's leadership. "While he didn't directly support us [HT]," Ali explained, "Awlaki took a hard, jihadi line on the matter."[58]

Like Abu Muntasir, Ali also recalls hearing of the closed-door jihadi discussions Awlaki was leading; at the time, he had little to disagree with him about. While Awlaki was by no means a supporter of HT, he also avoided criticizing the group, or indeed any Islamist and Salafi group in the West. Similarly, few criticized him. According to Ali, HT viewed him as "on the 'right' side—his lectures were 'safe' for us to use for Islamist ideological study." The type of accessible Salafism Awlaki drew upon, such as teaching the virtues of living like Muhammad and his followers, was largely unobjectionable to any Salafi or Islamist. As part of his desire to appeal to a broad base, he avoided complex doctrinal issues that divided these various factions. His message was non-sectarian, making him a rare figure who reached out to and appealed to a wider swath of Muslim believers at a time when Islamist and Salafi organizations vied for power and influence within Western Islam. "He was loved and used by everyone across the board—whether HT, JI, *Ikhwan* [Muslim Brotherhood], or various shades of Salafi and jihadi," explained Abu Muntasir, "because he was articulate, broad-based in his approach, but at times narrowly focused on jihadism."[59]

The first public warning of Awlaki's increasingly hardening views also took place in the United Kingdom. He produced a series of lectures translating a work called *Mashari al-Ashwaq ila Masari al-Ushaaq* (also known as *The Book of Jihad*), a book written by the fourteenth-century Islamic scholar and warrior Ibn Nuhaas al-Dumyati.[60] Some of the lectures were held in Dudley, near Birmingham, during the winter of 2003; among the attendees was Aimen Dean. A former al-Qaeda member, he was working as an informant for the British security services. He told me how he had been asked to monitor the meeting, not knowing who Awlaki was at the time, and was struck by the strident jihadist tone of the lecture.[61] The audience was "mesmerized" by the preacher, and Dean reports that it included three of the men who would go on to commit the July 7, 2005, bombings in London: Mohammad Siddique Khan, Shehzad Tanweer, and Germaine Lindsay.[62] If true, it is unsurprising that they were drawn to Awlaki at this time. Not only was he at the height of his popularity but Awlaki was also preaching a message of victimhood and violence that would have resonated with these angry young Muslims who by this point were involved in a milieu of British jihadists who were planning major attacks.[63]

Awlaki's popularity in the West was now reaching its peak, and he drew large crowds, according to Abu Muntasir and another man who knew and worked with him during this time. Usama Hasan, formerly an imam at the Tawheed Mosque in Leyton, East London, recalled that Awlaki "was one of the icons of Western Salafism and would pack out every venue he spoke at, people were excited to see him." Like Abu Muntasir, Hasan is now reformed but was also heavily involved in the British Islamist and Salafi scene of the 1980s and 1990s and is a veteran of the Afghan jihad. He also shared the view that even at this early stage, Awlaki was on the path to Salafi-jihadism, claiming that "there hasn't been much of a change in his basic theology and ideology."[64]

Usama Hasan also offered an interesting suggestion about why Awlaki later gravitated toward al-Qaeda. He noted that, unlike himself, Awlaki had never had the opportunity to fight jihad and, lacking this outlet, continued on a path that Hasan and Abu Muntasir came to reject: "I've got a feeling that he's always been yearning for it [to fight in jihad], and our yearning was satiated in a way, but he never got that outlet. Add to that his strong links to Yemen, which has extensive connections to al-Qaeda, and the pull to jihad was too strong."[65] However, while Hasan and Abu Muntasir were involved in a past form of Salafi-jihadism that was influenced by the fight to defend Muslims in Chechnya, Bosnia, and Afghanistan, Awlaki was to embrace the global al-Qaeda version focused on global terrorism.

Awlaki in Yemen

While he traveled back and forth to Yemen over the two years he lived in Britain and spent eleven years there as a child, in 2004 Awlaki took up permanent residence in Yemen, where he would reach the final stage of his development into a fully-fledged Salafi-jihadist. He soon began attending and teaching classes at al-Iman University in Sana'a, which was run by Abdul Majid al-Zindani, and also spoke at events in other educational institutions in the capital city. One of the attendees of a talk he gave at the Sana'a Institute for the Arabic Language (SIAL) was the future "underwear bomber" Umar Farouk Abdulmutallab, who traveled to Yemen in 2005 to learn Arabic.[66] This chance encounter introduced Abdulmutallab to the man who, four years later, would oversee his terrorist training with al-Qaeda.

In August 2006, while living in Sana'a, Awlaki was arrested and imprisoned by the Yemeni authorities. According to a U.S. Treasury Department statement released a few years later, Awlaki was arrested on "charges of kidnapping for ransom and being involved in an al-Qa'ida plot to kidnap a U.S. official."[67] Among Awlaki's Western followers, news of his arrest caused a large outpouring of anger and concern. Usama Hasan recalls that Awlaki's arrest was "the talk of the town" for his fellow congregants at the Tawheed Mosque and the wider Muslim community.[68] Popular Western Islamic forums lit up with comments such as, "Imaam Anwar Awlaki is deeply loved by so many people who listen to his lectures, May Allah free him soon and the other brothers suffering under the tawagheet [corrupt secular leaders] for nothing."[69] Cageprisoners, a British-based lobby group that offered support to Muslims convicted and imprisoned on terrorism charges, launched a campaign to secure his release.[70] In their promotional materials they stated that "reports indicate that Imam Anwar Al Awlaki, a prominent Muslim scholar highly regarded in English speaking Islamic circles, has been detained incommunicado for the past two months in Yemen and may face torture or ill treatment in custody."[71] The campaign called on supporters to write letters to U.S. Secretary of State Condoleezza Rice and President Ali Abdullah

Saleh of Yemen urging them to free the preacher. Eventually, Awlaki was released in December 2007 and did not face any further charges or convictions.

Awlaki's first public appearance after his release came in the form of an interview with the founder of Cageprisoners, Moazzam Begg. Contrary to the allegations made later by the U.S. Treasury, Awlaki claimed that he was initially arrested due to his involvement as an arbitrator in a tribal dispute and was then held for longer at the behest of the United States, which reportedly sent FBI interrogators to speak to him about his association with three of the 9/11 hijackers. Asked about what the future held for him, he replied: "I have a few opportunities open at the moment and I haven't chosen yet among them. I'm still sort of studying the situation at the time being."[72]

By June 2008, Awlaki was living in a part of Yemen's Shabwa governorate, which was a territory of his familial tribe, the Awalik. From this new base, he launched a widely read blog in which he began openly announcing his support for al-Qaeda and the global jihad movement. It was also during this time that he would become a figure of concern for American intelligence and security agencies. In October, the first official public pronouncement on the threat Awlaki posed was made by Charles E. Allen, the Undersecretary for Intelligence and Analysis at the Department of Homeland Security at the time. Speaking at the 2008 Geospatial Intelligence (GEOINT) conference in Nashville, Tennessee, Allen referred to Awlaki as a prime example of al-Qaeda's "reach into the homeland."[73] In a subsequent interview, Allen claimed that he chose to air his concerns in public because "I was impressed by what I was reading about his activities in Yemen. It became evident from what I saw and from talking to state and local government, that there was this individual who was bending the minds of people here in America." He also noticed a clear change in Awlaki's work and was struck that "he had changed from being a proselytizer among Western Muslims, to using his work to recruit for the global jihad." Though unable to reveal any details, Allen went on to mention that by 2008, "there was intelligence on him at the time that worried me."[74]

A 2009 report commissioned by the FBI also states that over the previous year Awlaki had become a figure of great concern to counterterrorism authorities. Defining him as a "prime example of a radicalization leader," the report went on to describe how Awlaki had "established and sustained an international reputation as a prolix, charismatic imam who provided Islamic guidance in English through sermons, lectures, publications, recordings, and a website." It also highlighted a worrying radicalization of his views, with an increase in calls for violence against the United States that were being spread via the internet. This, according to the report, had helped to provide the "stimulus and opportunity necessary for radicalization."[75]

Meanwhile, Awlaki's British supporters continued to promote him while he was in Yemen. First, in September 2008, Awlaki spoke live via video link at the London Wandsworth Council for a Ramadan event organized by Cageprisoners.[76] Though his output was steeped in jihadist ideology at this point, Awlaki's focus here was on the plight of Muslim prisoners in the West, and he made no calls for violence or other jihadist pronouncements. It is also unclear if Cageprisoners staff were aware of his more extreme pronouncements at this time. According to the official writeup of the event, he was "a big draw" and "there was pin drop silence as Imam Anwar reminded us of the favors Allah had bestowed on the prisoners and their position with Allah and the power of du'a [prayer] for the prisoners."[77] In the speech, he offered consolation to the families of Muslim prisoners by reciting *hadith* about the rewards in the afterlife for Muslims who suffered and sacrificed their lives for the *ummah*. He concluded that they should communicate to their loved ones behind bars that "your suffering is a sign that Allah loves you" and that "the imprisonment of your family member is good news, not bad."[78] Awlaki also encouraged the audience to help continue raising funds for Cageprisoners, which was doing "a great job in assisting every prisoner that they know about."[79]

A few months later, in January 2009, the East London Mosque held an event called "The End of Time," which was publicized using pictures of New York being destroyed by meteorites. At the event, an exclusive video sermon of Awlaki's was shown to the audience, again promoting him as a legitimate scholar despite his open support for jihadist terrorism.[80] This was not Awlaki's only appearance in East London that year. In April he was invited to teach a course via video for an Islamic education company called the Al Wasatiyyah Foundation in partnership with an associated company called the Tayyibun Institute. According to the course's promotional material, "this course will be based on the chapter: 'Virtues of the Sahabah' from the Sahih Muslim hadeeth collection and will be delivered by the world renowned orator Imam Anwar al Awlaki. . . . Imam Anwar's course tuition will be via professional private pre-recordings conducted under his supervision."[81] The event, which sold out its allocation of tickets ranging from £65 to £70, is another testament to Awlaki's continued popularity and profile as a respected Islamic scholar within certain circles of Western Islam at the time.

By this point, Awlaki had become a controversial figure, and the British media began reporting on his continued influence over British Muslims despite his now well-documented jihadist views. In the leadup to the start of the course, the *Daily Telegraph* highlighted that the event was scheduled to take place in a building owned by the local Tower Hamlets council called the Brady Arts Centre.[82] The piece included critical statements from the Conservative Party's shadow security minister Pauline Neville-Jones, who remarked that "I am shocked that a known extremist is being allowed to speak in a taxpayer-funded venue used by vulnerable young people . . . public funds and facilities, including local council funding and facilities, must not be given to extremist groups."[83]

The pressure was ramping up on the Tower Hamlets Council to act. "We suddenly got all this interest in the event," recalls Michael Keating, who at the time was a local government officer at Tower Hamlets tasked with locally implementing the government's new counter-extremism strategy known as Prevent.[84] Internal messages also came in from the U.K. Home Office asking Keating and his team to approach the event organizers and urge them to cancel Awlaki's impending lecture. However, they were not, according to Keating, willing to make the decision themselves: "the Home Office asked us if we could do something to prevent this event from taking place. But ultimately they weren't prepared to say, 'this is not going to happen.'"[85] Keating's visit with the organizers of the course, while cordial, did not go according to plan. He explained that the council feared that allowing Awlaki to speak on its own premises "was no good for the reputation of the borough, which at the time was perceived as a hotbed of extremism." However, Al Wasatiyyah's directors were not willing to cancel, apparently citing loss of revenue after paying for the venue and selling out the tickets, and the course went ahead as planned.

Following this, in August 2009, a similar controversy took place when Cageprisoners again organized an event featuring Awlaki via video. Entitled "Beyond Guantanamo," it was to be held at London's Kensington and Chelsea Council Town Hall, another official local government building. This time, however, the council took a harder line. In the preceding few weeks, Cageprisoners was informed by the council that Awlaki was deemed too extreme and that their event could only go ahead on their premises if they canceled his video address.[86] While it complied, the group also issued a statement on its site pointing out that Awlaki had never been charged or convicted of any terrorism offenses and claiming that it was unaware of any extreme pronouncements attributed to him.[87] On October 2, 2009, Cageprisoners republished on its website a defense of Awlaki by Fahad Ansari, one of its members at the time. Ansari was critical of the council's decision and referred to Awlaki as an "inspirational imam," writing that "one of the highlights of the event was to be a video message from the inspirational Imam Anwar al-Awlaki, who was himself detained without charge in Yemen for two years."[88] Three months after the official Cageprisoners response that claimed no knowledge of Awlaki's calls to jihad, Moazzam Begg also offered his views on the preacher following criticism directed at his organization for repeatedly hosting him, claiming that he and his organization were "strongly against his calls for the targeting of civilians."[89] Indeed, at no point did Cageprisoners appear to directly endorse Awlaki's violent views, which were widely known at the time.

After the cancellation of Awlaki's appearance at the 2009 event, Cageprisoners made the decision to post a recording of the talk on YouTube accompanied by the words "Banned: Anwar al-Awlaki's Speech for a Cageprisoners Event."[90] Similar to his 2008 address, the talk was not openly extreme and consisted largely of Awlaki reading from letters written by prominent Muslim prisoners. However, this time he could not avoid revealing himself to those with a trained eye for jihadist ideology. One of the readings Awlaki chose to recite was his translation of a poem written by Abu Muhammad al-Maqdisi, one of the most important and influential living Salafi-jihadist scholars who was serving a prison sentence in his native Jordan. He described al-Maqdisi as "one of the great scholars of our time," a statement that could only be uttered by either the innocently ignorant or, as is more likely in Awlaki's case, a committed Salafi-jihadist.[91] A figure who had influenced much of Awlaki's own work, al-Maqdisi had his own relationship to the global jihad movement, which will be explored in more detail in Chapter 2.

Cageprisoners was not the only group forced to cancel a pre-recorded Awlaki lecture that year. In April 2009, the Islamic Society of City University in London arranged for Awlaki to address their annual dinner. He was due to speak about the prophet's companions before the university's vice chancellor intervened and forced the organizers to withdraw plans to screen the video. Senior members of the Islamic

Society reportedly complied but also pledged to provide DVDs of Awlaki's lecture to audience members instead.[92]

As Awlaki continued to be celebrated as a leading scholar and victim of the war on Islam by his supporters in the United Kingdom, fears of his increased association with al-Qaeda were finally confirmed in late 2009. According to the U.S. Director of National Intelligence, James Clapper, he pledged allegiance to Nasir al-Wuhaishi, the head of AQAP, and began "playing a key role in setting the strategic direction" for the group.[93] Despite being based in Yemen, links between Awlaki and acts of jihadist terrorism in the United States began to emerge.

The first such link was in November 2009, soon after U.S. Army Major Nidal Hasan went on a killing spree at his base in Fort Hood, Texas, killing thirteen. It was revealed that Hasan had not only worshipped under Awlaki at the Dar al-Hijrah mosque during his time as an imam there but had also been in email contact with the preacher prior to his attack. Five days after the attack, Awlaki also posted an article on his blog entitled "Nidal Hassan Did the Right Thing," in which he praised the soldier's actions and called for further attacks.[94] From this point onward, Awlaki became a figure of great interest to Western governments and media alike. His name began to appear in connection with a number of Western jihadist plots. After the incident at Fort Hood, more concerning connections began to surface showing that at least two other Western jihadists had made direct contact with Awlaki via email in the years before Hasan's attack.

In a 2010 terrorism trial, it emerged that in mid-2008, American citizen Barry Bujol emailed Awlaki asking for advice on joining a terrorist group. According to court documents, he also asked for general advice on jihad. In response, Awlaki sent him a PDF of one of his most popular works, "44 Ways to Support Jihad."[95] Bujol would later be convicted of attempting to provide material support to AQAP, with which Awlaki was closely affiliated at the time of their communication. Four months before Fort Hood, in July 2009, Zachary Adam Chesser, also a U.S.

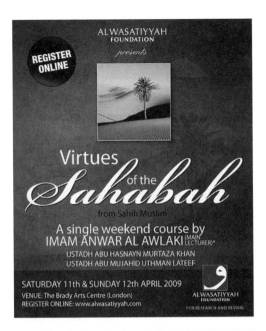

Figure 1.1 From top to bottom: Advertisement for Anwar al-Awlaki's 2009 Al Wasatiyyah Foundation course in London; advertisement for Awlaki's 2009 appearance at City University in London, which was canceled at the last minute; advertisement for Awlaki's 2009 appearance at Cageprisoners "Beyond Guantanamo" event in London, which was canceled by the Kensington and Chelsea Council (*Sources:* Al Wasatiyyah Foundation; City University Islamic Society; Cageprisoners)

citizen and resident, contacted Awlaki through his website asking for spiritual guidance and advice on joining the Somali al-Qaeda-aligned militia known as al-Shabaab. Chesser would later be convicted of attempting to join a terrorist group (al-Shabaab) and communicating death threats to Trey Parker and Matt Stone, two well-known American satirists and creators of the animated series *South Park*.[96]

The flurry of Western jihadist activity connected to Awlaki also continued after Fort Hood. A month following the attack, on Christmas Day 2009, Western-educated Nigerian Muslim convert Umar Farouk Abdulmutallab, himself a product of the British Islamist milieu that lionized Awlaki, attempted to detonate a bomb on Northwest Airlines flight 253 as it flew over Detroit on its way from Amsterdam. After his arrest, Abdulmutallab informed FBI agents that he had traveled to Yemen on his own volition so as to meet Anwar al-Awlaki, his inspiration and ideological guide. Together, they discussed martyrdom and jihad. Shortly afterward Awlaki approved his acolyte for a suicide mission, directly assisting him in the preparation of his martyrdom video and in the procurement of his sophisticated bomb before instructing him to use it to strike America on its own soil.[97]

Abdulmutallab's testimony puts beyond any doubt the operational role Awlaki was playing for al-Qaeda by late 2009, but this is only half the story. He was also by this point well established as a global jihadist ideologue among Muslims living in the West. That Awlaki was already considered a threat prior to the revelations of his operational involvement was confirmed at the time by the U.S. Director of National Intelligence, Dennis C. Blair: "He had been on the radar all along, but it was Abdulmutallab's testimony that really sealed it in my mind that this guy was dangerous and that we needed to go after him."[98]

Awlaki's stock now on the rise, Western jihadists continued to seek him out after the failed Christmas 2009 attack. In January 2010 a British-Bangladeshi British Airways employee named Rajib Karim emailed him to ask for advice on whether or not he should attack

Britain or travel to Yemen and live under strict *sharia* law. This time, Awlaki's response left no room for doubt, as he asked the young man to remain in his post at British Airways and help AQAP execute an attack on the airline.[99]

Awlaki's links with Nidal Hasan and his apparent involvement in planning and preparing Abdulmutallab's attempted bombing on Christmas Day 2009 led President Obama's administration to authorize his extrajudicial assassination in early 2010.[100] Later that year, the U.S. Treasury designated Awlaki as a Specially Designated Global Terrorist for his involvement in "acting for or on behalf of al-Qaeda in the Arabian Peninsula . . . and for providing financial, material or technological support for, or other services to or in support of, acts of terrorism."[101] In a move that publicly cemented Awlaki's relationship with AQAP, Nasir al-Wuhaishi released a statement in June 2010 through the group's official media wing, al-Malahim, in which he expressed support for the preacher in response to the negative attention he had begun to receive. In the video, the group's leader criticized the U.S. government's decision to target the cleric and also guaranteed his safety: "As for the Sheikh and Islamic preacher, Anwar Al-Awlaki, the likes of who we are proud to have in the Muslim *ummah*, he has not been deserted nor will he be, Allah willing, for he is amongst the Muslim masses who are spiteful of the oppressive tyranny of America. They will never surrender him. They know well that surrendering him to the infidels constitutes disbelief and hypocrisy, and that deserting him is humiliation and shame."[102]

Wuhaishi thought so highly of Awlaki that at some stage after the preacher's official involvement with AQAP, he sent a request to Osama bin Laden, asking if Awlaki might replace him as leader of al-Qaeda's Yemeni affiliate. This was a rather surprising revelation. Prior to this, it was widely assumed that Awlaki, while an effective communicator, did not possess the experience or gravitas to be a terrorist leader. For his part, it seems that Bin Laden was also not certain that Awlaki was ready for such a position. In a letter he sent in August 2010 to one of his senior commanders, Atiyah Abdul Rahman, Bin Laden asked that it be communicated to Wuhaishi that a more detailed profile of the preacher was required. Bin Laden also expressed doubts that Awlaki possessed the required battlefield experience, reminding Wuhaishi that "we here become reassured of the people when they go to the [front]line and get examined there." However, Bin Laden was well aware of Awlaki's work and his importance to the movement and was eager to maintain contact with him, writing that "the presence of some of the characteristics by our brother Anwar al-'Awlaqi is a good thing, in order to serve Jihad, and how excellent would it be if he gives us a chance to be introduced to him more."[103]

From his tribal base in the province of Shabwa in southeastern Yemen, Awlaki continued to coordinate terrorist attacks while also issuing statements about the global jihad which urged Muslims to do all they could to inflict death and destruction upon the United States and its allies. However, after he became America's public enemy number one after the assassination of Bin Laden in May 2011, the noose slowly began to tighten. Finally, after evading capture and assassination for over a year, Awlaki was tracked down and killed by a drone on September 30, 2011, while traveling through a desert somewhere between Yemen's northern al-Marib and al-Jawf governorates.

2

Awlaki and Activist Salafism

A N APPRECIATION for how and why Anwar al-Awlaki adopted Salafi-jihadism is vital to understanding him and the impact he had on the spread of the movement in the West. Because his early work contained no direct and explicit calls for violence, a common assumption about Awlaki's career is that, due to external influences related to the War on Terror, he transformed from a mainstream preacher into a cheerleader and recruiter for jihadist terrorism.[1] As with most radicalization trajectories, however, the story is not so simple.

While Awlaki was certainly affected by America's response to 9/11 and the treatment he received from the FBI shortly after the attacks, the ideological influences found within his early work are too often ignored. This chapter will address Awlaki's transformation by identifying where within the spectrum of Salafi thought he began his career. First, however, it is instructive to discuss the contours of this spectrum and how the various forms of Salafism manifested in the United States during Awlaki's time there. This will provide the context for an analysis of Awlaki's early work that will make up the rest of the chapter, identifying how he viewed Islam, how he chose to apply it in the modern world, and why these factors made him susceptible to a turn to violence.

This is not to suggest that he always supported global terrorism in the name of Islam. Rather, his eventual support for this approach may best be understood as an evolution that is mostly consonant with his early beliefs.

The Salafi Spectrum

Theologically, Awlaki's religious creed (*aqidah*) was closest to that of the Salafi movement throughout his career. He believed in relying almost solely upon the primary texts, called for Muslims to emulate Muhammad and his companions, and rejected the application of reason and philosophy to theological interpretation. He took on the outward appearance of a Salafi. His progression toward violence was a process that involved the crossing of boundaries between different forms of this belief system. Due to the evolving and fluid nature of this movement and the impact it has had on politics and political violence, in recent years Salafism has attracted the attention not only of Islamic studies scholars but also of political scientists and historians. It has been the subject of a variety of books that have demonstrated what an amorphous, transnational, and complex movement it has become.[2]

The theology of Salafism is rooted in the works of Ibn Taymiyya and his student Ibn Qayyim al-Jawziyya, fourteenth-century scholars of the Hanbali school of Islam. According to Ibn Taymiyya, Salafi beliefs are based on a literal interpretation of the primary Islamic texts that attempts to understand the physical aspects of God himself: "the way of the Salaf is to interpret literally the Quranic verses and *hadith* that relate to the Divine attributes, and without indicating modality and without attributing to him anthropomorphic qualities."[3] Ibn Taymiyya also believed that the introduction in Islamic thought of Aristotelian syllogisms undermined the revelations found in the Koran and the lessons of the *hadith,* or the sayings of the Prophet.[4] The need to make rational and reasoned arguments for the existence of God is therefore regarded by Salafis as an attack on the very concept of divine revelation upon which Islam is based. Thus, Salafis, rejecting all metaphorical approaches to reading the texts, believe that any description of God must be taken literally.[5]

Along with its call to bring Islam back to the authentic beliefs and practices of *al-salaf al-salih* (the first three generations of Muslims), Salafi theology is, according to Haykel, based on five further key claims. Arguably the most important and influential of these is *tawhid*, or the belief in the unity of God as the sole deity to be worshipped. The preservation of monotheism by speaking and acting against unbelief and idol worship (*shirk*) and by removing innovative beliefs and practices (*bida*) among Muslims make up the third and fourth aspects of Salafism. This system of belief is based on the claims that only the Koran, the *hadith* collections, and the consensus of Muhammad's companions can be relied upon as authentic sources of Islamic knowledge and that a literal interpretation of these texts is all that Muslims require to understand their faith, regardless of time or context.[6]

While the teachings of Ibn Taymiyya formed the basis for future Salafi thought, it was a theologian from the Najd region of the Arabian Peninsula who revived and refined them in a way that influences the movement today.[7] In the early 1740s, Muhammad ibn Abd al-Wahhab surveyed the Islamic landscape and concluded that most Muslims had strayed from the path of *tawhid*. He believed that contemporary Muslims in Arabia had reverted to a time of religious ignorance (*jahiliyyah*). In both their practices and beliefs, they took on elements of pre-Islamic idolatry and the influences of reason and critical thinking. Innovations such as this had destroyed the faith, and Muslims were committing idolatry by worshipping spirits (*jinn*), praying at grave sites, and making sacrifices to deities other than God. The answer, for Abd al-Wahhab, was a reapplication and renewal of *tawhid*, a doctrine designed to reinstate and purify Islamic monotheism after it was corrupted by these new practices and interpretations. Muslims had to profess belief in Allah and him alone and pray to him as the sole deity. In response Muhammad ibn Abd al-Wahhab developed three interrelated forms of *tawhid: tawhid al-rububiyya* (the affirmation of the oneness of God), *tawhid al-asma wa-al-sifat* (God is one in his names and attributes), and *tawhid al-uluhiyya* (God as the sole deity worthy of worship).[8]

Jihad, Abd al-Wahhab concluded, was the primary method to fight back against the growing tide of religious innovation. He led a revivalist campaign to cleanse Islam, sweeping through the Arabian Peninsula with a ferocity that in 1744 caught the attention of Muhammad ibn al-Saud, the emir of Ad-Diriyyah in what is today Saudi Arabia. He saw Abd al-Wahhab's ideas as an opportunity to lend religious legitimacy to his family's political ambitions to rule the region. The pact between Abd al-Wahhab and al-Saud led to the creation of the first Saudi state and eventually to the creation of Saudi Arabia in 1932. The descendants of Abd al-Wahhab, the Al al-Shaykh family, formed the religious establishment of the country, while the al-Saud family made up the political elite of the Saudi royal dynasty.[9] Followers of Abd al-Wahhab's teachings in Saudi Arabia, who make up much of the religious establishment, are commonly referred to as "Wahhabis," a term that is often erroneously used interchangeably with Salafi.

While all Salafis (Wahhabis included) share the same basic creed, which revolves around the centrality of *tawhid,* they differ in the methodology (*manhaj*) they pursue for its implementation and the form their proselytizing (*dawah*) should take.[10] Salafism in Western academic literature has traditionally been categorized into three strands: purists (also often referred to as quietists), politicos (also known as activist, or *haraki,* Salafis), and jihadis.[11] While imperfect, this framing is generally useful in explaining the similarities of and differences between Salafis.[12]

The purist, or quietist, Salafis are those who usually closely follow the Wahhabi Saudi religious establishment line and call for absolute obedience to the legitimate ruler (*wali al-amr*) of any Muslim country they are based in. They reject political involvement or political frames within their discourse, at least until a time when Islam is "purified" of innovation and other evils.[13] As part of this belief, they also often oppose the creation of formal groups, political activism, or fighting in circumstances where Muslims are being oppressed. The main practices they support are a process of grassroots education (*tarbiyah*), intended to prepare the masses for the organic creation of an Islamic state, and peaceful *dawah*. Due to their views on politics, quietist Salafis fiercely reject Islamist ideology, viewing it as a sinful innovation that must be purged from the faith. The most influential Saudi-based scholars with whom this strand is most closely associated are Muhammad Nasiruddin al-Albani, Abd al-Aziz ibn Baz, Muhammad ibn al-Uthaymeen, Muhammad Aman al-Jami, and Rabee al-Madkhali.[14]

In contrast to the quietists, politically activist Salafis represent a convergence between Salafi theology and Islamist ideology.[15] This category of Salafism is influenced by the Muslim Brotherhood and is more acquainted with the political process, elections, and geopolitics than those in the quietist category.[16] Due to their adoption of Islamism, activist Salafis believe that they are best placed to contextualize and frame Salafi *aqidah* so that it offers solutions and responses to contemporary political issues. They do not usually engage in, or call for, revolutionary violence in support of their cause, but in some cases they do call for the removal of "un-Islamic" regimes in the Arab world.[17]

Activist Salafis are often either involved in party politics, such as Egypt's Hizb al-Nour, or engaged in contentious political debate and activism, such as the *Sahwa* in Saudi Arabia during the 1990s.[18] While Lacroix has provided the authoritative account of the *Sahwa,* it is important to briefly discuss its ideological contours and global influence due to the impact its approach has had on activist and jihadi Salafism. Described as a "hybrid of Wahhabism and the ideology of the Muslim Brotherhood," it is arguably the single most influential activist Salafi movement.[19] Founded in the 1970s, movement members challenged the

Saudi state with demands to further involve religious figures in the running of government and to reduce the influence of the royal family. Their activism centered around petitions, letters, and the establishment of formal organizations.[20] The movement reached its peak in the early 1990s, when its members coalesced around their vehement rejection of the Saudi state's invitation to American troops into the Arabian Peninsula during the first Gulf War. While during the early phases of the *Sahwa* the Saudi government sought to coopt the activist power of the movement, the agitation it caused during the Gulf War led to a widespread crackdown in 1994 in which many of the leaders of the *Sahwa* were arrested.

During its early years, however, *Sahwa* members used a variety of methods to gain support from both the religious establishment and the royal family. Its main ideologues, for example, worked to find common ground between the country's rigid religious conservatism and Islamism's revolutionary political ideas. An important part of this effort was their argument that Islamist ideology had much in common with Wahhabi teachings and could be legitimated using the works of Ibn Taymiyya and Muhammad ibn Abd al-Wahhab. The central figures behind this movement, including scholars such as Salman al-Awdah, Safar al-Hawali, Muhammad Surur bin Nayif Zayn al-Abidin, and Mohammad Qutb (the brother of Muslim Brotherhood ideologue and leader Sayyid Qutb), helped to oversee this ideological cross-pollination between Salafist theology and Islamist/Muslim Brotherhood ideology and activism.[21]

Muhammad Qutb's main contribution involved reconciling his brother's ideas with Saudi Wahhabism. Arguably his biggest achievement was devising *tawhid al-hakimiyya,* which added a fourth component to Abd al-Wahhab's three forms of *tawhid.* A concept that drives both activist and Salafi-jihadist belief and practice today, it derived from Muslim Brotherhood ideologue Sayyid Qutb's formulation of the doctrine of *hakimiyya,* which he developed in his 1964 work *Milestones.*

Published in Egypt during the era of secular Arab nationalist President Gamal Abdel Nasser, the book argued that the root of the ills of the Muslim world was its embrace of secularism and the influences of imperial Western powers. He thus argued that God should be considered the sole sovereign (*hakim*) over the affairs of man. As such, Muslim societies must be ruled by laws set out in the Koran, otherwise they were in a state of disbelief (*jahiliyyah*) and the ruling government could theoretically be excommunicated and overthrown.[22] Two years after the publication of *Milestones,* Sayyid Qutb was executed by the Egyptian state after he was convicted of involvement in a plot to assassinate President Nasser.

However, Sayyid Qutb's revolutionary approach did not just present a threat to the Egyptian state but was also feared by the Saudis. His brother therefore needed to convince them that Qutb's teachings were in line with Wahhabi thought. Muhammad Qutb achieved this by arguing that *hakimiyya* is a form of al-Wahhab's *tawhid al-uluhiyya* (God as the sole deity worthy of worship) and that if God is the sole deity to be worshipped, he should also be the sole creator of law. Accepting laws other than those laid out by God in the Koran should, he argued, be seen as a sinful form of idol worship (*shirk*) that placed man-made law above that of *sharia.* This concept, Muhammad Qutb concluded, should not therefore be seen as an innovation but rather one that made al-Wahhab's teachings more explicit through emphasizing the sovereignty of God.[23]

Few of the *Sahwa* leaders or thinkers supported militancy in Saudi Arabia.[24] This fusion of Islamist political doctrine with Salafi theology did, however, lead to other alternative and more violent outcomes, namely the ideology of Salafi-jihadism.[25] The emergence of the activist strand was an important part of the creation of Salafi-jihadism because it injected political activism into traditionalist Salafism, which then opened up the possibility of a variety of different reactions to local and global events. Once contentious political activism was embraced as a legitimate method by Salafis, the shape that that activism could take also became open to debate. While much activism was based around vocal opposition, protests, and open letters criticizing the establishment, others took a more radical approach and decided that violence was the only effective form of activism to achieve real change.[26]

The jihadi and activist strands share a number of important similarities and are closer together than either of them is to the quietists. Jihadis and activists both see politics as integral to the faith. They are committed to *tawhid al-hakimiyya* and can therefore trace their ideological influences back to Islamist thinkers including Sayyid Qutb and Abul A'la Maududi, the founder of the South Asian Islamist political party Jamaat-e-Islami.[27] While activists do not practice violent *takfir* (the violent excommunication of Muslims who do not implement or follow *sharia* law), their affinity with Islamist ideology means that both strands also share the belief that a Muslim leader who rules by manmade laws is potentially an unbeliever. Some have argued that several of the original Salafi-jihadists are radicalized activist Salafis who initially supported nonviolent activism but later adopted violence after concluding that the former was either too slow or too ineffective in bringing about their desired changes.[28]

Salafis who fall into the activist category may issue genuine criticisms of jihadi groups, though they still hold underlying beliefs that condemn not the idea but rather the timing and nature of jihadi action. This is particularly significant in the context of understanding Awlaki's own evolution into a Salafi-jihadist. He and other influential Salafi sheikhs in the United States who went on to become supportive of jihad began as activist Salafis whose position on jihad was subject to a shift from theory to practice depending on the geopolitical context. This has not historically been a one-way street, however. In other cases, activist Salafis have moved from more radical ideas to relative moderation. One of the most cited cases of this is that of Salman al-Awdah, who, upon his release from prison in 1999, walked back on his earlier support for jihad against non-Muslim rulers and suicide bombing.[29]

The theological component of the Salafi-jihadist movement was also originally established by pioneering Salafi sheikhs influenced by the emergence of activist Salafism and the popularity of the approach adopted by *Sahwa*. These include Saudi-based clerics such as Hamud bin Uqla al-Shuaybi and Sulayman al-Ulwan and ideologues like Yusuf al-Uyayree and Abu Qatada, all of whom were influenced by the writings of Sayyid Qutb.[30] Yusuf al-Uyayree, an al-Qaeda ideologue whose work was an inspiration for Awlaki, was, according to Meijer, involved in constant dialogue with the *Sahwa* while he was active in al-Qaeda and "always regarded himself as part of that [*Sahwa*] movement."[31] While al-Uyayree criticized *Sahwa* sheikhs for not engaging in violent jihad against the Saudi state, he saw them as ideological brethren due to their willingness to comment on political matters concerning Muslims and saw al-Qaeda as a more militant expression of the same movement.[32]

Salafi-jihadism differs from quietist and activist Salafism primarily due to its ideological belief in the primacy and legitimacy of jihad over all other practices. Activist and jihadi Salafis also differ in the form of jihad they support and what represents a legitimate target for attack. The former may advocate for what is termed classical jihad as it has stronger roots in *sharia* law, while jihadis practice a more radical version, namely global jihad. Both of these support fighting against non-Muslims who are seen as occupying Muslim lands. However, the classical approach, which is most commonly associated with Abdullah Azzam and the jihad against the Soviets in Afghanistan, is rooted in guerrilla warfare waged against occupying militaries. Global jihadism, under the initial influence of Osama bin Laden and Ayman al-Zawahiri, places emphasis on mass-casualty terrorism against noncombatants within nations seen as spearheading the oppression of Muslims around the globe.[33] The global jihad approach is also much more open than the classical approach to the practice of *takfir*.[34]

Together with jihad, *takfir*, and *tawhid al-hakimiyya*, Salafi-jihadists also follow an extreme interpretation of the doctrine of *al-wala wal-bara*.[35] This doctrine and its specific application by Salafi-jihadists constitute perhaps the best example of a Salafi doctrine radicalized in Salafi-jihadist thought.[36] Within the wider Salafi movement, *al-wala wal-bara*, which denotes loyalty (*wala*) toward Muslims and enmity (*bara*) against and disavowal of non-Muslims, is one that is applied so as to define and activate boundaries between "rightly guided" Muslims on one side and "deviant" Muslims in addition to non-Muslims on the other. Quietists use it as a mechanism to prevent Muslims from allowing their religion and Islamic identity (*shaksiyah*) to be diluted or corrupted by other religions and cultures. They warn that Muslims must show their loyalty only to their fellow believers and avoid unnecessary contact with non-Muslims, rejecting their beliefs and practices as well as all "interfaith dialogue" with other religions.[37] Ibn Taymiyya, inspired by the work of earlier Hanbali scholars, developed it into a fully fledged doctrine with the purpose of preserving the purity of Islam as defined in the Koran and *hadith* and creating a devoted and ideological group of followers. Wagemakers also identifies *al-wala wal-bara* as a means used by modern-day Salafis of all stripes to clearly convey the war on Islam to their followers because it "establishes such a clear dichotomy between 'pure' Islam and everything else that it lends itself perfectly to the frequent attempts by Salafis to frame Islam as being under attack."[38]

This concept is especially relevant and popular among Western Salafis, whose audiences are often made up of Muslims who have daily interactions with Western culture and find themselves in a minority. Take, for example, the words of Abdur Raheem Green, a popular Western Salafi preacher who is considered a quietist: "The prophet warned us, be careful who you take as your friend, because you will take your *deen* [religion] from your friend. This is one of the reasons why Allah has warned us in his book: 'do not take the disbelievers as your *auliya* [allies], do not take the Jews and the Christians, or the *mushrikin* [polytheists] as your *auliya*.' . . . Do not prefer them to the believers, do not prefer their company to the company of the believers."[39]

On the other end of the Salafi spectrum, Salafi-jihadists apply *al-wala wal-bara* in an expressly political and violent fashion. Specifically, it is used to formulate the justifications for fighting jihad against rulers in Muslim-majority countries who do not fully apply the *sharia* and follow man-made laws. While Kepel informs us that Islamist thinkers like Qutb and Maududi already developed much of this legislative critique from a political and activist standpoint, a more theologically in-depth treatment was provided by the Jordanian Salafi-jihadist ideologue Abu Muhammad al-Maqdisi.[40]

In his work, al-Maqdisi, who drew upon Qutb's conception of *hakimiyya*, presented these rulers as polytheists and idols (*tawaghit*) due to their "worship" of mad-made laws over those of Allah. Unlike the Islamist thinkers who preceded him, al-Maqdisi added a new interpretation of the Salafi concept of *al-wala wal-bara* to bolster this line of argument.[41] According to Wagemakers, he "turned [the doctrine] from a quietist tool to purify the religion into an instrument for revolution."[42] Any Muslim who adopts man-made law is, according to al-Maqdisi, committing *shirk* and is an apostate who has pledged his or her loyalty (*wala*) to the forces of unbelief. Muslims are obligated to fight jihad against these rulers as a declaration of disavowal (*bara*) and in order to establish the law of Allah.[43] Al-Maqdisi's most influential work, *Millat Ibrahim*, begins with a "declaration of disavowal" that outlines the main targets of a pious Muslim's *bara*: "To the transgressing rulers [*tawaghit*] of every time and place . . . we say: 'Verily, we are free from you and whatever you worship besides Allah. Free from your wretched laws, methodologies, constitutions and values . . . free from your repugnant governments, courts, distinguishing characteristics and media. . . . We have rejected you, and there has become apparent between us and you, enmity and hatred forever, until you believe in Allah Alone.'"[44]

Salafi-jihadists in the West also place much emphasis on the various interpretations of *al-wala wal-bara*. Similar to the quietists, it is an important device for the identification and creation of inter-societal boundaries between Muslims and the non-Muslim majority. However, the purpose of this for jihadists goes beyond merely defining and protecting Muslim identity. It also assists in generating within radicalized Muslims a hatred and animosity toward non-Muslims who are the targets of terrorist attacks.

While the tripartite categorization of Salafism among the quietist, activist, and jihadi strands is an important contribution to our knowledge of the movement, the boundaries separating them remain fluid and open to significant overlap. Meijer, for example, warns that that the division "should not be regarded as rigid but as a sliding scale."[45] Hegghammer, who has argued for a more in-depth set of classifications of this wide-ranging movement, also acknowledges that attempting to apply any sort of typology to political Salafist thought "falls into the trap of excessive categorization of an inherently fluid and dynamic phenomenon."[46] In his study on jihadism in Saudi Arabia, he also found that that militant Islamists in the region are "usually linked, sociologically, discursively, or both, to the non-violent actors sharing the same dominant rationale."[47] Not only are Salafis very diverse, but, as we shall see in Awlaki's case, they also occasionally cross these boundaries depending on the situation they are faced with.[48]

Salafis in America

During Awlaki's formative years in the United States, the purist and activist strands of Salafism were manifested through two major umbrella organizations: the Quran and Sunnah Society (QSS) and the

Islamic Assembly of North America (IANA). Both operated as hubs for influential Salafi speakers and organized conferences and speaking tours featuring leading Salafi thinkers, often flown in from Saudi Arabia and other Arab countries.[49]

QSS was founded in the early 1990s by a student of the influential quietist Salafi sheikh Muhammad Nasiruddin al-Albani named Mohamed al-Jibaly.[50] As such, it was closely aligned with the quietists among the senior Saudi Arabian scholars, including al-Albani and his student Rabee al-Madkhali. In the 1990s al-Madkhali and his followers—often referred to as Madkhalis—emerged in response to the growing popularity of the activist approach and confronted Islamist ideologues they believed were polluting Islam with contemporary politics and other innovations.[51] Sheikh al-Madkhali not only passionately defended the Saudi religious establishment and ruling royal family but went on the offensive against its critics. He went so far as to label opponents as Kharijites (*khawarij*), a reference to a despised, seditious early Muslim sect.[52]

Rabee al-Madkhali has also led the way in authoring critiques of Sayyid Qutb and other Islamists, and he and his followers often refer to Islamist-influenced Salafis as "Qutbis" or "Sururis" (in reference to Sayyid Qutb and *Sahwa* scholar and former Muslim Brotherhood activist Muhammad Surur). For this category of quietist Salafis, Islamist thought is the root of extremism and violence and must be removed from the faith.[53] Madkhalis are also fiercely critical of Salafi-jihadist groups, seeing them as dangerous revolutionaries due to their opposition of Muslim rulers.[54]

As a result of its Madkhali influence, QSS was therefore deeply opposed to any sort of political engagement or discussion of current affairs. The sole interest of its scholars was in the study of *aqidah* (in particular *tawhid*) and Islamic jurisprudence (*fiqh*). As part of this, they would engage in lengthy and detailed theological debates that interested only the most ardent Salafis. According to former QSS member

Tariq Nelson, "they would literally sit around discussing how many an-
gels could dance of the head of pin."[55] While this may have fulfilled
the religious needs of a minority of American Muslims, this approach
never found any sort of widespread appeal.

By the time Awlaki came onto the Salafi scene in America, QSS was
undergoing a crippling internal discord based on issues of *aqidah* and
manhaj from which it would never fully recover. According to Shadee
Elmasry, the divisions between the Madkhalis and other quietists were
deep and permanent. Bitter leadership battles and tit-for-tat refutations
of the "deviant" beliefs of fellow Salafis regarded as having moved away
from the teachings of the Saudi establishment sheikhs came to define
the movement, eventually causing it to implode.[56] Many American
Salafis were put off by this approach. Their subsequent search for
new expressions of Salafism created an opportunity for preachers like
Awlaki who eschewed the divisive rhetoric of the quietists and were
willing to discuss politics and current affairs.

Partly in response to the struggles of QSS, IANA was founded in 1993.
Unlike its Madkhali counterpart, its leadership was heavily influenced
by the emerging activist Salafi movement and the *Sahwa*.[57] IANA's
founder Bassem Khafagi was not a Salafi and was more closely aligned
with Islamist activism as a member of the Council in American Islamic
Relations (CAIR).[58] Yasir Qadhi, who was involved with the American
Salafi movement at the time, notes how important this move was for
the development and spread of Salafism in America. It addressed one
of the main weaknesses of the quietist approach: "How can you expect
Muslims to ignore what is going on around them?"[59] Through a wider
engagement with politics and current affairs, IANA and America's activist Salafis were able to find a more widespread appeal for the
movement.

Given its activist approach, it is also unsurprising that IANA's output
was more closely aligned with modern-day jihad than anything produced by QSS. This included publishing in May 2001 *fatwas* in support

of suicide bombing in its magazine *Al Asr* (*The Era*), including one by Salman al-Awdah in which he stated that the tactic could be used to "gain supremacy for the work of God."[60] In addition, the most influential figure within IANA, an American-born preacher and imam named Ali al-Timimi, went on to become one of the first American Salafi-jihadist preachers. His work drew direct inspiration from a variety of Islamist thinkers, including the *Sahwa's* Safar Hawali (with whom he was often in close contact) and Sayyid Qutb.[61] Ali al-Timimi's popularity as an American, English-speaking Salafi preceded Awlaki after he gained a large following in the 1990s as the head of an Islamic center he established in northern Virginia called Dar al-Arqam.

After the 9/11 attacks, al-Timimi began to preach the renewed importance of fighting jihad to a small, trusted inner circle of acolytes, a shift in method and focus likely influenced by his initial activist Salafi outlook. On September 16, 2001, al-Timimi met a group of them—who were later to become known as the Virginia Jihad Network—in secret and encouraged them to travel to Afghanistan to join the Taliban and fight American forces who were soon going to be deployed there.[62] Ismail Royer, one of the attendees of the meeting, who joined and fought for the Pakistani jihadist group Lashkar-e-Taiba in 2000, recalls how al-Timimi held court and urged his followers to travel, telling them that they "had to be with the *mujahidin*."[63] The world, al-Timimi warned, was now going to be divided between Muslim and non-Muslim, and they had to choose the former if they were to be treated favorably on the Day of Judgment. The next day, al-Timimi told members of the network to travel to Afghanistan via Pakistan in order to receive training from Lashkar-e-Taiba before fighting U.S. forces in the region.

Royer, who has now been released after spending over a decade in prison for his involvement in the network, regarded al-Timimi as his spiritual leader. In his view, the preacher's decision to support jihad against America was due to his activist Salafi ideology and the influence of Hawali's writings. In particular, al-Timimi adopted Hawali's belief that 9/11 and wars in the Middle East were the harbingers of the final battle between belief and unbelief that would precede the apocalypse. As such, Muslims now had to side with any Islamic group that was fighting America. Discussing al-Timimi's change in rhetoric, Royer explains: "There's no question that Timimi's *haraki* [activist Salafi] orientation influenced his response to 9/11. One way that was so was Hawali's previous writings on the events leading up to the end of time, and how the events unfolding in the world today were those described in the Qur'an and *hadith*. When 9/11 happened I think Timimi interpreted things in light of that. Basically, it all boils down to the *ikhwan* [Muslim Brotherhood] influence on the Wahhabist and Salafist movements."[64]

In 2004 Ali al-Timimi was indicted in the Eastern District of Virginia for a variety of charges, including conspiracy to supply services to the Taliban, conspiracy to take part in military expeditions against the United States, and conspiracy to use, carry, possess, and discharge firearms.[65] He was convicted in 2005 on all charges and received a life sentence. IANA collapsed soon after, due both to its links with al-Timimi and the increased scrutiny it received from authorities after 9/11, who viewed it as a repository for violent jihadist thought.[66]

Awlaki, while not an official member of Dar al-Arqam, often associated with al-Timimi. In his book on Awlaki, *Objective Troy,* Scott Shane describes how Dar al-Hijrah hired Awlaki as a way of attracting the large Muslim population of the area away from Dar al-Arqam.[67] Along with al-Timimi, it was, according to Shane, regarded by the Dar al-Hijrah administration as a dangerous, more militant influence whose congregation was taught that voting was forbidden and that Muslims were not permitted to join the American military. Awlaki, it was hoped, would be able to rival al-Timimi, whose charisma and ability to speak about applying Salafism in America meant that he was able to draw much bigger crowds than his relatively out-of-touch rivals. However, it has been overlooked that Awlaki himself did not appear to object very much to al-Timimi's outfit. At least five well-known lectures of his were delivered at and produced by Dar al-Arqam, and Awlaki was also listed as a "lecturer" on the center's now defunct official website.[68]

There is another factor in the relationship between al-Timimi and Awlaki that has, thus far, been misunderstood. This relates to a specific meeting between the two that took place in October 2002, during a visit Awlaki made to America while he was living in England. Until now, knowledge of what took place during this meeting has been based on a November 2004 account given by Ali al-Timimi's defense team during his trial. According to them, Awlaki arrived at al-Timimi's house in Virginia unannounced and proceeded to ask him for advice on effective ways to recruit American Muslims to fight jihad overseas, a request that al-Timimi reportedly rejected.[69] This, in their view, suggests that Awlaki was working as an informant for the FBI, which was trying to entrap al-Timimi by allowing him the opportunity to discuss jihad recruitment with a seemingly trustworthy friend.[70] This assertion was further strengthened by the fact that, during this meeting, Awlaki was accompanied by a man named Nabil Garbeih, a peripheral member of the Virginia Jihad Network who would later appear as a government informant and gave evidence against al-Timimi during his trial. If proven, the claims of the defense would help al-Timimi's ongoing appeals against his conviction by demonstrating that the government withheld crucial information in the original trial and that the preacher rejected any discussion of recruiting for jihad when asked by Awlaki for advice.

There is reason, however, to doubt this version of events. First and foremost, it does not match up with the story al-Timimi himself told when first speaking to the FBI about his October 2002 meeting with Awlaki. In official documents that provide minutes (hitherto unreported) from a June 2004 interview Ali al-Timimi gave to the FBI in an attempt to convince them of his innocence before he was indicted, the

preacher gave a very different description of his interaction with Awlaki than that which was provided during his trial. He first stated that
the men knew each other due to a shared connection to JIMAS, in
which both men had been involved since the mid-1990s. Al-Timimi
claimed to have first met Awlaki in the United Kingdom during an August 2001 JIMAS conference; in his account, he was so impressed with
his knowledge and speaking ability that he recommended to JIMAS
head Abu Muntasir that Awlaki become a regular conference speaker
at future events.[71] This meeting was also the catalyst for al-Timimi's
later invitations to Awlaki to deliver lectures at Dar al-Arqam. Recalling
the meeting he had with Awlaki in October 2002, al-Timimi made no
mention of being asked about recruiting for jihad and did not express
that he felt in any way uneasy about their discussion. Instead, he claimed
that Awlaki appeared late at night to discuss his plans to move to Yemen
to avoid what he described as FBI harassment. Awlaki's concern, according to al-Timimi, was that the FBI intended to plant drugs in his
house in order to convince him to become an informant or face prosecution. After offering Awlaki some tea and a small gift, al-Timimi
claimed that the conversation went no further.[72]

While Awlaki was not directly involved with either QSS or IANA,
what is clear is that he maintained a close relationship with al-Timimi
and Dar al-Arqam, and there is little reason to view them as either professional or ideological rivals. Gaining a better sense of the nature of
QSS, IANA, and Ali al-Timimi also furthers our own understanding
of Awlaki's approach, allowing for a more accurate categorization of
his beliefs and an appreciation of the views of the American Salafi milieu of which he was a part. Awlaki's associations with Dar al-Arqam and
al-Timimi now clearly established, an analysis of Awlaki's early work
will also show how his politically charged sermons diverged significantly from the teachings of QSS and placed him closer to the IANA
activist Salafi approach pioneered in America by al-Timimi. In moving
from activist Salafism in America to Salafi-jihadism, Awlaki not only

followed a path originally forged by al-Timimi but also took it even further, toward violence and international terrorism.

An American Activist Salafi: Categorizing Awlaki's Early Approach

"Stories," according to Awlaki, "are a powerful method of teaching, they are memorable and filled with lessons."[73] No quote better captures how Awlaki approached his work as an Islamic preacher and later jihadist recruiter as well as why he was so popular. Above all, he was a storyteller who used the emotional power of this medium to motivate his followers, initially to become more involved in their religion and later to take up arms and fight jihad. The lectures of his that were recorded and disseminated during the early phases of his career drew heavily upon a selection of histories recounting the experiences of Muhammad and his closest followers during the most turbulent and violent phases of Islam's early history. He retold these stories using the most popular Arabic sources of the prophetic biographies (sirat) such as Al-Sira al Nabawiyya by Ibn Kathir, along with histories written by Islamic historians such as Abu Jafar Muhammad ibn Jarir al-Tabari.

Awlaki translated these sources into Americanized, idiomatic English, creating wide-ranging narratives that often drew parallels between the time of the Muhammad and his companions and the present day. Muslims living in the West, according to him, should not just take the early stories of Islam as metaphorical moral lessons but rather as literal blueprints for their own actions: "In his [Muhammad's] sira you would find situations and incidences that would help us in everything that we would need to know in our life."[74] This ability—to juxtapose key moments from the early history of Islam onto the present situation of Muslims—made him immensely popular and easily accessible. In his later, more openly Salafi-jihadist work, he employed this

skill as an effective mobilization tool, using the examples of more violent phases in the narrative of Muhammad and his followers to encourage modern-day jihad.

Studying the *sira* went beyond simply education, however. It was,
according to Awlaki, akin to an act of worship (*ibadah*) that came with
a great reward (*ajr*) from Allah.[75] He therefore took it upon himself
make these stories accessible to Westerners in ways that were not yet
widely available to them. This made him one of the first preachers to
popularize the storytelling approach to studying Islam among English-
speaking Muslims in the West. Yasir Qadhi, who has himself made a
significant contribution to making Islamic scholarship more widely
available in English, claims that "no one else presented Islam like this
in English, at least not in America."[76] The consistent focus on stories
both distinguished Awlaki from other similar preachers operating in
America during this time and does much to explain his popularity.

Sira best encapsulates Awlaki's early approach to teaching Islam, but
in order to grasp where Awlaki began on the spectrum of Salafi thought
discussed above, it is necessary to analyze his earliest lectures with a
focus on how he viewed the application of Salafi beliefs to politics and
current affairs. During this time, Awlaki's main diagnostic frames for
the challenges faced by Muslims in the West focused on three core
topics: the cultural and ideological war on Islam in the West, the physical war on Islam led by the U.S. military, and internal disagreements
between Muslims based on minor issues that in his view distracted
them from the existential threats they faced.

First, Awlaki believed that Islam was the subject of a direct ideological attack from Western culture, one that he presented as deliberately
diluting and damaging the religion and the Islamic identity of Muslims
living in the West. Like many other Salafis in America, he considered
Western secular culture to be a direct and metastatic threat to Islam
and Muslims. So-called Western values and ideas were presented as a
pernicious influence on Muslims, who had to protect themselves by

becoming more insular and devoting themselves to studying Islam. In one of his most famous early lectures that was based on *sira*, "The Life of Muhammad: The Makkan Period," Awlaki explained how this culture was being "forced down the throats of everyone on the face of the earth." Quoting directly from the work of the author and commentator Thomas Friedman, Awlaki argued that "the hidden hand of the market cannot survive without the hidden fist, and McDonald's will never flourish without McDonnell Douglas—the designer of F-15s [fighter jets]." This all-consuming culture, therefore, is not "benign or compassionate"; on the contrary, is it oppressive and violent: "either accept McDonald's, otherwise McDonnell Douglas will send their F15s above your head." It is also intolerant of other cultures, and deliberately "uproots" them. To illustrate the point, Awlaki drew from the work of Russian dissident and historian Aleksandr Solzhenitsyn: "to destroy a people, you must first sever their roots."[77]

However, in a number of important ways Awlaki's approach differed from that of many other Salafis operating in America at the time. First, he openly engaged with and discussed politics, something his quietist counterparts pointedly avoided. Islam, according to Awlaki, is "the only ideology that is standing up to this global [Western] culture." This suggests an early Islamist influence on Awlaki, who viewed Islam as an all-encompassing political ideology that formed the basis for opposition to the West. In addition, he was also comfortable making references to Western and non-Islamic sources such as Friedman and Solzhenitsyn. Such unconventional, Western intellectual sources are seen by Salafis as illegitimate because they have no Islamic backing and are not linked to the primary religious texts. This helps us to further comprehend the reasons behind Awlaki's mass appeal to Western Muslims compared to most other Salafis in America at the time. He was addressing modern geopolitical issues and engaging with the outside world in a way that would attract people beyond the core of inward-looking American Salafis, whose popularity and influence had begun to wane.[78]

Aside from its adversarial Islamist approach, there is another notable component of Awlaki's argument that helps to explain his contribution to the Westernization of Islamist and, later in his career, jihadist thought. His discussion of American power contains a clear nod to the type of anti-American politics often associated with radical anti-globalist movements. By fusing Islamism together with popular radical and conspiratorial anti-Americanism, he increased the reach of his message beyond simply curious young Muslims eager to learn more about their faith to include the growing numbers of youth who were suspicious of Western states and open to wide-ranging conspiracy theories about how the world is run.

The Muslim response to the threat they faced was, in his view, insufficient because "as Muslims and especially Muslims living in the West, we are suffering from a serious identity crisis. I mean you would find that even though the brother or the sister would be practicing Islam, but the identity itself, the Islamic identity itself is lost." Muslims in the West, he went on, knew more about their favorite basketball players and soccer teams than they did about their religion, and this had to change if Islam was to defend itself properly from the West.[79] Here, the link emerges between his diagnostic framing and the creation and promotion of collective identity, with Awlaki arguing that one of the reasons for Islam's ills was the failure of Western Muslims to define and uphold their identity.

After 9 / 11 and President Bush's declaration of the War on Terror, Awlaki's tone became more aggressive, and this influenced the second type of diagnostic framing he pursued. He began to present a more direct, physical war on Islam, using the examples of domestic counter-terrorism work and the wars in Afghanistan and Iraq. During a Friday sermon at Dar al-Hijrah, Awlaki drew on a specific event to frame the domestic war on Islam for his audience. On March 20, 2002, Operation Green Quest, a U.S. Customs interagency investigative entity tasked with stopping terror financing, carried out raids on members of the

SAAR network in Virginia. Named after its Saudi Arabian funder, Sulaiman Abdul Aziz al-Rajhi, SAAR was an umbrella organization of over a hundred Islamic charities, think tanks, and businesses, members of which were suspected of involvement in financing various terror networks.[80]

Speaking shortly after the raids, Awlaki exploited the incident to instill in his audience a sense of isolation and siege, framing any police or government counterterrorism efforts as part of the Western war on Islam and Muslims. These operations, he maintained, were part of an overall mission to "put out the light of Allah."[81] Using an argument that was gaining traction at the time—namely that the Bush administration's War on Terror was an attempt to mask a wider effort against all Muslims—Awlaki told his congregation that "this is not now a war on terrorism. We need to all be clear about this. This is a war against Muslims. It is a war against Muslims and Islam." Muslims in the West must therefore "wise up" and not take the government and media's comments about terrorism and Islam "at face value."[82]

If he was to get through to his audience, Awlaki needed to do more than just point to U.S. actions abroad. He had to make it vivid to them, and Operation Green Quest offered him the ideal opportunity to make this frame resonate with their experiences. This war was not just being waged abroad; but "it is happening right here, in America." He wove in familiar Western themes of liberalism and freedom, citing an apparent hypocrisy in the American approach that "is claiming to be fighting this war for the sake of freedom, while it is infringing on the freedom of its own citizens, just because they are Muslims." Awlaki also cited the history of minorities in America, aware that the plight of black Americans before the civil rights movement would strike a chord with his audience. In doing so, he drew deep comparisons with the situation faced by Muslims in America at the time: "Maybe the next day the Congress will pass a bill that Islam is illegal in America. Don't think that this is a strange thing to happen; anything is probable in the world of today, because there are no rights unless there's a struggle for those rights, and the history of America in that sense is very clear. African Americans in this country had to go through a struggle; their rights were not handed to them."[83] Muslims in America must therefore not be lulled into a false sense of security simply because they live far away from the battlefields where America and its allies are waging the war on Islam. While they may not be experiencing direct violence now, the warning signs of a coming threat were there for them to see, and Awlaki was endeavoring to identify and highlight them.

During his time in the United Kingdom, which began shortly after this sermon, Awlaki delivered a speech with a similar message, but this time it was tailored to a British audience. In December 2003, he took part in a campaign called "Stop Police Terror." This was founded following the arrest of a British Muslim named Babar Ahmed who reported that he had been severely mistreated by British counterterrorism police officers.[84] Backed by a number of British Islamist organizations, the stated aims of the campaign were to encourage Muslims to take action against "anti-terrorist police terror" and to raise awareness about "the deteriorating situation in the U.K. and the scale of arrests, raids and abuse meted out [against Muslims] by Anti-Terrorist Police."[85] The campaign statement also included an aggressive warning: "Britain's Muslims, as a community, will refuse to cooperate with the law enforcement authorities *if* this abuse continues."[86]

For a group that was founded in order to frame counterterrorism operations as part of the war on Islam, Awlaki was an obvious and useful partner. His involvement amounted to a forty-minute lecture that took place at the East London Mosque in London during a Friday sermon.[87] Islam's enemies, he contended, were taking advantage of the inaction of Muslims in the face of countless injustices: "We are watching one Muslim nation fall one after another and we're watching, sitting back, doing nothing. When Palestine was taken we did nothing and then one nation after another is entering into problems, we have Kashmir, we have Chechnya, the Muslims in the Philippines and now we have Iraq and the *ummah* is doing nothing. The *ummah* is watching while Iraq is being devoured."[88]

In order to align this frame with the experiences and concerns of his British audience, Awlaki reminded them that "we are not talking now about things that are happening in Iraq or Palestine, or somewhere else." Evidence of this war is also "in your own neighborhood, in your own city." That year, the British Parliament passed the Criminal Justice Act, which extended pre-charge detention of terrorism suspects from seven to fourteen days. This decision was the cause of much controversy in Britain at the time; many understood it as unfairly targeting Muslims.[89] It also provided an opportunity for Awlaki, who cited the detention without charge of British Muslims in the hope that it would resonate with his audience and lend credence to his claims that their government and society was turning against them. In doing so, he drew an equivalence to the hated Guantanamo Bay: "You know, when you talk about Guantanamo Bay and all that stuff, there is a Guantanamo Bay in this country. . . . You have over 520 Muslims who are locked up in jail and are left to rot in there, and there is no crime, they have not committed anything, there are no charges brought against them."[90] It was not only fellow Muslims in far-off lands who faced persecution as part of the anti-Islam conspiracy; the very same was happening in the purportedly enlightened homelands of Western Muslims, and they ignored such developments at their peril.

The East London Mosque was not the only place Awlaki delivered sentiments of this type. He also gave a variation of the lecture in late 2003 at the Tawheed Mosque in Leyton, East London. Usama Hasan, who chaired the talk as the mosque's imam, felt uneasy about Awlaki's tone and message, in particular his divisive and inflammatory language: "It was all very us and them, and I felt very uncomfortable about it . . . then he said we have to do something about it [police brutality]. He was very good at inspiring people, but then he would leave them with no practical suggestions about how to react or what to do."[91]

Aside from the threats coming from Western culture and politics, Awlaki looked internally for his third and final diagnostic frame, noting the pernicious effect of infighting and disagreements within Western Muslim communities. This was a common problem among the warring factions within American Salafism, which Awlaki was seeking to rise above. During the September 2001 convention of the Islamic Society of North America (ISNA) in Chicago, he gave a talk entitled "Tolerance: A Hallmark of Muslim Character." Infighting about what he saw as trivial issues of *fiqh*, such as how to dress or the appropriate length of one's beard, took Muslims' attention away from the major issues faced by the *ummah*: "We don't have our priorities straight. We shouldn't get into pitiful discussions and arguments about minor issues when the *ummah* is facing some serious problems. Iraq is being choked to death. . . . What are we doing for them? We should raise up the understanding of the *ummah* to a higher level. . . . The Palestinian issue should be something that we are concerned about day and night. We should participate in and support this uprising [a reference to the ongoing violence of Second Intifada] and let them know the American Muslims are with you."[92]

Awlaki's words here can also be read as an activist Salafi critique of the quietist Salafi strand in the West. Quietist scholars and preachers are notorious for the time they spend discussing and disagreeing over issues of *fiqh*. They are often criticized by activist Salafis and other Islamists for doing so at the cost of taking any action to help the *ummah*. For quietists, discussion and activism related to conflicts like that in Israel-Palestine is a waste of time. Not only does it achieve little, but it both distracts Muslims from studying their faith and plays to emotion instead of measured analysis.[93] Islam, according to this quietist approach, holds an eternal truth that is immune to the ever-shifting fortunes and pettiness of humankind, which Muslims must learn look beyond. Without a proper knowledge of the faith, which in the view of quietist Salafis very few Muslims possess, nothing can be achieved.

In his prognostic framing, so called because it offered solutions to the problems he identified, Awlaki suggested a number of options for Muslims to respond to the three challenges he laid out. In order to fend off the pernicious effects of Western culture on Muslim belief while also addressing current disunity within Western Muslim communities, Awlaki emphasized the importance of Islamic education (*tarbiyah*) and involvement in Islamic groups with a "political orientation."[94] This in turn would help form and protect an *ummah*-centric collective identity among his followers.

A true appreciation for Islamic history (described by Awlaki as "our umbilical cord") through the study of *sira* was one of the first steps in addressing this lack of unity. It was only through gaining this knowledge and attaching themselves to Islamic history that they could develop and strengthen this identity: "This is our lifeline, we are an extension of an *ummah*. . . . We are not severed from our roots, we are a part of a glorious *ummah* that we need to study about." This appreciation for the roots of Islam and its history would, he hoped, ensure that Western Muslims adopt an identity that centers on them being "part of the worldwide Muslim *ummah*." It was imperative that this identity form the core of a Western Muslim's persona, and they had to ensure that "local identity should not override our Muslim identity." Islam, according to Awlaki, required the abolition of the concept of the nation-state so that reverence was reserved solely for Allah; Muslims were not to be separated by arbitrary, man-made boundaries. Thus, "what happens in Palestine should concern every British Muslim. What happens in Kashmir should concern every American Muslim. What happens in every part of the Muslim world, should concern me as if it is happening within my own house."[95] Here too, we see Awlaki's activist Salafi tendencies in his calls for political activism and discussions of conflicts around the globe involving Muslims.

Awlaki's framing of the war on Islam and the question of Western Muslim identity were therefore inexorably linked. Muslims had to stop involving themselves in "pitiful" discussions about minor issues of *fiqh* while ignoring the demands of their collective global identity such as assisting their coreligionists who were suffering around the globe.[96] This need for the promotion and preservation of an *ummah*-centric Islamic identity was an acute concern in the West, where Muslims were faced with increasing personal dilemmas about where they fit into Western society.[97] In this way, Awlaki began to define boundaries between Western Muslims and wider society, hoping to draw them away from other influences and closer to the *ummah*.

As part of this, Awlaki's prognostic framing began to wed itself to the Manichaean binarism of *al-wala wal-bara*. The unity that Western Muslims required in order to progress could only be achieved, he argued, by developing boundaries between them and the rest of their society. He was at his most explicit about this during his speech for the "Stop Police Terror" campaign in London, in which he referred to the doctrine and its importance in helping protect Muslims from state counterterrorism measures: "If you have love of the Muslims you will be with the Muslims on the day of judgement. If you have love for the *kuffar* [non-Muslims] you will be with the *kuffar* on the day of judgement, that's how it works. That's the justice of Allah; somebody who loved the Muslims will be with the Muslims and will follow them wherever they go."[98]

According to Awlaki, there were "consequences of forsaking a Muslim" and not adhering to *al-wala wal-bara*. Referring to a *hadith* commonly cited in discussions of this doctrine, Awlaki reminded Muslims of their prophet's words: "A Muslim is the brother of a Muslim, he does not oppress him, he does not hand him over. . . . You don't hand over a Muslim to the enemies of Allah. . . . If you conceal the private sins of your Muslim brother, Allah will conceal yours on the day of judgement."[99] Awlaki's decision to translate this *hadith* using the term

"hand over" is significant given that the sermon was about British counterterrorism efforts at the time.[100] Muslims needed to resist working
with any facet of British security authorities because "as soon as you
allow one Muslim to be taken, Allah does not help you anymore." Any
assistance offered would, according to him, be tantamount to helping
shaytan [Satan]: "*Shaytan* has been our enemy since the time of Adam
and he will carry on being our enemy until the Day of Judgment. Don't
think that you will please him and keep him quiet by feeding him one
of your brothers."[101]

Awlaki's frames were strengthened by his use of *sira,* which filled
them with further religious legitimacy and injected the emotional and
mobilizing power of storytelling. At every opportunity, he placed his
audience in the role of the historic heroes of Islam who faced adversity
and bravely fought back. In a lecture series on the life of Umar bin-
Khattab, a companion of Muhammad and the second of the "rightly
guided caliphs," he gave an account of an experience of one of Umar's
companions, from which Western Muslims could learn when considering their interactions with non-Muslim fellow citizens.[102] Discussing
an episode where Abu Jahl, a Quraishi leader of pre-Islamic Mecca, deceived Umar's friend Ayyash ibn Abi Rabiah, Awlaki told his audience:
"Brothers and sisters, there is a very important lesson to learn here. . . .
Umar told Ayyash, don't believe them, they want to deceive you. The
important lesson to learn here is never, ever trust the *kuffar.* Do not
trust them."[103]

The period of Umar's life on which Awlaki focused took place during
the *hijrah* (migration) to Medina, when Muhammad and his followers
were transitioning from the Meccan period to the Medinan period of
Islam.[104] The hostility shown to Muslims in the West in modern times
was, according to Awlaki, the equivalent to what the faith's originators
experienced in Mecca, when Arabian tribes persecuted Muhammad
and prevented him and his followers from practicing Islam. This distinction between the Meccan and the Medinan eras and which of them

is more applicable to the present day is an important one for Salafis. A prognostic divide exists between those who see the present time as equivalent to either the Meccan period or the Medinan one. Both quietist and nonviolent political Salafis generally present the current context for Muslims as similar to the Meccan period, when Muhammad was preaching Islam peacefully through *dawah* while facing persecution from local tribes. This means that their prognostic frames revolve around methods such as study and proselytizing, similar to that pursued by Muhammad in the earliest years of Islam.

Political Salafis and Salafi-jihadists interpret the current situation for Muslims as similar to the Medinan period, when Muhammad and his followers migrated to Medina and began to participate in politics and waged military campaigns in order to realize the establishment of a caliphate. As such, Medinan period scholars are more inclined to call for a *manhaj* based around political activism or militancy.[105] At this stage, Awlaki was closer to the spirit of the Meccan period, acknowledging the suffering of Muslims but not yet calling for violence in response and focusing mainly on *dawah*. However, after 9 / 11, Awlaki was in the throes of moving away from this position and adopting an outlook more consonant with the Medinan period. He still shared elements of the prognosis of peaceful propagation and resistance but began to become more bellicose and confrontational in his rhetoric. However, he faced a clear obstacle to achieving the desired frame resonance.

For Muslims in the West, many of whom spend their lives working and living with non-Muslims, the lessons from Umar bin Khattab's life did not immediately relate to their experiences. Asking them to adopt such seemingly unnecessary enmity for their friends and neighbors was, on the face of it, a tall order. This did not go amiss, and Awlaki preempted what many in his audience may have thought about such a statement. He acknowledged that "you might argue and say: 'but my neighbor is such a nice person, my classmates are very nice, my coworkers, they're just fabulous people, they're so decent and honest.'" Such thoughts, he explained, were without foundation in Islam; this hatred and distrust should be held for the leaders of *kufr*, the ones who were "calling the shots." The leaders are "plotting to kill this religion," and one should not "make peace [with the state and society] based on your friend who is not a decision maker." The Koran says nothing and cares little for "the people who are just fillings and don't make any decisions." "Joe Six-pack and Sally Soccer mom," as he described them, are not those upon whom a Muslim should base their judgment of a society.[106]

Wider Western society did, however, also present a potential threat. To illustrate this, Awlaki relied on a contemporary example that would have been fresh in the minds of many in the audience. Referring to the Serbian genocide of Bosnian Muslims during the early 1990s, which was a potent contemporary recruitment tool for Islamist propaganda in Britain, he said: "You know, these nice neighbors, wonderful co-workers and friends, all that it needed was for [former Yugoslav president] Milosevic to tell them the Muslims are evil people, all that was needed, and they pounced on the Muslims like wild beasts. This is in twentieth century Europe." Modern Europe had already seen one recent atrocity against its Muslims, and for Western Muslims to believe they were now safe was, in Awlaki's view, a great folly. These unbelievers with whom Western Muslims must interact and forge relationships are no more than a few stirring speeches away from sanctioning, and even participating in, yet another mass killing of European Muslims: "So in Bosnia, that's what happened, they were very nice. . . . But then Milosevic tricked them, bringing up these false legends of history and these nationalistic songs. It inspired the people and they turned against the Muslims. They were so gullible and naïve that all it took were a few nationalistic songs and a few events in history that were fabricated and not true and they just attacked the Muslims, that's how easy it was to deceive these masses who were otherwise before that very decent and honest and nice people."[107]

Only by applying *al-wala wal-bara* and creating boundaries between themselves and their non-Muslim neighbors could Western Muslims ensure their survival. They had to emerge from their media-induced torpor and realize that it was only a matter of time before similar measures were taken against them. The Jews and Christians, through CNN and other media outlets ("the mouthpieces of the *shaytan*"), aimed to "deceive" Muslims into a false sense of security. They had, said Awlaki, echoing Malcolm X, been "bamboozled."[108]

As well as identifying social and religious boundaries for Western Muslims, Awlaki needed to further define the nature of the identity they needed to adopt. To this end, he deployed a concept found in the *hadith* and described by Muhammad as *al-taifa al-mansura*. Translated as "those who have been ordained victorious by God" or "the victorious group," this term is used as an identity marker by Salafis of all stripes. It describes the righteous Muslims who follow Islam as set out in the Koran and *hadith* and is especially popular with Salafi-jihadists who use this to define themselves in order to bolster and legitimize their claims of being the only group who have both the proper *aqidah* and are pursuing the correct actions to implement it.[109] According to Meijer, for Salafi-jihadists *al-taifa al-mansura* embodies these two aspects: "It is in this action and knowledge embodied in jihad that the vanguard, the 'victorious group,' manifests itself and sets itself apart from those who are not only weak, but are also theologically misguided and factually misinformed."[110]

"There will always be a core group," according to Awlaki, "who are on the straight path until the day of judgement." One of the benefits of being part of this group is that, unlike the majority of Muslims and non-Muslims on earth, they would not need to go through the ordeal of judgment after the grave and will go straight to *jannah* (heaven). Despite the importance of this group, however, its characteristics, as described by Awlaki, are vague, yet nonetheless revealing. Not only do they "follow the *sunnah* [sayings and deeds of the prophet]," but they also "do not fear the blame of the blamers." This is a popular line used by Western jihadists and is often found in global jihadist propaganda. It serves as useful defense mechanism for Westerners who are adopting this new identity and belief system in societies that widely reject and abhor their actions. God, they are told, has warned that those following the true path will face numerous challenges. They must be prepared for rejection from their societies and even those closest to them. In case his audience were at all unsure about what this meant, Awlaki expanded further, saying that "they don't care what anyone says about them, they don't care what the media says about them, they only care about what Allah says."[111]

Members of this ordained group were also "stern" toward non-Muslims while being "humble" toward their fellow Muslims, a formulation that echoes al-wala wal-bara. Finally, and perhaps most tellingly, Awlaki describes their most important and defining characteristic: "they fight jihad . . . for the haqq (faith), both defensive and offensive."[112] This may not necessarily demonstrate that Awlaki was trying to steer his audience toward Salafi-jihadism, but he made no effort to contextualize these statements or offer caveats about jihad being a nonviolent, spiritual struggle. While many Salafis refer to themselves as part of al-taifa al-mansura, quietists in particular stress that the defining feature of this group is that it follows the creed of Muhammad and his companions (the aqidah of Ahl as-Sunnah Wal-Jamaah), not that it pursues violent jihad. By contrast, Awlaki placed heavy emphasis on fighting in his breakdown of the characteristics of the group. This, it is important to remember, was during a period when Awlaki's work was by and large considered mainstream, and this represented an indication of the path he was later to adopt.

Few Salafis operating in America at this time would have discussed jihad in such a loose and ill-defined manner as Awlaki does here. Most would have offered caveats and warnings about practicing it in the modern context lest they run the risk of encouraging militancy, a concern that Awlaki apparently did not share. He concluded his comments on jihad by reminding his followers that "jihad is constant, it never stops." Taken in combination with his focus on al-taifa al-mansura, this belief is strikingly similar to that found in Saudi Arabian al-Qaeda ideologue Yusuf al-Uyayree's *Constants on the Path of Jihad,* which was written and made available online around the time Awlaki made these statements.[113] Roughly five years later, in 2005, Awlaki would endorse this work and translate it from Arabic into English, marking his public conversion to Salafi-jihadism. That he appeared to be quoting from it half a decade previously while still a preaching in the West raises a number of questions about his early beliefs and influences.

This is one of a number of examples of Awlaki expressing beliefs in his early years that are usually considered the preserve of Salafi-jihadists. He was, for instance, also open to the legitimacy of the tactic of suicide bombing and relied again upon a teaching most closely associated with al-Uyayree's writings in order to justify such an act. During his "Life of Muhammad" lecture series Awlaki provides various examples of important figures in pre-Islamic Christianity who died in defense of Abrahamic monotheism and turns to a story from a *hadith* in Sahih Muslim about the King and the Boy. This is a tale of a dying, idolatrous sorcerer-king in Yemen who, in the search for his successor, finds a young boy who is skilled in magic. The boy, however, soon converts to monotheism under the guidance of a Christian priest and rejects the beliefs of his king. When news of the boy worshipping only God reaches the king, he attempts on numerous occasions to have the boy killed, only to be thwarted by divine intervention. The boy finally informs the king how he could end his life—tie him to a tree and shoot an arrow at him after uttering the words "Bismillah [in the name of God], the Lord of the boy," all in front of a large audience. The king duly follows these instructions and the boy is killed. But the entire audience converts to Islam once the king utters the word "Bismillah," making the boy's death a noble act of martyrdom that assists in the spread of monotheism.

While this may not seem to be an obviously problematic story, it represents a significant red flag. The story of the King and the Boy is used almost exclusively by Salafi-jihadist theorists, who use it to justify the practice of suicide bombing. Indeed, Yusuf al-Uyayree had already used the same story to justify the tactic. In a pamphlet he wrote in 2000, "The Islamic Ruling on the Permissibility of Martyrdom Operations," al-Uyayree argued that suicide attacks do not go against Koranic injunctions against suicide and are legitimate both because they are a response to the larger forces of the enemy and because they offer benefits to the *ummah*.[114] In order to back this claim up, he referenced the *hadith* about the King and the Boy, claiming that "it is the strongest of evidences for this issue [the legitimacy of suicide operations]."[115] The boy tells the king to kill him with the intention furthering Islam, making it the death of a martyr and not an act of suicide.

This is, almost verbatim, what Awlaki also told his audience: "This is one of the many evidences given for the justification of what is referred to as suicide bombers. . . . There are restrictions on when it is allowed and where, but the conduct itself, of a person giving up his own life for Allah is a valid one. . . . The boy did it for a noble cause."[116] Awlaki would repeat this story again during his time in the West. While in the United Kingdom, he gave a series of lectures called "Companions of the Ditch," which was produced and distributed by British-based Islamic publication company called al-Noor. He was more explicit this time, telling his audience that the lessons taken from the tale of the King and the Boy were "especially important now."[117] When asked about the best methods available to Muslims in order to help spread Islam just as the boy had done, and cultivate their own faith, Awlaki responded that "every *ibadah* [form of worship] that is done contributes." He listed the various standard practices that are recognized as the five pillars of Islamic observance, including praying five times a day (*salah*) and making the pilgrimage to Mecca (*hajj*). He also, however, included the option to "go to jihad" without any effort to contextualize or offer further explanation. The inclusion of jihad as *ibadah* again reveals his increasingly Salafi-jihadist tendencies, as no other interpretation gives jihad such prominence.[118]

Similar to Awlaki's apparent reliance on *Constants on the Path of Jihad,* it is hard to imagine where else he would have drawn this if not from the work of al-Uyayree, a known jihadist scholar whom he would later rely heavily upon as he turned more openly to Salafi-jihadism. This raises further questions about what Awlaki's longer-term intentions at this stage were. While unlikely, it is not beyond the realm of possibility that this was his own jihadist version of *tarbiyah* in the West, reflecting his desire to lay the groundwork for a future, indigenous Western Salafi-jihadist movement.

Another problematic aspect of Awlaki's early teachings was his apparent sympathy toward the notion of *takfir* in relation to Muslim governments and leaders that do not implement *hakimiyya.* When asked by a member of the audience during a discussion on the Koran in the early 2000s how Muslims should regard those who do not rule by God's law, Awlaki replied that "the opinion of every Muslim scholar worthy of knowledge is that whoever does not rule by the Book of Allah has left the fold of Islam. That is an issue that is not up for debate."[119] This is a striking statement, one that again helps to place Awlaki at some distance from the quietist Salafi strands active in the United States at the time. This position is, however, also rare for activist Salafis who, while contesting Muslim states and their perceived failure to fully implement Islam, do not usually go so far as to excommunicate them. *Takfir* of this type is pursued almost exclusively by Salafi-jihadists.

While his discussion of jihad as *ibadah, takfir,* and suicide bombing certainly complicates matters, the most accurate categorization for Awlaki during his early years would be activist Salafism but with a propensity toward components of jihadi thought. Like other activist Salafis, he would often cite the teachings of Islamist ideologues and recommended them to students. When, during the recording of a lecture he gave in 2002, a student asked him for recommendations of reliable Koranic exegesis, his answer was as follows: "As for thoughts and ideas about the Quran which may not fall under the category of *tafseer*

[Koranic exegesis] but more of a contemplation of Quran [I recommend] *Fi Zhilaal-il-Quran* by Sayyid Qutb and *Tafkeem ul Quran* by Abul A'la Mawdudi."[120]

Qutb was especially influential on Awlaki's thinking at the time, and he relied upon the ideologue's interpretation of *jahiliyyah* to describe the world his audience was living in at the time. *Jahiliyyah,* as he understood it, "is a time period but it is also conduct, whenever you have a time that resembles the pre-Islamic era, it is called *jahiliyyah* and you will find that Sayyid Qutb uses this word a lot in reference to the times that we are living in. He says that there is a lot of resemblance between it and the early *jahiliyyah*."[121] In theological and historical terms, *jahiliyyah* refers to the period before the revelations of Allah through Muhammad and the subsequent foundation of Islam. However, taken up by Qutb, it became a methodical denunciation of the modern secular world that he used to attack the moral bankruptcy that was a product of man's denial of God's sovereignty (*hakimiyya*).[122] In Qutb's interpretation, *jahiliyyah* referred to any society, group, or individual in any period of time that rejected the implementation of God's law.[123] As with his discussion of jihad, Awlaki's reliance upon and recommendation of the work of ideologues like Qutb and Maududi again placed him apart from the quietist Salafis who were operating in America at the time, many of whom who were engaged in attacking the influence of Islamist ideology on Salafi creed, a mixture they regarded as the root of extremism.

Some of Awlaki's early contemporaries also note that he had a propensity toward Islamist ideology and believe that this heavily influenced his future ideological trajectory. Jamaal Zarabozo, one of the first American Salafi converts who was an influential figure in American Salafism during the 1980s and 1990s when Awlaki was emerging onto the scene, does not even class Awlaki as a Salafi. Instead, he regards him as more influenced by Islamism: "His work was never in-depth or sophisticated enough for me to consider him a Salafi, and I always regarded him as closer to the *Ikhwani* [Muslim Brotherhood] ideology."[124] Awlaki's appointment at the Islamist-influenced Dar al-Hijrah mosque also helps to place his early ideological influences. While other prominent American Salafis of the time were affiliated with openly Salafi mosques, Dar al-Hijrah was not a primarily Salafi institution. The mosque instead represented one of the main hubs of Muslim Brotherhood activism in the United States and was distinct from both the QSS and IANA strands of Salafism.[125] Ismail Royer, a regular Dar al-Hijrah congregant who had been involved with Islamist activism in Virginia through CAIR and attended some of Awlaki's lectures, also believes that Awlaki was more influenced by Islamism than Salafism. Recalling a conversation with a fellow activist about Awlaki's appointment in which Royer expressed his surprise at the hiring of an apparent Salafi, he responded that "you don't get a position like that at Dar al-Hijrah unless you are *Ikhwani* [Muslim Brotherhood]."[126]

Apart from Dar al-Hijrah, Awlaki's connections to other scholars and institutions help to further the argument that he was initially influenced by activist Salafism. In a blog post he published in 2008, Awlaki's own description of his religious training provides a complex picture.[127] He claimed to have studied with the Saudi Salafi "scholars of Makkah and Madina" for only a matter of months, also attending the study circle of Sheikh Ibn al-Uthaymeen, who was one of the leading quietist sheikhs of the Saudi religious establishment. In addition, Awlaki lists Salman al-Awdah as a person with whom he "spent a short time."[128] It is not clear when this was, but given Awlaki's own ideological leanings, this link with a leading *Sahwa* figure further distinguishes him from quietist Salafis, who are critical of Awdah's activism.

Further widening his ideological scope, Awlaki also wrote that he "benefited from the teachings of Shaykh Abdul Majid al-Zindani."[129] Zindani is the rector of the al-Iman University in Yemen and leading member of al-Islah party, a Yemeni Islamist political party with strong ties to the Muslim Brotherhood.[130] He has been described as a "Salafi

Islamist" and represents the activist Salafi trend in Yemen.[131] Awlaki's links to Yemeni Islamists in al-Islah go beyond just Zindani, and Awlaki also claims to have received religious training from Sheikh Hassan Maqbool al-Ahdal, who was a leading figure in al-Islah before his death in 2005. Al-Ahdal represented al-Islah in the Yemeni Parliament after being elected as an MP in 1993 and also served as part of the Judiciary Committee.[132] He is also considered an influential religious authority in the country and was the head of a family of Yemeni sheikhs from Yemen's al-Mahrah governorate in the east of the country. It is telling that Awlaki associated himself with the activist Salafi trend in Yemen. Awlaki made no mention of Yemen's well-established quietist Salafi movement, which was led, until his death in 2001, by the Saudi-trained cleric Muqbil bin Hadi al-Wadi'i, whose work has been carried on by his acolytes Muhammad al-Imam and Yahya al-Hajuri.[133] Harsh critics of the al-Islah current, these Yemeni quietists reject involvement in elections and are loyal to the rulers of the state.[134]

Awlaki claimed a number of ideological influences, but his level and depth of scholarly training was limited, despite the senior positions he found himself in as a young preacher in the United States. This, too, may help explain his eventual gravitation to jihadism. In the same blog post in which he discussed his Islamic education, Awlaki claimed that he had received *ijazah* from Maqbool al-Ahdal and other members of the al-Ahdal family. *Ijazah* (certificate) refers to a formal recognition granted to a student by a qualified scholar that demonstrates their competency in a field of Islamic religious knowledge. It also gives its recipient license to teach the topic to others. Awlaki lists a number of *ijazah* he claims to have received, but the validity of these assertions is very difficult to determine. In some cases, *ijazah* is granted after periods of brief study, while in others it requires a long process of genuine training. However, considering that Awlaki had not spent much time in Yemen by the time he wrote this article, there is reasonable cause to doubt the veracity of some of these claims. One of the *ijazah* he claims to have received is in the *hadith* collection of Sahih al-Bukhari. A multi-volume collection, it comprises thousands of pages and requires a great deal of time to study, often a number of years, with a recognized sheikh in order to be granted *ijazah*. Judging by Awlaki's known whereabouts, he did not spend the amount of time in Yemen required to receive a truly authentic level of training before publishing his most popular early works. Awlaki was, however, the son of influential Yemeni politician Nasser al-Awlaki, and it is possible that he was granted *ijazah* due to the connections he had in that country.

Awlaki's apparent lack of formal training is also reflected in his output, which is distinctly lacking when compared to the scholarly focus of his Western Salafi contemporaries. Throughout his body of work, there is no deep reflection on issues of *aqidah* (specifically the doctrine *tawhid*) or *fiqh* [Islamic jurisprudence], which are a staple for any true Salafi who has undergone religious training. By contrast, Ali Al-Timimi, Awlaki's closest contemporary in terms of ideology and influence, had a vast body of scholarly work and received formal training in Saudi Arabia for many years. He looked in detail at issues of *aqidah* and *fiqh,* giving talks with titles such as "Usul ul-Fiqh" (a seventeen-part series), "Tawhid and Shirk," and "Aqeedah Al Hamawiyah." Whether due to a lack of interest or a lack of ability, Awlaki never delved into this kind of detail, choosing to focus instead on retelling early Islamic history and discussing contemporary politics. These topics suited his storytelling skills, allowing him to use his eloquence to make up for (and perhaps cover up) his lack of in-depth knowledge.

While it was one of the reasons for Awlaki's widespread appeal, discussions of *sira* are considered by many Salafis as secondary to the importance of studying *hadith*. It is undoubtedly an important component of Islamic study, but *sira* is regarded as generally less reliable and cannot be used as the main source upon which to base one's understanding of the application of Islamic belief and practice.[135] The recognized scholars of *hadith* were concerned with verifying the authenticity of each story and saying of the prophet through establishing a chain of transmission from a succession of respected sources for each *hadith*.[136] Thus, when studying and teaching the most respected *hadith* volumes, such as those composed by Imam Bukhari, there is less room for interpretation and adjustment than in the study and teaching of Islamic history based on the work of the Islamic historians. Salafis argue that, unlike *hadith* scholars, Awlaki's favored Islamic historians were less concerned with establishing authenticity than they were with preserving any accounts they could find regardless of their accuracy.[137]

The proper teaching of *sira* therefore requires specialist knowledge and training in a range of Islamic scholarly disciplines and is viewed by quietist Salafis as one of the most difficult pursuits in the field. Thus, from the very start of his career Awlaki jumped into the deep end, taking on one of the most complex components of Islamic scholarship and presenting it to an audience eager for accessible, English-language Islamic teaching with an apparently strong scholarly foundation. Awlaki, put simply, was not at the level required to properly and responsibly convey the *sira,* but he identified it early on as the most effective method for his interests. Of all scholarly pursuits in Islam, *sira* is arguably the most effective medium through which to pursue political agendas under the guise of scholarship. Unburdened of the need to verify each claim, even while gaining access to a wealth of historical accounts from which to create a narrative, Awlaki offered personal interpretations to key moments in Islamic history and the actions of Muhammad and his companions that he was not qualified to produce. Accessible to the lay audience, steeped in lore, and malleable depending on one's interests, *sira* is the ideal vehicle for the preacher seeking to derive religious sanction for a range of political activism, including terrorism.

Many quietists also view a focus on *sira* as problematic due to the emotional responses it can elicit. To the quietist, emotion is one of the roots of extremism in Islam. Most Salafis base their study and interpretation of the faith only on evidence gleaned from the texts and the writings of a small group of recognized scholars. Purists regard interpretation and methodology based on emotion or personal experience as dangerous and misleading. Such an approach can erode the purity of the faith, cloud judgment, and lead to taking rash actions that go against core precepts.[138]

Abdullah Pocius, a young American Salafi who is now the imam of the Albanian Masjid in Philadelphia, recalls how Awlaki was viewed with suspicion by Salafis due to his intense focus on *sira*, lack of scholarly connections, and ability to elicit emotional reactions from his audience. During his early years as a convert in the period after 2002, Pocius regularly encountered American quietists in QSS mold who were concerned about Awlaki and his rise to prominence, warning followers to avoid his work: "There was this sense of, Who is this guy? Where did he come from? Who are his sheikhs?" While he may have received some training in Yemen, there is no evidence that he was taking advice or inspiration from any of the leading Salafi sheikhs in Saudi Arabia or elsewhere. In Pocius's eyes, Awlaki's lack of scholarly grounding or strong connections to recognized scholars, coupled with his skillful use of *sira*, made him "the most dangerous person who has ever existed in English-speaking Islam."[139]

Awlaki's possible lack of scholarly Salafi backing may also help explain how and why he later radicalized. As he was not anchored to any specific sheikhs or teachings, he was able to pick and choose his beliefs as it suited him without having to answer to anyone. This, combined with the clear activist Salafi influence on his preferred methods to achieve change, and inclination toward drawing on Islamist and Salafi-jihadist ideology, meant that his views on what form Salafi activism should take were subject to change depending on the fluctuations of geopolitics. Awlaki reacted to current events and personal experiences, changing his views on the importance and relevance of jihad as a result. The lack of stable grounding in a single doctrinal school of thought made the path to supporting violence more open to him than it would have been for many of his contemporaries.

Curious as it may seem, Awlaki's avoidance of the traditional Salafi topics that were the focus of his contemporaries helps to explain his appeal. Unwedded to any specific approach or scholar, his output was far more flexible and accessible, giving him the sort of mass appeal that quietist Salafism could never achieve in the West. His preference for a light, storytelling approach asked far less of its audience than the rigid and scholarly demands of other Salafi alternatives. Johari Abdul Malik, who refers to Awlaki's early work as "Salafi-light," recollects that during his time in the United States, Awlaki "did not pronounce himself as a Salafi because it would alienate and put off a large number of ordinary Muslims."[140] This was partly because by the late 1990s the term had begun to take on certain negative connotations in American Muslim circles, increasingly signifying the unpleasant and aggressive approach of the Madkhalis associated with QSS.[141]

The collapse of the QSS movement due to this outlook meant that by the late 1990s Salafism in the West needed a new, modern face. Awlaki, who was never focused on calling out and attacking "deviant" sects and practices, avoided labeling himself or harshly criticizing the beliefs of fellow American Muslims. Asked why he thought Awlaki found such success and popularity when he emerged, Yasir Qadhi suggested: "Right place, right time. Simple as that. He fulfilled a need."[142] This separation from traditional Salafism in America, combined with Awlaki's willingness to engage with politics and the wider world, endeared him to a much wider pool of American Muslims seeking an accessible expression of their faith that was relevant to their lives and offered solutions to the problems faced by Muslims in the modern world.

While IANA and its scholars did manage to fill some of the vacuum left by QSS and differed in their acceptance of political activism, they nonetheless produced work that was intellectually demanding and focused on traditional Salafi themes related to *aqidah* and *fiqh*. Awlaki, however, offered a form of activist Salafism that many different Islamic groups would agree with. He focused almost solely on the virtues of living like Muhammad and his companions while avoiding the more contentious topics related to belief and practice. This is also why, while in the United Kingdom, Awlaki was embraced by a wide variety of rival Islamist groups, from those influenced by the Muslim Brotherhood and Jamaat-e-Islami to the revolutionary Islamist political party Hizb ut-Tahrir and other various shades of Islamist and Salafi. He was able to transcend the factional divisions within Western Islamist and other conservative Islamic groups and as a result was able to attract Western Muslims from a variety of backgrounds.

Awlaki's approach and early popularity also help to explain the appeal of his later calls for jihad. He had already gained a large audience and following, many of whom saw him as the modern voice of Islam in the West. It is notable, therefore, that his early work is cited by radicalized Westerners as much as any of his later jihadist materials. As the analysis of Nidal Hasan in Chapter 5 will show, the Fort Hood shooter identified Awlaki's 2001 "Lives of the Prophets" lecture as the work that had impacted him the most, over and above the more explicit calls to jihad. Similarly, Dzhokhar Tsarnaev, one of the two brothers who carried out the Boston Marathon bombings in April 2013, was also influenced by Awlaki's work and recommended to his Twitter followers a month before the attack that they "listen to Anwar al Awlaki's (a shaheed iA) the here after series, you will gain an unbelievable amount of knowledge."[143] This was in reference to Awlaki's "The Hereafter" series of lectures in which he discussed the various stages of the afterlife—the series contained no discussion of politics or jihad. Other studies have also found that Awlaki's early, less explicitly violent work continues to be very popular among jihadists. In Donald Holbrook's analysis of media found in the possession of forty-eight individuals either convicted of terrorism offenses or killed carrying out attacks in the United Kingdom between 2004 and 2017, Awlaki's work was the most widespread among them; in that group, four out of his six most popular titles were his *sira,* history, and afterlife lectures.[144]

Had Awlaki emerged as a public figure after the 9 / 11 attacks and begun preaching jihad with no previous background as an imam, it is unlikely that he would have had the same traction with Western Muslims. His previous work provided the basis for his perceived legitimacy and helped convince many observers that Salafi-jihadism was an inherent part of the religion as he had already presented it. In contrast to the openly jihadist preachers operating in Britain around that time, such as Abdullah al-Faisal, Omar Bakri Muhammad, and Abu Hamza al-Masri, who were rejected by the majority of Western Muslims, Awlaki was not regarded as beyond the pale by mainstream Islamic organizations.[145] This meant that large numbers of Muslims were exposed to his work, as he had been presented to them as a legitimate scholar.

The preceding analysis of Awlaki's early works and ideological inspirations has sought to more accurately categorize his beliefs while simultaneously offering two interrelated factors that may have contributed to his future support for jihadism: the form of Salafism he chose and his lack of scholarly training and connections to a wider network of scholars. While there is no precise way to define Awlaki's ideology, and the current accepted categories of Salafism are themselves imperfect, an analysis of his work and ideological influences sets him distinctly apart from the quietist strand. This can be seen in his willingness to engage in politics and to urge his followers to take part in activism as well as his open criticism of Muslims who shun activism in favor of study. In addition, some of his earliest scholarly influences are derived from Yemeni sheikhs with strong ties to Yemeni activist Salafis and Islamists.

Although activist Salafism does not provide a direct pathway to Salafi-jihadism, in Awlaki's case it ensured that, rather that remaining constant, he had the ability to change his beliefs depending on how he viewed the political situation of Muslims in the West and beyond. This ideological malleability and openness to the use of violence is seen in his earliest sermons, in which Awlaki demonstrated a strong sympathy for components of Islamist ideology that also form the basis for Salafi-jihadist violence. He not only adopted the Qutbist interpretation of *jahiliyyah*, but his tacit support for *tawhid al-hakimiyya* also led him to pronounce *takfir* on Muslim leaders who did not fully implement Islam. He also relied upon a version of *al-wala wal-bara* that, while initially based only on separating Western Muslims and defining and protecting their collective identity, would gradually become more extreme as he moved toward jihadism. The most obvious signs of what was to come, however, were Awlaki's reference to jihad as *ibadah* and his use of the King and the Boy parable as a justification for suicide bombing. This places him among only a small handful of Salafis who support this tactic, the vast majority of whom are Salafi-jihadists. As we shall see in the following chapter, these ideological leanings meant that Awlaki's initial calls for nonviolent activism were subject to revision. This was especially the case in the years following 9/11, when he perceived the threat to Islam to be growing and evolving while also concluding that nonviolent activism was ineffective.

Although Awlaki was influenced and, according to his own account, trained by a well-respected family of sheikhs in Yemen, his lack of any strong and longstanding connections to scholars is the second factor to consider when assessing how and why he turned to global jihad. By contrast, the purist Madkhali strand that existed in the United States was largely inoculated from adopting Salafi-jihadist thought, and none of the movement's leadership figures in the United States changed their views in response to 9/11 and the War on Terror. This was largely due to their unquestioning devotion to the Saudi establishment sheikhs and visceral hatred for Islamist ideology and its influence on Salafism. Aw-laki's beliefs and their application, however, faced no such impediments. As a result, he had neither a clear ideological compass nor the skills (nor the inclination) to fully refute Salafi-jihadist ideology, making him more open to drastic changes in belief and methodology.

The question of where Awlaki initially fit into the Salafi spectrum aside, his early works also display the beginnings of a construction of a set collective action frames that would also evolve toward support for violence. Even in his earliest lectures, Awlaki used a mix of Islamic scripture, history, and current affairs to provide a diagnosis for the plight of Muslims in America and abroad. Western culture and society were engaged in an ideological and physical effort to undermine, change, and eventually destroy Islam. Meanwhile, Muslims were failing to respond appropriately due to a lack of knowledge about the history of Muhammad and the Salaf as well as a failure to take up political activism. While Awlaki was sympathetic to forms of classical jihad in Bosnia and Chechnya and supported the Hamas terror campaign against Israel during the Second Intifada, he had not yet adopted the prognostic frames of the global jihad movement. Muslims in America were not called upon to take up arms and commit terrorist attacks, as Awlaki would later encourage. They had to "deal with issues that are directly relating to our community, to our needs" by conducting *dawah*, learning Islamic history, and taking part in activist groups.[146] Thus, his prognostic framing was centered around *tarbiyah,* fostering a sense of Islamic brotherhood and, in doing so, adopting a collective identity defined by a shared faith and desire to help the *ummah.* While his diagnostic framing and method of teaching would remain largely consistent throughout his career, the discernible change in his framing could be seen in the actions he called upon his followers to undertake in order to change the plight of the *ummah.* His early sympathy toward elements of Salafi-jihadist ideology meant that he was able to shift from activist solutions to violent ones without any drastic change in the doctrines he preached or the sources he used.

This analysis notably lacks an emphasis on the influence of external factors on Awlaki's eventual embrace of jihadism. It is important to acknowledge that the War on Terror undoubtedly had a significant impact on him, as evidenced by his sermons during its incipient phases both at home and abroad. Similarly, his apparent ill treatment by the FBI while still in America would have helped confirm his long-held suspicions about the West's animosity toward Islam and contributed to his support of those Muslims whom he saw as willing to fight back. Nonetheless, given what has been uncovered in Awlaki's earliest works, it is reasonable to argue that his eventual turn to violence was deeply influenced both by his view of the world and his willingness to modify his religious positions depending on the geopolitical context. As events relating to Muslims changed after 9/11, so did Awlaki. From the very start of his career as a preacher, he expressed a significant level of animosity toward America and an acceptance of some of the main pillars of Islamist and Salafi-jihadist thought. Over the coming years, these would only fester and grow.

3

Awlaki and Salafi-Jihadism: Theory and Praxis

As Awlaki's activist Salafi ideology came up against the War on Terror era, he began to conclude that political activism would not be enough to stem what he saw as the rising tide of anti-Islam activity both at home and abroad. Concepts and doctrines he had previously adopted and introduced to his audience—most notably jihad, *al-wala wal-bara,* and *al-taifa al-mansura*—would now begin to take on increasingly radical forms as his perception of the immediacy of the threat changed. His willingness to adapt his activist methodology in response to a shifting political and social environment, along with a preexisting sympathy toward Salafi-jihadism, meant that his move toward this belief system faced few serious ideological impediments. Awlaki's output up until this point, while politically oriented and at times sprinkled with Salafi-jihadi sentiment, offered his audience only a vague set of solutions. He pushed them to the edge with constant warnings of an existential threat that were often interspersed with stories glorifying jihad campaigns during the early years of Islam. However, it was not until 2005 that Awlaki would explicitly call upon his followers to take part in violence.

Despite this change, Awlaki's diagnostic framing remained consistent with his earlier work. Still focused on the Western war on Islam, he continued to update his frames so that they remained relevant to the evolving discourse on Islam, terrorism, and the West. Of special interest was the emerging discussion about what constituted "moderate" or "mainstream" Islam and whether the religion was compatible with, and could adapt to, what are understood to be liberal democratic values.[1] As Western societies continued to grapple with the challenges posed by the radicalization of their Muslim citizens, this formed part of the backdrop for the political and social engagement of many Western Muslims. Awlaki was able to exploit these emerging concerns of his audience by attaching them to his diagnostic frames.[2]

As he began to solidify his collective action framing, a more marked change can be seen in how Awlaki framed what he believed should be the appropriate Muslim responses to the threats they faced. In contrast to his previous work, he now began to offer prognostic and motivational frames designed to encourage his audience to participate in various forms of global jihadist activism, including terrorism. In the process of developing methods to make the ideology appealing, he also contributed to a new strategic approach based on lone-actor terrorism and a Salafi-jihadist reimagining of the propaganda of the deed concept.

During this period, Awlaki pursued five key objectives that will be explored in the coming pages.[3] The first was to widen the reservoir, also known as the "mobilization potential," of possible Western recruits to the global jihad movement.[4] He did this through several means, including translating and providing a Western-centric commentary on influential Salafi-jihadist texts. In order to mobilize these supporters, Awlaki also provided arguments that weighed the perceived costs and benefits of participation, positing that there were both individual and collective gains to be had in fighting jihad.[5] Third, once they were convinced of the merits of fighting jihad, his audience still faced considerable physical and ideological barriers to participation, which Awlaki attempted to remove. Fourth, he helped to construct a militant collective identity underpinned by Salafi-jihadist ideology that appealed to a Western audience. This identity was defined by a set of shared grievances, blameworthy targets, and an agreement upon the necessity of a violent response, all of which Awlaki would articulate through his various frames. This collective identity provided the glue that bonded together informal networks of sympathizers in the West. These became the focus of Awlaki's attention during his later years when he and a team of followers based in Yemen used emerging communications technologies to forge contacts with like-minded individuals at a time when face-to-face interactions and the creation of formal networks for international terrorists was becoming increasingly difficult. Finally, he also identified, and in some cases created, a variety of opportunities for engaging in collective action on behalf of the global jihad movement.

Awlaki's previous experience in packaging Islam for Westerners also proved useful during this phase of his career, and his preaching style remained similar to his previous works. Initially, he continued to produce lengthy lectures, often interspersed with *sira*, only this time with a much more explicit focus on jihad. This first set of lectures laid the foundations for his later work, which took the form of short articles, blog posts, and brief lectures that continued to link the ideology with specific current events affecting Western Muslims.

Translating Jihad

The first step in making Salafi-jihadism more accessible to Westerners and increasing the reservoir of potential recruits was ensuring that works of influential ideologues, many of which were only available in Arabic, were translated into English. In 2009, Awlaki would explain his motivations for translating and analyzing jihadist tracts in the following

terms: "Most of the Jihad literature is available only in Arabic and publishers are not willing to take the risk of translating it. The only ones
who are spending the money and time translating Jihad literature are
the Western intelligence services . . . and too bad, they would not be
willing to share it with you."[6]

After moving to the United Kingdom, Awlaki began this process by
providing a full oral translation of *The Book of Jihad* by fourteenth-
century Islamic scholar and fighter Ahmad Ibrahim Muhammad al-
Dimashqi al-Dumyati, also known as Ibn Nuhaas.[7] His choice of focus
here is revealing. This is not a work that would have been familiar to
the majority of his audience. Jihadists, however, had long considered it
to be an important contribution, frequently citing Ibn Nuhaas in their
justifications for jihad in modern times.[8] No effort to translate this text
into English had ever been made before Awlaki embarked on the
project, and no one has done so since. Quotes from Awlaki's translation remain popular and are often deployed by Western IS supporters
who, during their online conversations, regularly refer and link to audio
clips of a section called "Advice to the Ones Who Stay Behind."[9] In this
context, the passage was used to encourage Western Muslims to travel
to the battlefields of jihad in Syria and Iraq.

In the book, Ibn Nuhaas set out to inspire participation in jihad by
using the Koran and *hadith* to refute arguments against fighting jihad
and remove other obstacles to taking part such as fear of death, concerns for one's family, and a devotion to the material world (*dunya*). He
also provided a number of arguments against defining jihad as primarily a nonviolent, personal, and spiritual struggle. Reinterpreting
jihad in this way is a common theological argument used by some Islamic scholars to discourage Muslims from fighting modern-day jihad.[10]

First delivered in closed-door meetings during his time in London
in 2003, Awlaki's translation pursued similar aims to those of the original and was not simply an academic exercise. He too was concerned
about reinterpreting jihad. Such efforts by some mainstream scholars

were framed by Awlaki as an obstacle to participation that must be overcome.[11] The true meaning of jihad, according to Awlaki, faced an assault in the post-9/11 confusion and subsequent search for answers about Islam and global terrorism. Although *The Book of Jihad* is roughly six hundred years old, Awlaki argued that its messages about the importance and legitimacy of violent jihad were still relevant for Western Muslims today. The book's many references to the words of Muhammad and his followers made it the best source for Muslims who wanted to understand jihad in a time when Islam was being altered and misunderstood: "[Jihad] is an integral part of *fiqh*. . . . However, because of the circumstances today it has become a very obscure issue. This issue of jihad has accumulated many misinterpretations. . . . It is not clear in the minds of . . . Muslims. That's why we want to go and study an old book rather than a new one, because with the *Salaf,* the old Muslims, most likely they would have it right, unlike *ul-khalaf* [later scholars], who among them you would find an accumulation of different influences."[12]

The definition of jihad, according to Awlaki, was the biggest victim of the gradual dilution of Islam since the time of Muhammad and the first three generations of Muslims. He explained that in the original Arabic, the linguistic meaning of jihad is "to strive" but since the introduction of Islam, it had also taken on a more important *sharia* meaning: "Striving to the limit in fighting in the sake of Allah directly or by money, or intellect, or by increasing the numbers [of Muslims] or other means."[13] Using this along with sources from the Koran and *hadith,* Awlaki clarified that jihad refers primarily to physical fighting in the path of God as well as any other act that directly assists this deed.[14]

Despite this, he warned that "nowadays, it is very common to find among Muslims the understanding that jihad is primarily jihad al-nafs [internal struggle] and the secondary meaning is the fighting of the kuffar [nonbelievers]."[15] Much to the chagrin of many Islamists and Salafi-jihadists, the *hadith* in which this statement can be found is widely used by mainstream Muslims, including many in the West. They are, however, greatly mistaken, according to Awlaki, as this teaching is based upon an unreliable "fabricated *hadith*."[16] Ibn Nuhaas's work, then, which provides a classical justification and explanation of jihad, supplied Awlaki with a platform that he could use to introduce the theological underpinnings of violent jihad to his audience.

Although he attempted to lend the book modern relevance, Awlaki needed something newer to place jihad in a more immediate context for Western Muslims. This was provided to him in the form of *Constants on the Path of Jihad,* a book written by the late Saudi Arabian Salafi-jihadist ideologue Yusuf al-Uyayree. Unlike Ibn Nuhaas, al-Uyayree was a modern Salafi-jihadist who was introduced to activist Salafism by the *Sahwa* movement in Saudi Arabia during the 1990s and later trained at al-Qaeda's infamous al-Faruq camp in Afghanistan during the Taliban era.[17] At the time of his death in 2003, he was the founding leader of al-Qaeda in Saudi Arabia, a predecessor of AQAP.[18] His book on jihad is a contemporary jihadist work that explicitly places Ibn Nuhaas's ancient teachings into a modern context.[19] Similar to *The Book of Jihad,* al-Uyayree's text would not be accessible to English-speaking audiences were it not for Awlaki. As discussed in Chapter 2, it is likely that he had already been inspired by al-Uyayree in the early phase of his career. During his time in the United States and Britain, he had touched on a number of important themes found in al-Uyayree's work. This included conceptualizing violent jihad as an act of worship that will remain constant until the end of time, touting the legitimacy of suicide bombing, and highlighting the role of *al-taifa al-mansura* and the Koranic prophecy of their eventual victory.

Since Awlaki's oral translation in 2005, *Constants on the Path of Jihad* has served as a useful resource for Western jihadists.[20] Arguably Awlaki's most popular lecture, it has been cited as an inspiration for violence in numerous terrorist trials. In 2008, the United States Department of Homeland Security (DHS) was provided with an assessment by its Extremism and Radicalization Branch warning that "English language transcripts and recordings that are circulating on the Internet and in hard copy of . . . 'Constants on the Path of Jihad' command U.S. Muslims to conduct violent attacks in the Homeland and against U.S. targets abroad. . . . The sermon also attempts to inoculate readers against popular counter-violence messages."[21]

The audio and transcript of this lecture were distributed on numerous jihadist websites at the time, and they remain available online today. For a time they were also disseminated on mainstream Islamic forums and other websites. When it came to the attention of U.S. authorities in 2008, the lecture was found on one of the most popular of these, www.ummah.com, a website that according to the assessment received approximately 48,300 visitors per month from the United States alone.[22]

In contrast to his work on *The Book of Jihad,* where Awlaki rarely strayed from direct translation to provide commentary and analysis, the most revealing parts of *Constants on the Path of Jihad* are the areas where he departed from the original text and reframed it so that it resonated with his audience. Al-Uyayree provided a relatively dry and scholarly justification for jihad, but Awlaki peppered his translation with American idioms and his trademark storytelling style, lending the work an emotional and cultural depth that the original lacked.

Awlaki was in awe of al-Uyayree's contribution to Islam, describing his books on jihad and martyrdom as "masterpieces." More specifically, he lauded the scholar's skill in applying ancient religious teachings to modern times, noting that al-Uyayree displayed "knowledge of the text and also knowledge of present day, and that is what is needed by the Mufti, by the scholar, it's to be able to use the text and apply it to our present day."[23] This was also how Awlaki saw himself, but in a Western context. His work displays a desire to do in English what al-Uyayree did so skillfully in Arabic: not only justify the religious mandate for violent jihad against the "enemies of Islam" but also successfully align global jihadist frames so that they would apply to a modern context.

Al-Uyayree's treatise identified six "constants" in the Salafi-jihadist interpretation of jihad: Jihad will continue until the Day of Judgment; jihad does not rely on a specific individual or leader; jihad is not tied to a specific land; jihad does not depend on a certain battle; victory in jihad is not defined solely by military triumphs; and military defeat does not mean the end of jihad. These are themes that will, according to al-Uyayree, remain unchanged from the time of Muhammad until the End of Days and formed the basis for how Muslims should respond to the war on Islam.

Al-Uyayree's claim that the war on Islam was gathering pace—one echoed by many other Salafi-jihadists—relied upon the increased emphasis Western nations placed on waging war on jihadist groups in Muslim-majority countries after the 9/11 attacks. Because jihad and the establishing an Islamic State are regarded by Salafi-jihadists as integral and undeniable components of the faith, any effort to prevent or fight against this impulse is framed by them as part of the worldwide aggression against Muslims. Jihad, al-Uyayree argued, was a form of *ibadah,* a "ritual" of Islamic worship that the enemies of Islam attempted to delegitimize by calling it "terrorism and criminality."[24] This presentation of jihad as a form of worship is perhaps the most contested claim made by Salafi-jihadists about the religious legitimacy of jihad. Jihad is important for all Salafis, but for jihadists it is equal to, if not more significant than, the five obligatory pillars of Islamic worship.[25] The addition of this "sixth pillar" is accepted only by a small, usually Salafi-jihadist–oriented, minority of Muslims. By 2005, when he translated *Constants on the Path of Jihad,* Awlaki had fully embraced this belief, arguing that the divine instruction for Muslims to fast is found in Surah al-Baqarah, the same chapter of the Koran in which jihad is also prescribed, yet Muslims often treat these two obligations differently: "Allah says, 'Fighting has been prescribed upon you and you dislike it, but it is possible that you dislike a thing which is good for you and you love a thing which is bad for you. But Allah knows and you know not [Koran 2:216].' This *ayah* [verse] says that fighting is prescribed upon you, so it is a *fard* [obligation], it's an instruction from Allah. . . . They [jihad and fasting] are both in Surah al Baqarah. Fighting is prescribed upon you and fasting is prescribed upon you; so how come we are treating them differently?"[26]

Awlaki's embrace of this concept may, for some, demonstrate a dramatic departure from his previous beliefs. However, we have seen that years earlier, while he was still living in the West, Awlaki had already defined violent jihad as *ibadah* during his "Companions of the Ditch" lecture. Applying al-Uyayree's interpretation of jihad, Awlaki argued that the West's fight against terrorism was religiously motivated. To illustrate this, he drew on what was by then a widely cited and infamous quote attributed to President George W. Bush: "You can find that the Christians and the Jews are using religion to justify what they are doing. . . . It is interesting to see at a very high level in American politics. . . . For example, [Palestinian Authority head] Abu Mazen: he said that he had a meeting with [President George W.] Bush and that Bush told him that God has instructed him to invade Afghanistan."[27]

The war on Islam was not simply a physical, military effort, however. It also had political, cultural, and ideological components that Western Muslims needed to recognize. On the political front, Awlaki argued that NATO, the European Union, and others were developing and discussing strategies to fight jihad and are united in fighting Islam: "Diplomacy around the world now is revolving around a central idea, and that's fighting Islamic terrorism. . . . On the political level . . . every single government in the world is in line to fight Islam." The Western mainstream media, meanwhile, was leading the cultural charge by presenting a negative image of the religion and its adherents: "We find that the media is doing an excellent job in deceiving the people, the masses, to what Islam really is. They are giving Islam a face in this country [reference to the United States] which is a very deceptive one."[28]

Most concerning for Awlaki, however, was the ideological component of the war on Islam. As a Salafi, the preservation of core elements of the creed, or *aqidah,* was of the utmost importance to him—without this, the religion itself would lose meaning and fall apart. While in the original text al-Uyayree expressed his frustration at the "blurring of the features of jihad," Awlaki went further, drawing on a number of examples that were relevant to his audience.[29] The most glaring of these were attempts by Muslims and non-Muslims in the West to define a mainstream Islam that rejected violent jihad. He framed this as an attempt to "customize" and thus destroy the religion from within by reinterpreting its core doctrines so that it conformed to the norms of secular democracy: "Many Muslims today, they say that, since we are living in the West, we have to customize an Islam that is suitable for the West. No, that's not how you should practice Islam—if you feel that Islam needs to be customized for a particular area, that means you need to make *hijrah* [migrate] from it, and go and find a place where . . . you can live Islam in its entirety."[30]

Western Muslims needed only to look at the prophetic model for inspiration. Muhammad, Awlaki explained, rather than migrating to Medina, could have stayed in Mecca and altered Islam in order to satisfy his enemies, but this would have been an affront to the revelations of God. In another of his familiar turns of phrase, Awlaki exclaimed that "Muhammad did not customize Islam based on his location, no, he customized the location based on Islam!"[31] This is the example Western Muslims should follow, and the war-on-Islam conspiracy was leading them astray.

Although Awlaki updated his references to ensure that his diagnostic frames remained relevant to the evolving discourse, his presentation of the threat of Western culture remained as it did during his "Life of Muhammad: The Makkan Period" lecture many years earlier. His views on how to solve this, however, had moved closer to the Salafi-jihadist prognosis. Now, Muslims had only two options: Make *hijrah* as Muhammad did during the Meccan period in order to escape persecution, or fight back. As he would explain five years later, Awlaki shifted his prognostic framing after observing how the situation of Muslims in the West and beyond had deteriorated to such an extent that he deemed education and nonviolent activism as no longer effective.[32]

Alternative approaches to preserving and protecting Islam provided by quietist Salafis and other Muslim groups were now framed by Awlaki as ideological obstacles to fighting jihad that needed to be overcome. These included the *tarbiyah* methodology. Translated as "education," *tarbiyah* defines the approach of most quietists and Meccan-period Salafis who see *dawah* and Islamic education as a long-term tactic for constructing a religious identity and preparing the ground for the organic emergence of an Islamic society governed by the *sharia*.[33] The pursuit of this goal through the use of revolutionary violence, especially before Muslims have gained an in-depth knowledge of their faith, is regarded by quietists as foolhardy and ineffective; they see it as the cause of many of the current ills of the *ummah*. This teaching was, in Awlaki's view, based on a mistaken reading of how the primary Islamic texts described varying forms of worship, including jihad: "A lot of people and a lot of *jamaa* [Islamic groups] . . . say the following: '*Tarbiyah* is a prerequisite of jihad. So without *tarbiyah* you cannot make jihad.' They don't say that it is something that is needed, they don't say that it is something good to have, they say that you cannot fight jihad without *tarbiyah*. Is there justification for delaying jihad *fi-sabi-lillah* [in the path of God]? If somebody starts practicing Islam . . . would you tell them that you would have to have *tarbiyah* before you start fasting [for Ramadan]? . . . Nobody would say that, it's a joke. So what's the difference? Why do we say that about jihad? How come we are treating them differently?"

Adding a further rhetorical twist to al-Uyayree's original text, Awlaki asked whether in the time of Muhammad his followers were required to undertake years of study before fighting, suggesting that this was an absurd claim: "When somebody would embrace Islam, would *Rasool* [Muhammad] tell them that 'you have to go and study under the

Shuyookh [sheikhs], and then after that you can fight *fi-sabi-lillah?*'"[34] In one sentence, Awlaki lifted one of the most important jurisprudential impediments placed upon Muslims wishing to pursue violent jihad. The concept of *tarbiyah* before jihad was, according to him, used by Muslims who wanted to "bail out" of fighting. It is the product of a flaw within the human condition that causes an aversion to fighting, and it needed to be overcome for the sake of Islam and the *ummah*. While a seemingly radical move away from Awlaki's past calls for patience and study, this is primarily a change of method, rather than of a core belief (*aqidah*). Awlaki's activist Salafi tendencies, combined with an emotionally driven approach and preexisting sympathy for Salafi-jihadist ideas and groups, left him open to adjusting his view on the preferred method of change to be pursued by the *ummah*.

How one viewed, interpreted, and practiced jihad also formed the basis of the militant collective identity Awlaki sought to define for his audience. It was therefore significant that he identified and created boundaries between the "true" Muslims who pursue jihad and the "deviant" or "misguided" sects who adopt different interpretations of when and how it should be fought, if at all.[35] In order to help define the militant parameters of this identity, Awlaki also gave significantly more attention than al-Uyayree to *al-taifa al-mansura*. It is telling that while the original work includes brief mention of the "victorious sect," al-Uyayree does not dwell on how to define or identify it in the way Awlaki chooses to.

Al-taifa al-mansura was a subject of interest to Awlaki since the late 1990s when, in lectures such as "Stories from the *Hadith*," he laid out the parameters of this group. What is perhaps most remarkable about his revisiting of this concept here is how little his description of the group differs from his presentation of it during his early career in the West. While he is more explicit in his calls for immediate violence, it is by no means a dramatic change in his outlook. Awlaki noticed that, among his followers, there was a commonly expressed concern over which Islamic groups were the most legitimate: "In lectures, brothers and sisters will often ask the question . . . 'Oh Sheikh, there are so many Islamic groups today, tell us which one to join.' . . . They don't know which *jamaa* [group] to join. . . . The issue shouldn't be confusing at all because . . . Allah has made it clear. If we look in the right place, we will find the answer. Rasool Allah [Muhammad] has told us in *hadith* that there is a *taifa* [group or sect], there is a victorious group called *al-taifa al-mansura*. . . . He told us what the qualities of this victorious group are. If we look at these characteristics it will be as clear as the sun at noon, you will know which *jamaa* fits these qualities."

Aligning the qualities set out by Muhammad with modern-day Salafi-jihadist groups, Awlaki identified a few of the required characteristics found in the Koran and *hadith,* applying them to modern examples. First, he described them as "humble towards the believers." Taken on its own, this requisite feature of *al-taifa al-mansura* can be interpreted in numerous ways. Awlaki offered a specifically militant take: "This means they are concerned with the believers, they love the believers. . . . They feel that a Muslim in the East is my brother . . . and if that Muslim in the East is killed, it is my responsibility to defend him." Muslims in the West, however, were turning on each other, and Awlaki used this to continue his boundary activation work, identifying a clear distinction between "rightly guided" Muslims and the "deviants" who were willing to compromise their beliefs in order to build closer alliances with their governments: "You find that there are some people who claim to be Muslim, but they have the opposite of this trait. . . . You find that they are willing to give *fatawa* [religious edicts] to the government to detain Muslims, to interrogate Muslims . . . to allow Muslims to spy on Muslims. You find that they are willing to stand alongside the *kuffar* to fight against Muslims. So they represent the opposite though they claim to be Muslim."[36]

In order to protect the *ummah, al-taifa al-mansura* also had to be "stern towards the disbelievers." This is a reference to the requirement found in *al-wala wal-bara* to renounce both non-Muslims and Muslims who ignore the call to jihad and to establish Islamic law. Awlaki, now adopting an increasingly radicalized version of this doctrine, knowingly asked: "Who are the ones who are harsh against *al-kufaar* [nonbelievers]? Who are the ones who are willing to stand up against the oppression of the *kufaar*? Who are the ones who are willing to terrorize the *kuffar*?" Referring to Koran 8:60, which in one translation reads: "Against them [the disbelievers] make ready your strength to the utmost of your power, including steeds of war, to strike terror into [the hearts of] the enemies," Awlaki also pointed out that the Arabic word *irhab*, meaning "terror," is used in this verse. This is an authority that Awlaki uses to his advantage: "The word *irhab* in Arabic, which is the translation of terrorism, is actually a word in Koran." Again defining the boundaries between *al-taifa al-mansura* and other Muslims, Awlaki identified those who are "very critical of the Muslims, but at the same time they are very humble towards the *kuffar*."[37] They do this for the purposes of *dawah* to convert the disbelievers to Islam, but by refusing to accept the Salafi-jihadist interpretation of *irhab*, Awlaki argued that they are presenting a skewed version of their religion.

Finally, and perhaps most importantly, those true members of *al-taifa al-mansura* "fight in the path of Allah," just as Awlaki told his British audience years earlier during "Companions of the Ditch." With more than a hint of sarcasm, Awlaki, again straying from al-Uyayree's script, told his listeners to "take your torchlight" and look around the modern world to find out "who are the people who are fighting *fi-sabi-lillah*, is that too difficult to do?"[38] Once a Western Muslim has done this, the question of which group to join should become clear. Awlaki did not, however, specify that Muslims should join al-Qaeda or any other jihadist group. As was common in Awlaki's work, he allowed the audience to feel as if they were coming to their own conclusions after being presented with evidence from the texts. He was rarely explicit about what specific groups Muslims should participate in, preferring to let them retain a sense of individual agency even as he was simultaneously pushing them in a certain direction.

Awlaki used Western references throughout, aligning the qualities and experiences of *al-taifa al-mansura* with the knowledge and experiences of his audience. Using Koran 5:54 ("they [*al-taifa al-mansura*] do not fear the blame of the blamers"), Awlaki reminded them that God himself warned that *al-taifa al-mansura* would be attacked and criticized by the enemies of Islam. He identified the modern perpetrators of such infractions as the Western media: "The *kuffar* are going to speak about them. The *kuffar* are going to write about them in their papers, they're going to speak negatively about them on TV and radio. But do these brothers care? . . . They don't care what CNN would say, or the BBC or ABC. They wouldn't care what *The New York Times* would write about them, or what *The Washington Post* would say about them. . . . They don't care at all, as long as it pleases Allah."[39]

Muslims were warned by their prophet that they should expect betrayal from the *munafiqeen* (hypocritical or false Muslims who profess to follow the faith while concealing their disbelief) within their own ranks, as well as from the Jews and the Christians, and there was plenty of evidence of that in the modern world. In the original text, al-Uyayree offered reassurances that, despite their hardships, those who stayed true to the ideals of *al-taifa al-mansura* were destined to prevail. God has ordained the victory of this group, and the Muslims should remain steadfast, concerning themselves only with gaining his pleasure while ignoring the battlefield defeats of jihadist groups and the criticisms they may receive. Awlaki was also certain that the prophecy will be realized and claimed that it was happening before their very eyes. "In fact," he exclaimed, "[the *mujahidin's*] numbers keep on multiplying." Awlaki added his own examples here too, referring to the U.S. Defense Secretary Donald Rumsfeld's leaked 2003 internal memo about what the United States could do to reduce an expanding threat from global jihadism.[40] Awlaki's answer was simple: "Well, Mr. Rumsfeld, the reason [you have not won] is because you are fighting *al-taifa al-mansura,* which Allah promised that he will protect. No matter how many you kill and how many you arrest, they will carry on. You can never win this war . . . because you are fighting the *auliya* [chosen ones / saints] of Allah and Allah says: 'whoever fights my *auliya,* I will wage war against them.'"[41]

This, he hoped would strengthen the will of his audience, as would the claim that fighting jihad ensured that they would be properly practicing Islam and pleasing Allah. Taking a moment away from translating al-Uyayree, he offered his own motivational message:

> I just wanted to mention one thing regarding what I said about the qualities of the righteous group which you should join: I think after mentioning these qualities, it's very clear who are the people who carry these qualities. And since they carry these qualities, they would also carry the other two qualities, which is, Allah loves them and they love Allah. Now, a lot of people would want to be loved by Allah, and a lot of Muslims want to develop a love of Allah, and they're looking for the magic pill that they could swallow, and suddenly they would love Allah. . . . If you want Allah to love you and you want to love Allah, then this [joining *al-taifa al-mansura*] is how to do it.

As the global jihad movement continued to thrive and produce various groups and influential leaders, al-Uyayree stressed that jihad was not dependent upon a single individual or organization. In the post–Bin Laden era of global jihad, this is an important area of concern, one that al-Uyayree foresaw and made ideological provisions for. Here, al-Uyayree relied on Koran 3:144: "Muhammad is no more than a messenger, messengers [the like of whom] have passed away before him. If he dies or is killed, will you then turn back on your heels as disbelievers?

And he who turns back on his heels, not the least harm will he do to Allah." For al-Uyayree, this verse was a message to those who questioned the longevity of the global jihad movement. The death of the religion's founder and most important figure, far from ending the defense and spread of Islam, served to strengthen the resolve of his followers to continue fighting.

Referring to the aftermath of the Battle of Uhud (A.D. 625), during which there were widespread (but false) rumors about the death of Muhammad, al-Uyayree described the actions of those who reacted in accordance with the words of Allah and continued to fight. This is the example that Muslims should continue to follow, safe in the knowledge that they fight not for any man but for Allah, who is immortal. He also noted that after Muhammad's death, the *Sahaba* continued fighting without interruption, and Islam thrived: "The death of the Prophet did not change the approach of the *Sahaba* in Jihad, and increased their conquests."[42]

Al-Uyayree went on to name a number of the most influential jihadist leaders, including Osama bin Laden, who "is not an individual, but represents a method that all the *ummah* believes in."[43] While Awlaki followed the original text closely here, he avoided making any such references to specific individuals in his translation. There are two possible reasons for this. It is most likely a reflection of his desire to present global jihad as a movement that went beyond a reliance on specific organizations and leaders. However, Awlaki might also have been wary of linking himself directly with terrorist figures out of a fear of making himself a target of U.S. counterterrorism efforts. This is less likely, however, considering that he had already lavished praise on al-Uyayree, who was himself a known al-Qaeda leadership figure.

Because the global jihad is a movement that transcends formal groups and personalities, al-Uyayree also argued that it is not subject to formal understandings of victory and defeat. Victory could be defined in numerous ways that went beyond battlefield triumphs. One form of victory was the maintenance of the purity of the Salafi-jihadist creed through individual sacrifice and fighting in the face of overwhelming odds: "the slave of jihad will have achieved another victory when he sacrifices himself and his money for the sake of his principles and support for his religion." Even if the fighter is defeated, according to al-Uyayree, a form of moral victory has already been achieved. In their willingness to face an enemy that is technologically superior and in possession of more resources, the *mujahidin* defeated both those Muslims who stray from the path and reject jihad and the nonbelievers through a demonstration of devotion to their beliefs and principles: "[The *mujahid*] won by applying his principles in the face of those who doubt Islam and practice heresy, apostasy and atheism."[44]

Awlaki gave special attention to this "victory of the idea" approach, expanding on citations made by al-Uyayree to create a compelling narrative with broader lessons. It is here that Awlaki diverged most from the original text, using artistic license to enliven and enrich al-Uyayree's arguments through storytelling and the use of direct Western references. He used this discussion as a platform to make specific requests of Western Muslims by aligning jihadist frames to match a sociopolitical context that was more familiar to them. He also offered a number of cost-benefit analyses, explaining the collective benefits that could be reaped for the *ummah* through personal sacrifice.

In the original text, al-Uyayree uses the Koran and *hadith* to tell the story of the People of the Ditch (sometimes also referred to as "the Trench"), a favored reference point for both al-Uyayree and Awlaki. An extension of the King and the Boy story, it tells the tale of the people who witnessed the boy's death and converted to monotheism. In his attempts to force them to renounce their newfound beliefs, the King tells them to reject Allah or be thrown into a flaming ditch. After they choose to die for their faith, one woman, cradling a baby, hesitates until God speaks through the infant, telling her to hold firm for the sake of her faith. After relating that the woman chose to die with her baby, al-Uyayree wrote that this "showed the meaning of victory and clarifies the misunderstanding of this concept." Awlaki added his own flair to al-Uyayree's version, injecting more detail and pathos: "The method of their death in itself is so horrific that we can only appreciate how great their steadfastness was. They were told to jump alive in trenches filled with burning wood. And they were jumping one after another in these trenches, burning to death. They chose the fire of this *dunya* [material world] rather than the fire of the hereafter."

Awlaki also claimed that this story demonstrated how, if a Muslim even takes one step toward jihad, Allah will help them. The woman took the first step and "Allah helped her. . . . If you take that first step towards Allah, Allah will make many steps towards you. If you walk towards Allah, Allah will run towards you."[45] This was intended to provide encouragement to those who, while sympathetic to the jihad movement, were hesitating out of fear or lack of faith. The story would already have been familiar to those who were closely following Awlaki while he was still in the West. He had already used it in his "Companions of the Ditch" lecture, which made almost identical arguments while (at that time) avoiding explicit and immediate calls for violence.

The stories of the People of the Ditch and the King and the Boy were also useful for Awlaki as they helped him provide an important cost-benefit analysis for this audience. He presented the Boy as a role model for Muslims today, as his actions reaped collective rewards for Islam and the *ummah*. While the boy "paid the price with his own blood," his actions were the most powerful form of *dawah* possible, ensuring mass conversion to monotheism. Awlaki also cited modern examples of Muslims who had done the same, including Sayyid Qutb, whose words were "brought to life" by his execution at the hands of the secular Nasser regime in Egypt.[46]

These instances of self-sacrifice allowed Awlaki to turn the spotlight on Western Muslims. Using examples culled from news stories about the perceived disrespect shown toward Islam and Muslims by their

fellow countrymen, he attempted to shame them into acting. Earlier
that year, for example, *Newsweek* broke a story claiming that the interrogators and guards at the Guantanamo Bay military prison had flushed
down the toilet or otherwise desecrated copies of the Koran.[47] This was
part of a rash of reports about similar incidents that dominated Western
news cycles, causing protests in Muslim-majority countries and among
Muslims in the West and forcing world leaders to issue public condemnations.[48] At this juncture began the controversy over the cartoons of
Muhammad drawn in the Danish newspaper *Jyllands-Posten,* an act that
some Muslim activists also regarded by as an egregious attack on
Islam.[49] Only a year before these events, in April 2004, the pictures of
the abuse of Iraqi prisoners at the hands of U.S. soldiers in the Abu
Ghraib prison also gained worldwide attention. Exploiting the febrile
atmosphere created by this dark moment in the history of U.S. relations
with Islam, Awlaki erupted into a furious critique of Western Muslims:

> How can you dare say that you love the religion of Allah and
> you know well that the enemy has desecrated the book of Allah
> and you do nothing? When you know that they have flushed
> the Koran down a toilet and you don't pick up your weapon and
> fight for the sake of Allah? When you know that they have in-
> sulted *Rasoolullah* through pathetic images of him? When you
> know that they are torturing Muslim POWs both physically and
> mentally? When you know that they have embarrassed and hu-
> miliated the Ummah by stripping naked the Muslim POWs
> and capturing filthy images?[50]

Inflammatory and steeped in emotion, this message was also part
of Awlaki's diagnostic framing efforts. Muslims in the West had to be
made aware of the multifaceted nature of the war on Islam and react
with violence in order to survive. They had plenty of reasons to be
angry, and the threat they faced was an immediate one, yet they did

not mobilize in large numbers: "Do you need a bomb to drop on your house to give you a reason to get up and fight?! It will be too late by then."[51] Too many Muslims in the West continued to ignore the model of behavior provided by Muhammad and the *Sahaba*. If Islam was to survive, this had to become a defining element of their identity. Referring to how Muslims should react to the Muhammad cartoons, Awlaki pointed out that "the *Sahaba* have done assassinations, under the command of the prophet, against those who spoke ill of Muhammad." Replicating the ways of the greatest generations of Muslims, he argued, should be all the justification and motivation they needed.

While he railed against them, Awlaki welcomed these attacks on Islam because they meant that a line in the sand had been drawn. They helped to "show us truth from falsehood" and clearly demarcated the boundaries between "who the true *momin* [Muslim] was and who the *munafiq* [hypocritical Muslim] was." Before this, there was a "gray area," and Muslims could be excused for a lack of awareness of who their true enemies were. Now, however, "events like these reveal true *iman* [faith] from *nifaq* [hypocrisy]." This removal of doubt, the "gray area," is something Awlaki would later highlight in more detail as a way to frame the choices Muslims had to make and the identity they needed to adopt. As will be explored in more depth in Chapter 8, over a decade later, it would also form the basis of the Islamic State's early outreach to Westerners.

In 2006, shortly after the release of his translation of *Constants on the Path of Jihad,* Awlaki was imprisoned in Yemen; he was not released until late 2007.[52] While some have argued that it was his experience in prison that radicalized him,[53] analysis of his output up to this point suggests that he had already endorsed the global jihad program. Notably, while Awlaki later wrote about his experiences in prison, he did not claim that he was severely mistreated or that it influenced his own embrace of al-Qaeda.[54] Upon his release, Awlaki became more active on the internet, broadcasting his latest sermons through various online platforms and also launching his blog, which ensured that all of his output was easily accessible online and also allowed his followers to contact him directly.[55] Although no official statistics are available about the traffic the blog received, it had a significant readership and was even referenced on occasion by influential Western Muslims. In Britain, for example, Azad Ali, then a member of the British Government's Civil Service Islamic Society and one of the leading members of the Islamic Forum of Europe,[56] referenced Awlaki's blog on his own website, describing him as "one of my favourite speakers and scholars."[57]

Awlaki's articles regularly attracted hundreds of comments, mainly from people claiming to be Western Muslims who considered Awlaki their best source of information on Islam. Howard Clark, a former senior intelligence analyst for the Department of Homeland Security who monitored Awlaki's blog for the DHS Office of Intelligence and Analysis, attests that the daily traffic statistics for it were very high, with the majority of users coming from Britain and the United States: "By this time, al-Qaeda had begun to put huge stock into the Internet as a perfect conduit for their messaging and propaganda. By August 2008, Awlaki was all over YouTube and the rest of the Internet, and his website was skyrocketing in readership. The statistics were extremely concerning, particularly the number of visitors from the United States and Britain."[58]

Filled with messages tailored specifically to appeal to English-speaking Muslims in the West, the blog was a final and unambiguous announcement of Awlaki's full public conversion to Salafi-jihadism. The format he now chose—short-form blog posts that could provide rapid analysis of current events—indicated a new stage in his development. It reflected a desire to make his ideas even more easily digestible, and in the process cast as wide a net as possible in his attempts to recruit for global jihad and increase the size of the movement's mobilization potential. Putting his work on a more interactive online platform also helped Awlaki create a network of sympathizers, linking him to the pool of potential recruits he was helping to create.

One of his most prominent blog posts—"44 Ways to Support Jihad"—was yet another translation, adaptation, and update of a famous jihadi document. After setting out the ideological case for participating in jihad in *Constants on the Path of Jihad*, Awlaki drew upon a document called "39 Ways to Serve and Participate in Jihad" by prominent AQAP member Isa al-Awshan to provide the basis for a discussion of the ways Westerners could become involved in the fight against oppression.[59] As with any social movement, the global jihad movement was being propelled by a multitude of different forms of participation that were presented through a variety of prognostic frames that Awlaki claimed "is what Clausewitz would refer to as 'total war' but with the Islamic rules of engagement": "Jihad here is not just picking up a gun and fighting. Jihad is broader than that. What is meant by Jihad in this context is a total effort by the *ummah* to fight and defeat its enemy. *Rasulullah* [Muhammad] says: 'Fight the disbelievers with yourself, your wealth and your tongues. . . . It is a battle in the battlefield and a battle for the hearts and minds of the people.'"[60]

While physical, violent jihad was at the forefront of his thinking, Awlaki believed that mobilization potential in the West could be increased by lowering the bar for what was considered to be meaningful involvement in the movement. The more someone was made to feel that they were contributing to the global jihad movement through activities other than fighting, the higher the likelihood that they would later move on to other forms of participation. This introduction to the movement through taking part in what can be described as forms of low-risk activism (such as creating and disseminating propaganda or taking part in nonviolent protests) could, Awlaki hoped, mark the start of a journey toward an individual taking more high-risk actions. A person who may engage in forms of low-risk activism due to their budding and minimal level of support for a given movement, once there, is susceptible to becoming more sympathetic to its goals and may forge links with a range of movement activists.[61] In some cases, the alterations to identity brought on by involvement in low-risk activism combined with an introduction to new networks of like-minded individuals can lead individuals to take part in costlier and higher-risk forms of activism such as political violence.[62]

Awlaki's aims and intentions when he translated this document are also better understood when comparing his version with the original "39 Ways." The comparison enables one to determine what he added to the work so that its message could fit with the experiences and capabilities of a Western audience. He placed extra emphasis, for example, on the "financial jihad" that provides the movement with the resources required for its survival: "Probably the most important contribution the Muslims of the West could do for Jihad is making Jihad with their wealth." The Western media, a long-time target of Awlaki's, was also identified as an enemy to be resisted. As he had stated in *Constants on the Path of Jihad,* Western media outlets were directly involved in the cultural component of the war on Islam. Muslims therefore must take it upon themselves to raise awareness of this among their coreligionists and "encourage them to be careful and critical of the Western media." Part of this fight should also include the provision of alternative media sources that would not only counter the Western media but also provide Muslims with information about "the *mujahidin* and their scholars."[63] This was most effectively done, he suggested, through the creation of websites that would publish Salafi-jihadist texts and lectures.

Other additions to the original text included calls to learn Arabic in order to translate jihadi literature into as many languages as possible. As Awlaki understood it, increasing the availability of the intellectual and religious arguments for participating in jihad would precipitate the success of the movement: "Every movement of change is preceded first by an intellectual change. It is said that the time of Salahudeen [twelfth-century Sultan of Egypt and Syria and leader of the Muslim campaign against the Crusaders] was preceded by an upsurge in writings about Jihad. We are seeing this happen today. This revival of Jihad needs to take place among Muslims of every tongue."[64]

Together with the blog, Awlaki began to produce short audio lectures and videos that were disseminated on various online platforms. However, none of his work from this time onward was to come near his previous output in terms of length or depth of discussion. These briefer offerings fulfilled two of Awlaki's main messaging goals. First, they allowed him to begin presenting and framing Salafi-jihadism in simpler and more accessible terms. In addition, his online presence allowed him to provide rapid "real-time" reactions to issues and events of interest to Western Muslims.

Rather than undergoing a marked shift in his messaging, however, Awlaki expanded on frames, themes, and arguments he had already developed in *Constants on the Path of Jihad*. His translation and adaptation of al-Uyayree's work thus formed the basis for the majority of his future output. Unsurprisingly, jihad remained his primary concern. However, Awlaki also expanded upon other important components of Salafi-jihadism. In order to lend further religious legitimacy to his calls for jihad while also strengthening his framing efforts and further cultivating the global jihadist militant collective identity, he focused on two other concepts: *hijrah* and *al-wala wal-bara*.

Hijrah: Leaving the West

While Awlaki touched on the topic of *hijrah* as an integral part of jihad in *Constants on the Path of Jihad,* he now needed to provide a more detailed account of this idea and its relevance. The term refers to a period soon after Muhammad began preaching Islam in pagan Mecca, where he was persecuted by local tribes.[65] According to the Koran and *hadith,* God commanded Muhammad to leave Mecca in A.D. 622 in order to avoid assassination. He and his followers who made the journey—referred to as the *muhajiroon*—fled to what is now Medina, and this emigration became known as the *hijrah.* Once in Medina, Muhammad began to oversee jihad campaigns against the tribes.[66] This is one of the single most important moments in the history of Islam, and *hijrah* has been operationalized and given modern relevance by Salafi-jihadists wishing to encourage Muslims to leave their homes and travel to fight jihad. In light of the unprecedented numbers of Muslims around the world who traveled to join the Islamic State after the start of the Syrian Civil War in 2011, the impact and relevance of this idea remains significant.[67]

Writing in 2010, Awlaki offered the following explanation of the importance of *hijrah* and its link to jihad, arguing that it was only after this event that Islam experienced its greatest success in both converting new followers and achieving military victory: "When the Messenger of Allah was giving da'wah [the call to Islam] in Makkah for thirteen years, only a few hundred became Muslim. When he made hijrah to Madinah, within ten years, over a hundred thousand became Muslim. So how come his da'wah in Madinah was much more fruitful than his da'wah in Makkah? That was because he was using a superior form of da'wah in Madinah and that is the da'wah of the sword."[68]

Less than a year earlier, Awlaki gave a short lecture devoted to the topic via audio-link to an Australian Salafi group called Ahl Sunnah wa'al Jama'a (ASWJ). At the time, ASWJ was well known in Australia as the headquarters for the Australian-Lebanese Salafi-jihadist preacher Feiz Mohammad.[69] He is often seen in the same mold as Awlaki due to his command of English and his ability to translate rigid Salafi ideology to Australian Muslim audiences. Awlaki therefore fit neatly into the overall aims of the ASWJ mission, and his lecture at the time was one of the most authoritative and lengthy available on the subject in the English language.

Awlaki's desire to establish the relevance of *hijrah* in Western Islamic belief was clear from the outset as he explained that it was among the most referenced topics in both the Koran and *hadith* and during the early history of Islam was "one of the central issues of being Muslim."[70] During Islam's more dominant phases, the topic faded from the attention of scholars and the wider *ummah*, he argued, due to the lack of any large Muslim population living outside of Islamic land, often referred to as *dar al-kufr*. Unlike modern times, Muslims during the era of the Salaf lived almost exclusively in *dar al-Islam* (Islamic lands). Now, it was important that *hijrah* would be understood by Western Muslims who, surrounded by nonbelievers, were not only losing their *iman* but were missing the opportunity to take part in jihadist conflicts overseas.

While Awlaki was certainly not the first English-speaking jihadist leader to discuss *hijrah*, his appreciation of its significance to a Western audience was arguably the most acute. He recognized that this idea could be used to exert pressure on his audience to act in support of Muslims worldwide by joining the global jihad movement. As part of this, he deployed *hijrah* as a tool to explain and reshape the identity of Western Muslims who felt both angry about the plight of Muslims around the world and ashamed at their own inaction. In this way, the concept was indelibly tied to the principles of *al-wala wal-bara*, helping to define and activate boundaries of identity. Harking back to Islam's incipient phases under Muhammad when he fled to Medina, Awlaki presented the act of *hijrah* itself as a boundary-creating mechanism. It was, he argued, the "distinguishing factor between *iman* and *kufr*" due to the fact that all of those who fled with Muhammad to Medina were no longer able to live as Muslims in Mecca. Only those who were in Medina were "part of the *auliya* [protectors of Allah's words]," while those in Mecca would have to face the consequences on the Day of Judgment.[71]

This effort by Awlaki to breathe new life into *hijrah* was also an integral component of lending contemporary relevance to the foundational years of Islam and transforming ancient concepts into actionable tools for the creation and establishment of a militant social movement. It allowed him yet again to juxtapose the early history of Islam and Muhammad's actions with the modern-day lives of Muslims in the West. Awlaki achieved this by presenting Western Muslims in the same situation as Muhammad before his flight to Medina. In the face of the perceived onslaught upon Islam that was the War on Terror, Muslims had no choice but to act as Muhammad did when faced with similar circumstances. It was not enough for Muslims to simply "feel" part of the *ummah,* they had to back those feelings up with action, either by making *hijrah* themselves or by fighting back through conducting terrorist attacks at home.

Although an important part of Salafi-jihadist ideology more widely, *hijrah* holds a distinct significance in the Western context. For a movement leader addressing an audience who did not live in or near war zones where jihadist militias were engaged in combat and are personally unaffected by the conflict, the challenge of providing a convincing argument to take up arms was particularly acute. When he began to call Muslims to jihad, Awlaki therefore focused much of his attention on explaining the importance of *hijrah,* and the resultant pressure he brought to bear on their identities became a factor in motivating some Western jihadists to travel to jihadist war zones or commit attacks at home.

Al-wala wal-bara: Dividing the West

Awlaki relied on the *al-wala wal-bara* doctrine throughout his career, but rarely did he directly refer to it in his earlier years. This may be because he was aware of its controversial nature in the context of the divisive U.S. Salafi scene at a time when he preached the importance of Muslim unity above all else. However, as his calls for violence and criticism of Muslims who rejected jihad increased, he came to rely upon it as a mechanism to encourage a separation from and hatred and violence toward Western society. Like most other Salafis, Awlaki defined *al-wala wal-bara* as "a creed that a Muslim should have loyalty towards Allah, His Messenger and the believers, and should disavow the disbelievers." While Western influences divided people into "races and ethnicities, tribes and nations," *al-wala wal-bara* reduced this divide to a much simpler and sectarian one between Muslim and non-Muslim. The concept of nation and nationhood was reimagined: "the believers, irrespective of their ethnicities, are one nation and they are separate from the non-believers." This, according to Awlaki, must be adopted as a "central issue" for every Muslim and is vital for the protection of the Islamic *aqidah* and development of a militant collective identity.[72]

Although it constituted "a central element of our military creed," Awlaki was concerned that *al-wala wal-bara* had not received "its fair share of attention" in the West. Western Muslims needed to continue propagating and developing it within their communities if the movement was to prevail. Otherwise, by lacking a proper appreciation of the level of hatred one must have for the *kuffar,* "Allah will not grant us victory."[73] Awlaki took this reasoning to its most violent conclusion, claiming that killing non-Muslim American civilians was not, as some Salafis argue, an act of apostasy because it did not go against the principles of *al-wala wal-bara:* "If a Muslim kills each and every civilian disbeliever on the face of the earth he is still a Muslim and we cannot side with the disbelievers against him."[74]

By encouraging Western Muslims to disavow the ways of their non-Muslim compatriots on an individual and societal level, Awlaki was attempting to further increase the possibility that they would begin to consider Western civilians as a direct threat. This, in turn, could make them more open to conducting attacks against them in Western countries. The dehumanizing aspect of this doctrine can also contribute to a process that the social psychologist Fathali Moghaddam refers to as "social categorization." This allows recruits to perceive non-Muslims as part of an "out-group" whom they can psychologically distance themselves from and simultaneously come to perceive as legitimate targets. This, in turn, helps them to sidestep "inhibitory mechanisms" that usually prevent a person from committing an atrocity.[75]

Awlaki relied on a number of *hadith* and Koranic passages to convey the centrality of this doctrine to Islamic belief, but he focused on Koran 60:1.[76] This verse describes the importance of remaining true to Islam despite the desire of its enemies to force Muslims into disavowing components of their *aqidah*. Awlaki explained that in this verse, "Allah is telling us about the intentions of America . . . of the U.K.," and about cultures and governments that are working to force Muslims "to leave part of the religion."[77]

Current events in the West, especially democratic elections, provided Awlaki an opportunity to demonstrate the proper application of *al-wala wal-bara*. During the 2008 U.S. presidential election he took to his blog to explain why Muslims should not participate and in so doing helped construct a militant collective identity. As he argued, democracy is "a Western system that was founded and developed in the West and today the West, not the Muslims, have full authority and right to tell the world what democracy is and how it should be practiced and implemented. We have our own system of government and likewise it is the Muslims who are going to define it and will not allow non-Muslims to meddle with our religion and teach us what is right from wrong."[78]

By taking part in elections, Muslims risked diluting their identity by bringing about the "breaking down of the psychological barrier that should exist between Muslims and non-Muslims, the erosion of the *aqidah* of *wala* and *bara*."[79] This opened Western Muslims up to "the risk of losing one's religion." Muslims who adopted these values were therefore framed as traitors or "sell-outs." Despite its chief utility as a tool to divide Muslims from non-Muslim influences, *al-wala wal-bara* could also be used to help define intra-Muslim boundaries.

Shortly after the elections, Awlaki complained that "many American Muslims still insisted on voting" and continued "chasing a mirage that somehow the new president [Barack Obama] will improve their lot." He was reminded of the experience of Muslims living in al-Andalus during the fall of Muslim Spain, who despite being oppressed "still had hope that their situation would improve, even after the Catholic monarchs showed them the worst treatment." During that time, he argues, Muslims mistakenly pinned their hopes on the return of the Mahdi to save them, and today Muslim Americans foolishly looked to democracy and the liberal rhetoric of Barack Obama for answers.[80] Like the Muslims of al-Andalus, American Muslims who continued to accept the status quo would gradually lose their identity until Islam as they knew it ceased to exist.

The American system, in his eyes, was misleading American Muslims by continuing to allow them their spiritual practices of prayer and fasting while preventing them from being Muslims "in the full sense of the word." Muslims who support American democracy must realize that their government will never allow them to fully practice Islam because "the issues of Sharia law, Jihad, wala and bara, hudud [sharia-based punishments], khilafah, the Quranic teachings concerning the Jews and Christians, and support of Muslim resistance fighters around the world will not be tolerated."[81] Soon, the spiritual aspects of Islam would also come under attack by an American society emboldened by its government's war on Islam. Here Awlaki reiterated a concern he first expressed during his early series on the life of Muhammad: "American culture will destroy their families. It will deprive their children and grandchildren of their identity."[82] According to this line of argument, no matter what American Muslims do, from taking part in the democratic process to forsaking components of their faith, they will not satisfy the demands of their tyrannical masters, "unless you do one thing: give up your religion."[83]

In a May 2008 lecture given via phone link to a South African Islamic conference, Awlaki coined the phrases "Rand Islam" and "Rand

Muslims" to describe those Muslims who were either led astray or had "sold out" to Western demands. The RAND Corporation, based in Santa Monica, California, had recently published two reports cited by Awlaki as a perfect example of the Western desire to dismantle Islam. Titled "Building Moderate Muslim Networks" and "Civil Democratic Islam," the studies offered a number of basic criteria for what they considered to be moderate Islam.[84] These included a commitment to democracy, a rejection of violence, and support for internationally recognized human rights, including those of religious minorities. Making sure to point out that RAND "is a . . . non-profit organization that provides analysis to the U.S. Department of Defense," Awlaki framed these studies as an attempt to weaken and defang Islam by bringing it in line with secular, liberal values:

> So a Muslim who defends his lands, a Muslim who refuses occupation, a Muslim who wants to live according to Islamic rule, is an extremist. And the moderate Muslim is a Muslim, who invites the U.S. army to come and invade his land, and is happy to follow manmade laws and is a person who has no honor and dignity to defend himself against aggression. This is a moderate Muslim! So from what you see, a moderate Muslim to them, is in reality a non-Muslim! Because according to these four definitions, the definitions that they gave, this is Kufr this is not Islam! So from now on, I am not going to call it a moderate Muslim but I think a more appropriate term would be a "Rand Muslim."[85]

Studies such as those produced by RAND provided yet more evidence of "the active involvement of the U.S. in defining what Islam means today," which has led to "a gradual decline in the standard of *wala* and *bara*."[86] The title of the lecture—"Battle of Hearts and Minds"—was itself an indication of one of the ways in which Awlaki wanted to frame this issue for his audience. Using terminology that was made popular by the Bush administration during the 2003 invasion of Iraq, Awlaki provided his own take on the battle for hearts and minds as a war of ideas that Muslims in the West must fight in order to preserve the tenets of their religion. He went so far as to suggest that Western Muslims "should be more concerned, about what is in the hearts and minds of Muslims rather than what happens on the battlefield!"[87]

The mobilizing effect of the combination of Awlaki's deployment of *hijrah* and *al-wala wal-bara* and the pressure it brought to bear on Muslims in the West to act is well illustrated by the case of Rajib Karim. In late February 2011, Karim, a British Airways employee, was convicted in the United Kingdom for conspiring with Awlaki to assist in orchestrating an attack on an airliner in addition to passing along critical information on airport security measures.[88] Email correspondence in early 2010 with both his Yemen-based brother, Tehzeeb, who was helping him make contact with the preacher, and Awlaki himself provides a rare and valuable insight into the mind of an Awlaki disciple.

Upon reading the messages, the reverence on the part of Rajib and Tehzeeb for the "Sheikh" they regarded as a spiritual leader is beyond doubt. Moreover, their resolve to assist in or carry out an attack in the West was immeasurably strengthened after making direct contact with him. In a message to Awlaki, Tehzeeb described how they both saw him as a legitimate interpreter of God's will: "it fills our heart with happiness to be in direct communication with you. only allah knows what we feel about you. and this is from the honor which allah bestows on those who honor his words and his deen [religion] and its sanctities."[89]

Similarly, Rajib told Awlaki how much "respect and love" he had for him, adding that hearing directly from him was a "blessing from allah" that "gave me hope." Upon offering to take a job as a flight attendant, he informed Awlaki of his concerns about the likelihood that this role would involve taking part in activities that are *haram* (forbidden) in

Islam, such as serving alcohol and non-halal food. Karim placed significant emphasis on gaining religious sanction for his actions, something he believed that Awlaki had the authority to provide. He therefore asked the preacher to provide him with a *daleel* (Islamic scriptural evidence) proving that taking the job was acceptable for a Muslim if undertaken in pursuit of "the jihadi cause."[90]

The email also contained information on what particular elements of Awlaki's message resonated with Rajib, who, unlike his brother, lived in the West. The stark choices of either *hijrah* or jihad offered by Awlaki had an impact on Rajib, as did the strict requirements of *al-wala wal-bara*. He wrote to Awlaki describing his fears of becoming a *munafiq* due to having coexisted peacefully with non-Muslims in Britain for so long and not observing the teachings of loyalty and enmity. He also explained that he was depressed because he was still living in Britain: "I hate myself for not making hijrah and also not being able to do anything here." His intention was never to "make a living here and start enjoying my life in the country," which Awlaki framed as a betrayal of the *ummah;* rather, "from the moment I entered this country my *niyah* [intention] was to do something for the *deen* [religion]."[91]

These feelings of guilt increased "as month after month and then slowly years went by without anything happening," so much so that he felt that his "*iman* was getting affected" and he "started feeling like a real munafiq." He ignored the tenets of *al-wala wal-bara* by "living here away from the company of good brothers and spending a good part of my working day with the kuffar."[92] This is what prompted him to reach out to his spiritual guide and offer his support to the global jihad movement. Rajib could no longer ignore the demands of the militant collective identity and felt he was turning his back on both his religion and his fellow Muslims by living peacefully in the West. Having adopted Awlaki's various frames, he saw violence as the best way to rectify this and fulfill his duties as a "true" Muslim. Awlaki responded to Rajib, encouraging him not to make *hijrah* and instead requesting that he use his position as a staff member at British Airways either to plant a bomb on a plane or to pass on crucial details about new airport security measures.[93]

The email conversation was being monitored by British intelligence, and Karim was arrested in February 2010. He was later convicted and sentenced to thirty years in prison. This case demonstrates yet again that Awlaki was seen as a leadership figure among Western Salafi-jihadists. He had not only created the frames through which Karim and others came to understand their situation as Muslims in the West, but he also identified different opportunities for them to take part in the movement depending on their situations.

Global Jihad and Assassinations in the West

While Awlaki welcomed the "battle of ideas" between the West and Islam, his deployment and framing of *hijrah* and *al-wala wal-bara* served primarily to strengthen his ever-increasing calls for Muslims in the West to take part in violent jihad by exerting pressure on them to act. *Constants on the Path of Jihad* provided the ideological and religious basis for Awlaki's support for global jihad, while "44 Ways to Support Jihad" gave general directives on acting upon these beliefs. All that was needed now was the identification of specific mobilization opportunities for Western Muslims, both at home and abroad.

For those wishing to make *hijrah* and help the *mujahidin* establish an Islamic state, Awlaki gave two contemporary examples of groups that were properly applying the correct methodology at the time: the Afghan Taliban and the Islamic Courts Union (ICU) in Somalia (a precursor to al-Shabaab). Writing on his blog in August 2008, Awlaki argued that both groups demonstrated beyond any doubt that the most successful Islamic movements are those that "reached to power not through elections or debates but through war."[94] The eventual demise of the Taliban and the fall of the ICU did not represent a failure of the jihad methodology but rather a failure on the part of the *ummah*, which did not offer sufficient support through participating in jihad.

He offered a similar motivational frame some months later in a December 2008 post, "Salutations to al-Shabaab in Somalia." Written during a period of relative success for the al-Qaeda–linked Somali militia that had recently emerged from ashes of the defeated ICU, Awlaki presented it as an example of the triumph and effectiveness of violent jihad in establishing the law of Allah: "al-Shabab not only have succeeded in expanding the areas that fall under their rule but they have succeeded in implementing the *sharia* and giving us a living example of how we as Muslims should proceed to change our situation." In a direct attack on democracy, he declared that "the ballot has failed us but the bullet has not."[95]

Jihad in faraway lands, while important, was not Awlaki's primary interest. The doctrine was, according to him, not just a tool for establishing the Islamic state but also served as an act of vengeance against the West that would restore the dignity of the *ummah* and its prophet. The most important example of this is a lecture Awlaki gave in the midst of the Muhammad cartoon controversy in Europe. In May 2008 he used *Paltalk,* an online live audio chat forum popular with English-speaking Salafi-jihadists, to deliver a lecture titled "The Dust Will Never Settle Down." During the course of the talk, he drew on examples from the history of Islam to call for targeted assassinations of people who had insulted the religion.

Awlaki was not the first jihadist to address this issue. Two months prior, Osama bin Laden released an audio through the group's media wing as-Sahab in which he briefly addressed the cartoon controversy. However, while he issued a veiled threat to European nations—"if there is no check on the freedom of your words, then let your hearts be open to the freedom of our actions"—Bin Laden did not provide any discussion of why a violent response would be permissible or legitimate in

Islam.[96] In comparison, Awlaki's lecture represents the most comprehensive effort by a Salafi-jihadist to provide a religious justification for the killing of those deemed to have insulted Muhammad. Today, it remains a popular reference point on the topic for Western jihadists and has been translated into multiple languages.[97]

Awlaki framed the unflattering depictions of Muhammad as another aspect of the ideological war on Islam, one component of which was the defaming and ridiculing of Muslims in wider Western discourse. Publicity for the sermon, which could be found on a number of popular Islamic forums, presented it as a scholar's guidance on how Western Muslims should react to this issue. Listeners were promised that they would receive the required information on "what is the ruling of *Shari'a* on such incidents [insulting the prophet] and how did the *Sahaba* deal with such people and what do our scholars say about them."[98]

Referring to the original fiasco, triggered by the cartoon of Muhammad published in the Danish daily *Jyllands-Posten* in 2005, Awlaki stated that "the Muslim world was on fire." Yet the reaction to the subsequent drawings by Swedish cartoonist Lars Vilks in 2007 was unacceptably lethargic, partly because "our enemies have successfully desensitized us."[99] Unlike the *Sahaba* before them, Western Muslims were not displaying sufficient love and devotion for Muhammad, and this had to change. In their search for answers, he suggested that they again draw inspiration from the early history of Islam: "Let's go back [to the time of the prophet and *Sahaba*] and see how things were then. . . . That is the way we should follow, the way of the *Sahaba*."

Drawing again upon the power of narrative, Awlaki focused on figures from Islamic history who showed their devotion to Muhammad and held them up as examples for Western Muslims to follow. He told the story from a *hadith* found in Sahih Bukhari about Kaab ibn al-Ashraf—a poet and Jewish tribal leader in pre-Islamic Mecca who wrote poems insulting the prophet and lamenting the victory of the Muslims over the tribe of the Quraish in the Battle of Badr—Awlaki informed listeners that Muhammad had sanctioned his murder.[100] One of the *Sahaba*, Muhammad ibn Maslama, volunteered to assassinate al-Ashraf, and Awlaki praised him for his zeal and devotion to Muhammad. But what of modern-day Muslims in the West? "How concerned are you?" he asked, "how concerned are we when it comes to the honor of *Rasool*, when it comes to the honor of Islam, when it comes to the book of Allah? How serious do we take it? . . . We want the spirit of the *Sahaba*."[101]

Awlaki avoided direct incitement to murder here, a feature that characterizes much of his work until the latest stages of his career. However, it is difficult to read this message as anything other than a call to kill those deemed to have ridiculed or insulted Muhammad. This suspicion is further bolstered by Awlaki's reference to (and translation of) a section of a book by Ibn Taymiyya called *As-Saram Al-Maslool Ala Shatim Ar-Rasul* (The Drawn Sword and the One Who Curses the Messenger), which includes an account of Muhammad's justification for violence against those who defame him: "He [al-Ashraf] spoke against me and he defamed me with his poetry. And then he made it clear to the Jews—if any one of you . . . try to defame me through your words, [the sword] will be the way we deal with you. There is nothing between us and you except the sword. There will be no dialogue, there will be no forgiveness, there will be no building of bridges, there will be no attempts of reconciliation, there will only be the sword between me and you."[102]

Awlaki's call for assassinations has influenced a number of attacks in the West against people jihadists have deemed to be defaming or attacking Islam through art, and its reach has also expanded beyond the English-speaking world. In January 2015, more than three years after his death, Awlaki's name emerged in connection with what at the time was France's biggest terrorist attack in decades, when two brothers, Chérif and Saïd Kouachi, stormed the Paris offices of the French satirical magazine *Charlie Hebdo*, killing twelve people. The attack was in response to the publication's regular lampooning of Muhammad in various cartoon strips. In a live interview given by Chérif Kouachi while he was on the run, he asserted that Awlaki had helped coordinate the attack and that it had been planned years earlier.[103] This claim was later backed up in a statement issued by AQAP in which senior official Nasser bin Ali al-Ansi took credit for the attack and referred to Awlaki's involvement.[104] In April 2015, during the trial of Nigerian citizen Lawal Babafemi, who was a member of AQAP and was close with Awlaki, the prosecuting U.S. Attorney at the time, Loretta Lynch, provided further details about Awlaki's direct involvement in the planning of the attack. In a previously sealed court document, she revealed that Chérif "met and trained with Awlaki," who also provided him with $20,000 in cash before sending him back to France.[105]

"The Dust will Never Settle Down" was one of Awlaki's last longform lectures. From 2009 until his death in 2011, his output in English fell into two categories: short and concise audio and video digests of his previous works and articles in a magazine named *Inspire* that he had set up after joining AQAP in 2009. It was in the latter venue that he and a cadre of followers who had joined him in Yemen would begin to formulate and communicate a new strategy for attacking the West.

4

"And Inspire the Believers . . ."

I n October 2017, a car veered off Exhibition Road in West London, mounted the sidewalk, and plowed into a group of pedestrians.[1] The incident was a traffic accident, but in the immediate aftermath the Metropolitan Police felt compelled to announce via Twitter that it "is not being treated as a terror-related incident," even as the British media scrambled to report minute-by-minute developments.[2] This chain of events has been replayed several times in major Western cities over the past decade. No longer can this type of car accident or a random act of violence be reported without at least a mention of or hint toward terrorism. This reflects the profound impact a certain form of jihadist terrorism has had on the Western psyche. Jihadism lingers in the backs of our minds at all times. In this sense, it continues to achieve key strategic aims of any terrorist group, namely injecting a perpetual state of fear among the target population and conveying the message to sympathizers that the movement remains strong. The global jihad movement owes much to Awlaki and some of his most influential followers for their role in creating this situation.

As Anwar al-Awlaki's output became increasingly violent and specific in its choice of targets, he formalized his efforts by joining AQAP in 2009. This allowed him to engage in a more organized strategic effort to implement the methodology he had been preaching for the preceding four years. At the time, the group's focus was regional—even before its official creation in January 2009 as a result of a merger between al-Qaeda's Saudi Arabian and Yemeni branches, its members, in a fragile alliance with various Yemeni tribes, had been involved in a bloody insurgency against the Yemeni state for at least three years.[3] Awlaki's arrival offered the group an unexpected new dimension: the ability to project its activities into the West and in particular into the United States, which, compared to West European nations, had a far less dynamic and active jihadist scene. By the time of Awlaki's death in 2011, AQAP had grown into the most dangerous of all the al-Qaeda franchises involved in plotting international terrorist attacks against the West. This was in large part due to the impact Awlaki had on their propaganda output and international terrorist strategy.

Awlaki's dual contribution is perhaps best encapsulated in the creation of *Inspire* magazine in mid-2010. The English-language online magazine represents the culmination of all of Awlaki's work after his translation of *Constants on the Path of Jihad*. Rather than simply focusing on ideology, however, it was used to cement a new strategy based on his teachings, for which a new term, "open source jihad," had been coined. In creating this publication, he and a close group of loyal followers believed that they were continuing and implementing the work of Salafi-jihadist strategists who came before them. Since the founding of al-Qaeda, these individuals wrote about the necessity to develop effective ways of communicating their ideology and inspiring action. This not only allowed them to instill a shared sense of grievance and injustice within a given target audience but also helped to convince them that change was possible.[4] The most influential of these thinkers, including Mohammed Atef, Abu Hudaifa, and Abu Musab al-Suri, observed that many of history's successful global movements had benefited from the creation of an alternative media apparatus and argued that the Salafi-jihadist movement must follow suit. In order to achieve this, they recommended the creation of units of devoted media specialists who would work in tandem with military operations so as to achieve maximum propaganda impact.

Writing in 1990, Mohammed Atef (also known as Abu Hafs al-Masri), a senior al-Qaeda commander, laid out the basic framework for the movement's media strategy.[5] He recommended a global expansion of recruitment efforts that targeted the entire *ummah* through messaging that offered a clear diagnosis of the problems faced by Muslims together with prognoses for how to respond as well as reasons designed to motivate people to act. In order to achieve a significant level of mobilization in favor of the jihad movement, he believed that it had to elucidate for Muslims "the reasons of this war between the Mujahidin and the idol, as well as the goal of this war." He regarded the success of this messaging as equal to, if not more important than, battlefield victories.[6]

A decade later, in June 2000, Abu Hudaifa, who was a close confidant of bin Laden's, wrote his friend a lengthy letter on this subject. The letter contained many similar arguments to Atef's while also including criticism of what he saw as a failure on the part of the movement to use alternative media to its advantage. Written in the form of a *nasiha* (a sincere criticism to a figure of authority), the text is polite yet stern. His strongest criticism was reserved for the failure to capitalize on the disastrous American military effort in 1993 to capture clan leaders linked to local warlord Muhammad Aidid in Mogadishu, Somalia. Eighteen American soldiers were killed at the hands of an assorted group of militia men supportive of Aidid's claims to the Somali presidency, some of whom Osama bin Laden later claimed were trained by al-Qaeda.[7] Abu Hudaifa wrote that "we did not invest these events politically to serve the jihad program. Most of the people inside [the country] are unaware of the great effort the mujahidin made against the American forces." A properly functioning media network would have used such an event to "motivate and encourage the [Islamic] nation." This, in turn, would have helped followers to overcome the "barrier of fear" preventing them from acting by giving "a live and actual example of the recent experiment in which the mujahidin succeeded in achieving the target and driving the enemy away."[8]

Atef and Abu Hudaifa's ideas for a jihadist media strategy were among the first of their kind. The most extensive work on this, however, was to come in Abu Musab al-Suri's 2004 treatise *The Call of Global Islamic Resistance*. Al-Suri, whose current status is unknown beyond reports in 2009 of his imprisonment in Syria, remains one of the most important strategic thinkers for the global jihad movement, and his work contributed significantly to its strategic direction.[9] Updating and refining the ideas of his predecessors (he reserved special praise for Abu Hafs), he wrote in detail about the importance of jihadi media while also looking beyond the constraints of formal organizations.[10] The struggle against the West was to be executed, according to al-Suri, on a global scale, and the jihad movement required a detailed strategy to pursue this. This was to be centered on using jihadi media to "transform this confrontation into an *Ummah*-wide battle, after the *Ummah* has been ignited by the jihadist elite."[11]

The 1,600-page document called for a radical restructuring of global jihadism toward a popular revolution model. Al-Suri argued that the post-9/11 era was distinctly uncharitable toward organized and hierarchical jihadi groups, believing that in order to survive al-Qaeda had to transform into a diffuse international movement connected mainly through Islamic solidarity and ideology. Accordingly, al-Suri recommended that al-Qaeda increase its efforts to project its ideas and solutions across the globe. By encouraging this new, decentralized version of the group, he hoped to spark the creation of numerous "self-starter" individuals and terrorist cells with no organizational connections to the group. This "school of individual jihad" as he referred to it, was free from the constraints of conventional warfare.[12] It could also effectively

subvert the military superiority of the West on the battlefield while ensuring that members could now avoid the dangers of being arrested
when traveling to epicenters of jihad in Afghanistan, Iraq and
elsewhere.

The jihadi "resistance" could be implemented by small groups or individuals anywhere in the world, and jihadi internet media was to be
the cornerstone of this approach. Building on his predecessors' concept
of small specialist jihadi media units, al-Suri called for the creation of
"clandestine incitement brigades . . . made up of one to three members,
who are well-versed in Shari'ah, politics, and letters and possess media
expertise, knowledge of activism, and expertise in using the Internet
and electronic communication networks."[13] One of the primary utili-
ties of such a group would be to help foment "individual jihad" by providing jihadi media consumers with the requisite ideological, strategic, and operational materials to carry out attacks within their host
nations. Each group would tailor its material based on the region it was
targeting for recruitment, and al-Suri's strategy required an effective
interpreter if it was to work in the West. During the latter stages of his
career, this interpretive responsibility was taken on by Awlaki who,
with the assistance of a group of people who coalesced around him after
he joined AQAP in 2009, began production of *Inspire* under AQAP's al-
Malahim imprint. The editors, led by Awlaki's protégé Samir Khan,
saw their work as a direct extension and realization of al-Suri's vision
and regularly reproduced sections of his book in the pages of the
magazine.[14]

While it received much attention from Western analysts and media
when it was first released, it is often overlooked that *Inspire* was an updated version of *Jihad Recollections,* an online product created by Samir
Khan in 2009 while he was still living in America. According to Jesse
Morton, one of the most prominent American jihadist propagandists
of the time (who was then known by his jihadist *nom de guerre* Younis
Abdullah Muhammad) and a friend of Khan's, he began producing

Jihad Recollections after receiving specific instructions from Awlaki via email to do so.[15] Morton explains that *"Jihad Recollections* was really the precursor to *Inspire,* it uses the same quotes, the same analysis and was one of the first systematic efforts to create high-quality English language jihadist propaganda."[16] This ability to create media that, in terms of quality, was comparable to that produced by mainstream Western outlets was very appealing to their audience, "all these young Western jihadis were like 'wow you guys can compete with the kuffar.'"[17]

Morton, according to his own account, was involved in radicalizing Khan in the early 2000s during meetings Khan attended that were organized by the Islamic Thinkers Society, a Salafi-jihadist group Morton was leading in New York that modeled itself on the British organization, al-Muhajiroun.[18] Morton recalls how, during their initial discussions about creating *Jihad Recollections,* he originally advocated for it to be more text-heavy, but Khan and Awlaki "saw and understood the power of imagery and they definitely got that right."[19] Morton also contributed to *Jihad Recollections,* writing an article for the first issue titled "The Predications of the Conquering of Rome," arguing that al-Qaeda should focus its efforts in Arab nations and avoid terrorist attacks in America.[20] According to Morton, Awlaki was not happy about this, commenting that "he was pissed off because he still thought the priority should be to attack America."[21]

After leaving his home in Charlotte, North Carolina, to join Awlaki in Yemen in the summer of 2009, Khan would soon be joined in his propaganda work by other like-minded individuals whose devotion to Awlaki led them to travel to Yemen and offer him their services. One of the first known cases is that of Vietnamese-born British national Minh Quang Pham, who traveled from the United Kingdom to Yemen in late 2010 with the intention of pledging an oath of allegiance (*bayah*) to Awlaki and AQAP. During his time there, Pham worked closely with Khan to produce a number of issues of *Inspire.* A skilled graphic artist, he was involved in graphic design and image editing.[22]

In a lengthy handwritten statement to the judge in his trial, Pham gave a number of details related to his involvement with Awlaki and Khan, while also expressing regret for his "erroneous judgement." His original intention was "to help fellow Muslims who were hurt by wars or deprived of rights from tyrannical leaders."[23] After a difficult adjustment period when he first moved to England, he converted to Islam in 2004 at the age of 21. The religion offered him a new, stable identity after years of depression and drug use—he was "enlightened by the belief system and the way of life it [Islam] has to offer." His first experience of Islamic activism came when he joined the Tablighi Jamaat, a conservative Islamic movement inspired by Salafism that focuses on *dawah*. While Pham's time with the group was very formative, it seems that his desire to help the cause of Islam was not quite satiated by proselytizing.

Pham's pledge of allegiance to AQAP in January 2011 was made, according to him, out of a desire to be part of "an Islamic army raised to liberate all Muslims countries of injustice + oppression + to restore Islamic territory which was established from the 7th century up-till the Ottoman Islamic rule." Pham began his time with the group as an "assistant artist" for *Inspire*, working under the editorship of Samir Khan for the production of issues four and five of the magazine, but they did not get along. Pham indicated that they disagreed about various "petty" issues and on one occasion had to even be physically separated after an argument about Pham's previous group, the Tablighi Jamaat, which Khan saw as heretical and was "strongly opposed to." Pham eventually left AQAP for the United Kingdom in July 2011, just two months before his former colleagues were both killed by an American drone.[24]

Upon his return, Pham was immediately arrested at Heathrow airport and held until his extradition to the United States in early 2015. Before his trial, he gave a voluntary interview to the FBI in which he revealed that he was involved in more than just propaganda, admitting to his participation in a terrorist bomb plot he had planned with Awlaki.

Pham approached Awlaki in the weeks before his trip back home and "offered to conduct a suicide attack and 'sacrifice himself' on behalf of al-Qaeda upon his return to the United Kingdom." As part of the plot, Awlaki provided Pham with £6,000 and told him to use it to purchase the chemicals needed for the bomb and to rent a house where he could construct it. Awlaki also trained Pham in how to make the bomb, showing him "how to build an explosive device using readily available household chemicals and other materials," while also instructing him to tape metal bolts around the explosive container so as to ensure maximum casualties upon detonation. He instructed Pham to target the arrivals area at Heathrow during times when passengers were arriving from either Israel or the United States.[25] In 2016, Pham pleaded guilty in an American court to a number of terrorism-related charges, including providing material support to AQAP and conspiring to receive military training from the group.[26]

In the months before Pham left Yemen, he and Samir Khan were joined by Nigerian citizen Lawal Olaniyi Babafemi, who traveled from Nigeria to Yemen in January 2011 with the specific intention of joining Awlaki's propaganda team. After meeting an AQAP facilitator in the Abyan governorate, he pledged allegiance to AQAP and adopted the *kunya* Abu Abdullah. While at a safe house, he first met Pham and Khan, who were joined by a British AQAP member named Sami Ali al-Fadli. Together they traveled to Shabwa, where Awlaki was based at the time. Their primary focus was on creating products for *Inspire* magazine, and in its fifth issue Babafemi is even pictured holding an AK-47 next to Khan, Pham, and al-Fadli. Babafemi would later recount how Khan explained to him that the primary purpose of the magazine was to inspire Western, English-speaking Muslims to plan and carry out terrorist attacks in their home countries without any central direction or coordination from al-Qaeda.[27] Among Babafemi's contributions to the magazine was writing pro-jihad rap lyrics, which he hoped would appeal to young Westerners.

Figure 4.1 Image reportedly depicting Samir Khan, Lawal Babafemi, Minh Quang Pham, and Sami Ali al-Fadli in Yemen, 2011 (*Source:* al-Malahim)

Alongside his work for AQAP's media operations team, Babafemi also received weapons training and eventually met Awlaki in a number of one-on-one meetings. In these exchanges, Awlaki stressed the need for the recruitment of more English speakers who could help him reach out to Muslims in the West. He eventually tasked Babafemi with going back to Nigeria to find more people like him to bring to Yemen. After receiving almost $9,000 in cash from another AQAP member, he returned to his home country where he was arrested in August 2011 and turned over to American custody before being charged with providing material support to al-Qaeda. In April 2014, he pleaded guilty and received a prison sentence of twenty-two years.

Under the stewardship of Awlaki, this team of propagandists used *Inspire* to pursue two interrelated goals. The first was to act as an extension of the messaging Awlaki conducted in the years after his translation of *Constants on the Path of Jihad*. It therefore continued to link jihadist ideology and frames with current events, offering swift reactions to issues which concerned Western Muslims. In pursuit of this, numerous articles were written by Awlaki and others in which they provided their view of major global events that likely garnered the interests of their readership. Due to ease of production, an issue of the magazine could be released soon after a major event and thus provide Awlaki with a platform from which to offer an alternative, global jihadist assessment to that provided by Western media.

One of the first global events that Awlaki wrote about was the wave of uprisings in the Middle East that began in Tunisia and then moved to Egypt and several other countries in 2011. In the initial phase, protesters called for more democratic, accountable, and representative government to replace decades of dictatorship. As such, many Western analysts suggested that these developments might be a hammer blow to al-Qaeda and Salafi-jihadist ideology; according to that premise, al-Qaeda had consistently argued that the only way to remove secular Arab dictatorships was through violence, but the youth showed this was not the case. In the view of some, the initial success of what became known as the Arab Spring fatally undermined the goals and methods of the global jihad movement.[28]

A new, positive spin was therefore required. For his part, Awlaki formulated a response to the Arab uprisings designed specifically to appeal to Western Muslims. Referring to comments and analysis claiming that al-Qaeda was now on its heels, he constructed motivational frames that depicted these developments as a win-win situation for the movement. The fall of Ben Ali in Tunisia and Hosni Mubarak in Egypt "brought a change to the collective mind of the *Ummah*" by demonstrating that it was possible to bring down seemingly impervious regimes. This, in turn, helped to break "the barriers of fear in the hearts and minds that the tyrants couldn't be removed." Despite support for these figures from America and the West, then, nothing could stop the "tsunami of change."[29]

Awlaki and the *Inspire* contributors also focused on issues closer to home for Muslims in the West. Drawing inspiration from his 2008 lecture of the same title, the first issue announced the "Dust Will Never Settle Down Campaign." An entire section of the magazine was devoted to discussing the necessity to respond to the Muhammad cartoons with violence, culminating in an article on the subject by Awlaki.[30] It began with a detailed timeline listing various instances where Muhammad was "attacked" and Muslims in Europe responded with violence. The list included the initial controversy sparked by *Jyllands-Posten* and attempts made by Muslims in the West to kill cartoonists such as Lars Vilks and Kurt Westergaard. Here is also found the infamous "hit-list" containing the names of people whom AQAP identified as the main instigators behind the campaign to malign Muhammad, including Salman Rushdie, the Kashmiri Muslim author of *The Satanic Verses,* and outspoken Somali-born author and activist Ayaan Hirsi Ali.

In his accompanying article, Awlaki attempted to subvert Western liberal ideas, couching his justification for killing people who insult Muhammad in terms of individual and collective "rights": "If you have the right to slander the Messenger of Allah we have the right to defend him. If it is part of your freedom of speech to defame Muhammad, it is part of our religion to fight you." As with his lecture on the matter two years earlier, Awlaki framed this controversy as a symptom of the West's war against Islam, writing that the production of the cartoons was part of "a deeply rooted historic hatred for Islam and Muslims. . . . [During the Crusades] it was in the name of Christianity; today it is in the name of Democracy." These cartoonists and satirists were just a symptom of a secular Western political system that was designed with the intention of destroying religion. Attacking this system through any means possible was therefore a necessary act of survival:

> These perpetrators are not operating in a vacuum . . . they are operating within a system that is offering them support and protection. The government, political parties, the police, the intelligence services, blogs, social networks, the media . . . are part of a system within which the defamation of Islam is not only protected but promoted. The main elements in this system are the laws that make this blasphemy legal. Because they are practicing a "right" that is defended by the law, they have the backing of the entire Western political system. This would make the attacking of any Western target legal from an Islamic viewpoint. The entire Western system is staunchly protecting and promoting the defamation of Muhammad and therefore, it is the entire Western system that is at war with Islam. Assassinations, bombings, and acts of arson are all legitimate forms of revenge against a system that relishes the sacrilege of Islam in the name of freedom.[31]

How a Muslim chose to react to this would be a defining component of their identity. Those "patriotic American Muslims" living peacefully in America wrongly believed that they were enjoying the benefits of the "rights" afforded to them, including the freedom of religion. They had either chosen to ignore or were unaware that "this right includes his duty to fight against those who blaspheme his prophet." These attacks on Islam, according to Awlaki, should therefore "serve as a mobilizing factor for Muslims," and help to galvanize support for violent jihad as the only effective and legitimate response. "The medicine" prescribed by Muhammad in the *hadith* is "the execution of those involved. . . . We will fight for him, we will instigate, we will bomb and we will assassinate." Jihad fought in defense of the honor of Muhammad was, according to Awlaki, the "pinnacle of all deeds." The fight for Islam was open to all Muslims and "should not be limited to a particular group of Muslims such as the *mujahidin* but should be the effort of the . . . entire ummah."[32] In this way was the door of action also now opened for those supporters living in the West.

Beyond addressing current events and justifying violent jihad in the West, the second aim of *Inspire* was more novel: to solidify, explain, and facilitate a strategic shift within al-Qaeda toward promoting an individual jihad model for terrorist operations in the West. This approach was influenced in large part by the propaganda of the deed theory developed and adopted by some of the earliest modern terrorists.[33] The basic premise was that terrorist attacks, no matter the scale, are themselves acts of propaganda. Conceptualized by Russian and Italian anarchists during the mid-nineteenth century, it refers to a belief in the didactic power of violence, which is seen as necessary not only to draw attention to a cause but also to inform and educate people about a specific movement in the hope that it will encourage increased recruitment.[34] It has been an important part of almost all terrorist strategies ever since. The Italian revolutionary Carlo Pisacane, one of the early adopters of the approach, described propaganda of the deed most succinctly when he wrote that "ideas result from deeds, not the latter from the former, and the people will not be free when they are educated, but educated when they are free."[35]

Inherently smaller in scale and usually less deadly, the aim of individual, unconnected attacks was not mass-casualty spectaculars like 9/11. While committing major attacks remained the ideal scenario, Awlaki adopted a pragmatic approach, recognizing that the survival of the movement in the West would have to rely upon the communicative power, propaganda value, and motivational nature of acts of terrorist violence. He, like other terrorist leaders before him, believed that violent acts held the potential to fend off and divide the enemies of the movement while inspiring sympathizers to act. Vital to the success of such an endeavor was a strong sense of collective identity, which bound adherents together in the absence of their membership to a formal organization. Awlaki's relied upon his past efforts to construct and promote this identity in the pages of *Inspire*. Readers are encouraged to practice *al-wala wal-bara* and, as part of this, commit attacks in the West to demonstrate their loyalty to Muslims or else make *hijrah* and participate in jihadist formations overseas.

In its first issue, released in June 2010, the editors introduced the term "open source jihad" as the tactical framework Westerners should employ to implement the new strategy. They defined this as "a resource manual for those who loathe the tyrants" which includes "bomb making techniques, security measures, guerrilla tactics, weapons training and all other jihad related activities." The editors claimed that this would be "America's worst nightmare" because it "allows Muslims to train at home instead of risking dangerous travel abroad."[36] For Westerners, jihad was "now at hands reach." This call was accompanied by specific targeting suggestions as well as instructions on how to make bombs. The second issue, for example, suggested attaching butcher blades to the front of a pickup truck, near the headlights so that "the blades strike your targets at the torso level or higher," and driving through large crowds of people.[37]

However, the focus was less on the success of a terrorist operation than it was on the message it sent to both supporters and adversaries. Even when discussing the failed attempt at a large-scale attack by Umar Farouk Abdulmutallab, it was framed as a success in the hope that it would inspire other Western Muslims to follow suit. While the bomb may not have detonated, the young Nigerian convert demonstrated the ability of the *mujahidin* to overcome the vast counterterrorism apparatus of Europe and North America: "He [Abdulmutallab] managed to penetrate all devices, modern advanced technology and security checkpoints in the international airports bravely without fear of death, relying on Allah and defying the great myth of the American and international intelligence, and exposing how fragile they are, bringing their nose to the ground, and making them regret all that they spent on security technology."[38]

More important, Abdulmutallab's act demonstrated the "unity of *aqidah* and brotherhood in Islam" and the power of a shared collective identity based on an ideology that demands violent action. Other Muslims should take encouragement from this act and that of Nidal Hasan, who also received a special mention in the statement as an example of a Western Muslim willing to "stand up and kill all the crusaders by all means available to him." Abdulmutallab's failed attack was presented as an act of propaganda, and the targets of its message were not only Western Muslims. America's leaders were also told that "if our messages can reach you by words, then they wouldn't have travelled by planes. And indeed the message we intended to send you through the plane of the hero Umar al-Faruq . . . is: America will never live in peace until we live its reality in Palestine."[39]

Other failed attacks were given similar treatment. In East London in May 2010, Roshonara Choudhry attempted the murder of her local MP, Stephen Timms, in revenge for his support for the Iraq War in 2003. She later claimed to have been inspired by Awlaki and acted alone.[40] After Choudhry was convicted, the fourth issue of *Inspire* praised her attack and used it as a vehicle to communicate the creed of *al-wala wal-bara*. She proved herself as a "follower of the borderless loyalty." Fusing the jihadist collective identity with *al-wala walbara*, the article explained that, "through her actions, she proved to the world the power of a borderless loyalty: Islam. The ummah . . . [is] waiting to see more people of her caliber. . . . We say to the *kuffar*: the borderless loyalty is a religious sentiment of the people in your midst. As long as the Muslims remain in your focus, you will remain in ours. No matter the security precautions you may take, you cannot kill a borderless idea."[41]

Likewise, after a failed attempt by Awlaki and AQAP in October 2010 to use plastic explosives hidden in printer cartridges to bring down two UPS cargo planes bound for the United States, the magazine offered a positive spin.[42] While the bombs never detonated, the magazine's producers took heed of Abu Hudaifa's suggestions about using media to capitalize on the propaganda value of jihadi operations. In November 2010, they released a "special edition" issue that contained detailed coverage of the plot. According to an unnamed author referred to as "head of operations"—likely Awlaki himself—the attempted bombing had two aims. Firstly, AQAP wanted to demonstrate again that Western governments were failing to keep their citizens safe despite the vast sums of money they were spending on security. Related to this, the second aim was to "hemorrhage" Western economies by forcing them to spend additional billions on counterterrorism and security, which would now also have to include the economically significant international cargo industry.[43] As part of this propaganda effort, the magazine made much of the low cost of the operation, which was nonetheless able to cause a chink in the armor of multi-billion-dollar counterterrorism strategies. The front cover of the online magazine was also emblazoned with the figure "$4,200," referring to the apparent cost of the attack, a negligible sum when compared to the money spent by Western governments in response.[44]

This focus on propaganda impact over the size and success of an attack was also evident in Awlaki's video output during this time. In March 2010, while attempting to mine a propaganda advantage from the aftermath of Abdulmutallab's failed Christmas Day bombing in 2009 and Nidal Hasan's Fort Hood shooting, which had taken place a few weeks earlier, Awlaki released two short audio lectures. In the first, he suggested that the attacks targeted two separate audiences: wider American society and American Muslims. The actions of Abdulmutallab and Hasan demonstrated to Americans that "they are paying the price" for the actions of their governments. Whereas they once "enjoyed the blessings of security and peace," today, despite all the money and effort their country spends on security, "you are still unsafe, even in the holiest and most sacred days to you: Christmas day." Similar to the framing of the failed printer cartridge bombings, Abdulmutallab's attack was presented as a success because he "succeeded in breaking through the security systems that have cost the U.S. government alone over $40 billion since 9/11." This type of messaging, aimed at the American people about the inevitable, divinely ordained victory of their enemy, is designed to wear down and eventually break their spirit. "America cannot, and will not, win," Awlaki explained, "the tables have turned and there's no rolling back of the world-wide jihad movement."[45]

The American government was so alarmed at the growth of the movement that, according to him, it was attempting to cover up the extent of the threat "in order to cushion the reaction of the American public." Awlaki pointed out that, at the time of the attack, American officials did not release the details of his email exchanges with Nidal Hasan and intentionally downplayed the significance of the Christmas Day bombing. Shortly after the attack, President Obama urged the public to avoid "jumping to conclusions" about the motives of the perpetrators.[46] As Awlaki was likely aware, political rivals of the president and sections of the American media had been criticizing the Obama administration for precisely this tendency.[47] However, these efforts failed to dampen the propaganda power of the attacks and, unlike the Americans, "we are transparent and open in proclaiming our message to the world: our objective is to bring Islam back to life, we seek to remove the tyrannical and parasitical rulers of the Muslim world and replace them with men of God."[48]

For an American Muslim audience, the attacks carried a message centered on encouraging mobilization. Abdulmutallab and Hasan demonstrated that, no matter the obstacles in place, it was possible to achieve the goals of the movement if one had the sincere intention to help one's fellow Muslims. In addition, these attacks demonstrated the correct way to respond to the "ominous clouds gathering in your horizon." In a message that was reminiscent of the warning he issued to his congregants in Virginia nine years earlier during his "War on Terror" sermon, Awlaki claimed that America was turning against its Muslims. They must not longer "be deceived by the promises of preserving your rights from a government that is right now killing your own brothers and sisters."[49]

To further strengthen the emotional appeal of his claim, Awlaki also told a story about himself that he hoped would resonate with his followers. It followed the standard narrative arc of a hero who faces injustice and is eventually forced into violence after exhausting all other options. Referring to his own days as an activist Salafi in America, Awlaki explained how he came to the realization that "nonviolent Islamic activism" was ineffective: "I could not reconcile between living in the U.S. and being Muslim, and I eventually came to the conclusion that jihad against America is binding upon myself, just as it is binding on every other able Muslim." It was now unacceptable for a Muslim to live in America without taking action, either by making *hijrah* or following the examples of Hasan and Abdulmutallab. The pressure Awlaki exerted on American Muslims to fulfill the requirements of their collective identity and practice jihad and *al-wala wal-bara* was only increased by these attacks. By remaining in the United States without carrying out an act of jihad, Muslims were *de facto* pledging their loyalty to an American government that is leading the *kuffar* in the war on Islam while also implementing man-made law: "How can your conscience allow you to live in peaceful co-existence with the nation that is responsible for the tyranny and crimes committed against your own brothers and sisters? How can you have your loyalty to a government that is leading the war against Islam and Muslims?"[50]

Days later, another related audio lecture appeared on jihadist internet forums and YouTube. Though only a few minutes long, it carried a

similar set of messages while also using language about the movement that would be instantly recognizable to anyone who followed
Western media reporting on terrorism. Using the now-familiar term
to describe the phenomena of Western Muslims participating in
jihad, Awlaki pointed to attacks and plots by Muslims in the West demonstrating that "jihad is not being imported but is being homegrown."
Despite the efforts of the most powerful nations in the world, the
jihad movement continued to flourish, as "the two capitals of the
war against Islam, Washington D.C. and London have also become
the centers of Western Jihad." He also included a sentence that he
knew would delight headline writers throughout the English-speaking
world: "Jihad is becoming as American as apple pie and as British as
afternoon tea."[51]

Some months earlier, a case of homegrown radicalization caught the
attention of the media due to the apparently unexpected form the
plotter took. Colleen LaRose, a white American female convert to
Islam, was arrested after her plot to kill Swedish cartoonist Lars Vilks
was uncovered by American investigators.[52] Before a recent surge in
research and analysis on female jihadists, spurred to some extent by
the flow of Western women to the Islamic state since 2011, female involvement in jihadism was largely seen as a novelty.[53] Dubbed "Jihad
Jane" by the press, Awlaki reveled in the propaganda value of her case:
a "blond, blue eyed, small framed, middle-aged female" pursuing jihad
perfectly demonstrated the movement's transcendent qualities and
widespread appeal. Her desire to protect the honor of Islam by targeting
someone who had produced insulting images of Muhammad made her
an even more compelling example for others to follow. Comparing her
actions to the killing of Kaab ibn al-Ashraf, which was "the most famous of all special operations carried out during the lifetime of the
Messenger," Awlaki urged that "even if we fail in the attempt," it was
the idea behind the act itself and the message it conveyed to the West
that was more important. Referring to both LaRose and the case of

Muhammad Geele, who attempted the murder of Danish cartoonist Kurt Westergaard on New Year's Day 2010,[54] he proclaimed that: "The West will come to realize that when the honor of the Messenger of Allah is at stake, the dust will never settle down." He referred again to the 2003 Rumsfeld memo, as he did in his translation of *Constants on the Path of Jihad,* to establish that the *mujahidin* have repeatedly stymied the best efforts of a superpower to stop them. The Americans had come to the realization that there was a group of Muslims (*al-taifa al-mansura*) whose victory was divinely ordained. There was no stopping them, and no amount of "RAND Muslims . . . would be able to block the light of the truth from reaching the hearts of those courageous brothers and sisters."[55]

What is most notable about the plots or attacks that were triumphantly cited in *Inspire* is that none of them succeeded in the immediate objective of killing their targets. Their value was not, however, based on their operational success but rather their propaganda impact; acts of violence in the name of global jihad, it was hoped, would have force-multiplying effects. They carried a message that was meant as both a morale booster and inspiration for Western jihadists who may have begun to lose hope in the global jihad project. They also served as a warning for the enemies of Islam who, despite their best efforts, were unable to stop the *mujahidin* from planning attacks.

The popularity and perceived success of this strategy was also eventually recognized by the leadership of al-Qaeda, which also endorsed it, albeit grudgingly. The older generation of leaders, including Bin Laden and Zawahiri, still placed great value in sophisticated terrorist spectaculars that achieved high casualty numbers. They regarded the indiscriminate and low-tech lone-actor approach as a defilement of the noble methods of the elite jihadist vanguard represented by al-Qaeda. In a number of letters recovered in bin Laden's Abbottabad hideout after his assassination in May 2011, the al-Qaeda leader expressed his concern about the unrestrained and apparently disorganized nature of the type of attacks called for by Awlaki. He feared that they would not only serve to cheapen the nature of the movement but also backfire due to the likelihood that Muslims may end up being victims of such random attacks, leading to a loss of support from within the *ummah*.[56]

Another concern brought up by Bin Laden related to *aqd al-aman,* or the covenant of security. An ideological sticking point for more traditional jihadists, this refers to a belief that when they accept citizenship or a visa from a non-Muslim country, a Muslim enters into a contract whereby they have taken an oath before God not to harm the nation in question.[57] If an American citizen follows the instructions in *Inspire* and conducts an attack inside America, they could be acting in breach of an agreement with God himself. This issue was addressed by Awlaki in the fourth issue of *Inspire,* in which he provided a ruling that dismissed this obstacle to fighting jihad, arguing that Western nations are at war with Islam and can be classified *dar al-harb* (land of war) rather than *dar al-ahd* (land of covenant). As such, "Muslims are not bound by the covenants of citizenship and visa that exist between them and nations of *dār al-ḥarb*."[58]

This was not a view shared by Bin Laden, however, who apparently continued to respect this notion until his death. In a letter written to senior al-Qaeda member Attiya al-Libi, he noted the case of Faisal Shahzad, a naturalized American citizen who attempted to detonate a bomb in Times Square in May 2010 after being inspired by Awlaki's work.[59] Bin Laden closely followed the ensuing court case and noticed that Shahzad claimed to have lied when he took his oath before receiving his American citizenship. Bin Laden criticized this, writing that "it is not permissible in Islam to betray trust and break a covenant . . . getting the American citizenship requires taking an oath to not harm America." He was concerned that such an approach would tarnish the reputation of the movement, warning that "we do not want *al-Mujahidin* to be accused of breaking a covenant."[60]

It seems, however, that other leadership figures began to adopt Awlaki's approach to attacking the West. In mid-2011 as-Sahab, the official al-Qaeda media outlet, released a video featuring Awlaki and a number of leading al-Qaeda members and respected jihadist scholars including Ayman al-Zawahiri, Abu Yahya al-Libi, and Attiya al-Libi, all of whom were shown endorsing individual jihad in the West. Attiya al-Libi, the recipient of bin Laden's letter urging that the movement adhere to the covenant of security, specifically rejected that it could be applied in the West today: "the opinion that we follow is that the visa is not considered an agreement of security." In addition, he claimed that even if one were to accept the existence of such an agreement, "it can be broken if the disbelievers commit aggression against Islam and Muslims."[61]

The video also depicts a variety of other jihadist leadership figures presenting ideological and tactical justifications for Western Muslims to take up arms against their home countries on their own, with no organizational support or religious sanction. While also providing the usual claims centered around a global war on Islam lead by America, the video is mainly concerned with providing possible solutions to this problem and offering a motivation for Western Muslims to participate in the movement. Religious verses are used to justify the individual jihad approach, and the title of the video is itself a translation of a verse in Koran 4:84: "So fight in the cause of Allah, you are not held responsible except for yourself. And encourage the believers [to join you] that perhaps Allah will restrain the [military] might of those who disbelieve." In the video, the narrator explains that in response to this global aggression, Muslims in the West must "pursue all means approved by the Islamic law to put an end to this barbaric aggression that knows no limit and is not confined to a particular location. . . . When the *mujahidin* call on Muslims, all Muslims, each one according to his ability and capacity, to engage in an open war against these countries that declared war on Muslims, they must know that this is a legitimate demand."[62]

Individual jihad is described by al-Qaeda ideologue Abu Yahya al-Libi in the video as "one person or a small group of *mujahidin* carrying out a military operation according to the limits of the *Sharia* to harm the enemy and to encourage the Muslims in accordance with the circumstances." Adding an Islamic historical perspective to such acts of violence in the West, he contends that, "this is not new or an innovated action. . . . Individual jihad was performed at the time of the Prophet in a number of operations and some of the heroes of the companions of the Prophet performed it too following the invitation of the Prophet."[63]

The adoption of Awlaki's approach by members of the core al-Qaeda leadership via the as-Sahab media organ suggests that he had more influence over the thinking of the group than previously thought. That this happened despite bin Laden's views on preserving the covenant of security and maintaining operational control of attacks is a testament to Awlaki's growing influence at the time. Taken together with AQAP leader Nasir al-Wuhaishi's letter to Bin Laden requesting that Awlaki be made head of AQAP (which bin Laden rejected), there is reason to believe that Awlaki gained a significant amount of respect among senior members of the group. Had he not been killed soon after, it is possible that Awlaki's reputation would have continued to grow in the eyes of the jihadi elite, earning him further seniority within the al-Qaeda leadership.

This official endorsement from al-Qaeda also represents the apex of Awlaki's career, which was to be cut short just three months later. His journey from popular mainstream preacher to leading jihadist ideologue and strategist, while complex and containing many unanswered questions, is one best defined by circumstance, context, and a fluid ideology. Despite the changes he underwent, his diagnostic framing remained largely consistent. From his earliest works until his final utterances, the problem Muslims faced were presented as the product of a multifaceted war-on-Islam conspiracy led by America. As circumstances changed, particularly after 9/11, so did Awlaki's views on how to solve the problems of the *ummah*. Muslim-majority countries such as Afghanistan and Iraq became the targets of military operations while Western Muslims faced increased scrutiny and new laws designed to fight domestic terrorism. Apart from governments, wider Western society and culture, in his view, became increasingly hostile to Islam. Its art was used to defame the prophet, while its media was little more than an anti-Muslim propaganda organ, pumping out misinformation and lies aimed at turning the population against Islam. The entire West had become openly hostile to Muslims, and the faithful were foolish to ignore the warning signs.

This elicited a change in Awlaki's prognostic framing. His earlier sermons, influenced by activist Salafism, called upon Western Muslims to put aside their minor differences and join together to push back against the tide of Islamophobia. This, in his view at the time, was to be done through participating in politically active Islamic organizations that used nonviolent means to contest the state. In order to protect their faith, he also urged Muslims to develop a strong Islamic identity through religious education focused on the early history of Islam. After concluding that nonviolent activism was insufficient, he argued that his audience must follow suit by adopting more radical versions of the Salafi doctrines than he had been pushing. Jihad, initially presented as a noble struggle conducted by the Salaf or, in modern times, an endeavor limited to defending Muslim lands, was now a vengeful global project with few rules of engagement. Western civilians, deemed to be complicit in the war on Islam, became legitimate targets and could be pursued and killed anywhere in the world.

Similarly, his deployment *al-wala wal-bara* began as a tool to protect Western Muslim's Islamic identity from Western secular culture. By 2005, it had evolved into a justification for murder. It was no longer enough for Muslims to separate and define themselves against their non-Muslim neighbors. By exploiting their preexisting fears about a rise in anti-Muslim sentiment, Awlaki encouraged them to develop a deep-seated hatred for non-Muslims that ultimately had to manifest itself into acts of extreme violence. Awlaki saw this use of *al-wala wal-bara* to create in-groups and out-groups, an important component of the recruitment efforts of a variety of extremist groups, as an important first step toward encouraging mobilization.

Hijrah, meanwhile, was only introduced in detail during the latter stages of Awlaki's career. It complemented his evolving presentation of *al-wala wal-bara* by further exploiting the identity crisis that some Western Muslims were collectively undergoing and exerting pressure on them to choose an identity and then act upon it. As their countries supposedly turned against Muslims, Awlaki portrayed Western Muslims as involved in a tug-of-war between their Western and Muslim identities. While *al-wala wal-bara* defined the divisions, *hijrah* offered two stark choices: Leave the hostile West or stay and fight back. Muslims who remained in the West and sat on the fence were living in limbo (or, as he called it, a "gray area"); he framed their actions as a betrayal of the *ummah* and their duties to God. By adding a sense of shame to the pressure his audience already felt, he hoped to push many of them to act.

The form this fight-back could take went beyond physical, violent acts. Unlike other Western jihadist preachers, Awlaki paid specific attention to the importance of low-risk activism by offering a variety of prognostic frames related to jihad that did not involve fighting or risking one's life. Works such as "44 Ways to Support jihad" highlighted the myriad actions through which one could become involved in the movement at the ground floor. He hoped that this would spark a gradual progression toward more high-risk ventures, the pinnacle of which was jihad in the form of terrorist attacks in the West.

Awlaki's motivational framing efforts varied. Like other ideologues, he explained the promises of the afterlife in heaven for those who took part, and in this way differed little from others. Similarly, he spoke of the collective benefits reaped for the *ummah* by taking part in violent action. It was in his appreciation of the power of violence, however, where Awlaki made his biggest motivational contribution. At a time when al-Qaeda was still hoping to replicate its achievements on 9/11, he had a different mission, which he rapidly convinced much of the al-Qaeda leadership to adopt. Through calling for individual attacks with no centralized organization, he helped to increase the amount of violent jihadist activity in the West, albeit while also reducing the scale and complexity of the attacks themselves. He did not perceive this to be a significant concern, however, because he framed any attack carried out by a Western Muslim in a Western country as evidence of the power and eventual success of the movement. Like terrorist strategists of the past, he recognized the motivational and propagandistic power of the violent act itself. Awlaki believed that such attacks, no matter the scale or success, would have a self-multiplying effect. Similar to the "contagion" phenomenon seen with mass shootings, he hoped that as more attacks were carried out, more jihadist sympathizers would be inspired to follow suit.[64]

Awlaki pursued a variety of frame alignment strategies that ensured that his arguments would resonate with his target audience. His intimate knowledge of what issues mattered to them allowed him to provide urgency and relevance to the global jihad project. He would therefore link his frames to touchstone events concerning Muslims in the West in order to prove the war-on-Islam conspiracy as well as to provide the impetus to fight against it. While this perception was often isolated to the foreign entanglements of Western militaries in Muslim-majority countries, Awlaki sought to make this idea more urgent and personal for his audience by providing examples of its domestic, often ideological, components.

The salience of these frames was also reliant upon Awlaki's long-standing reputation as a respected Islamic scholar. Without this authority, his messaging would have had much less of an impact. Part of the reason for his popularity, a trait that set him apart from other Salafis in the West, was his style of Islamic teaching, which relied heavily upon *sira.* The *sira* method used storytelling to help create a narrative that was deeply embedded in Islamic history and had recently been expanded to include the activities of Western Muslims. Pivotal, and often violent, periods of Islamic history such as the *hijrah,* which involved the religion's most respected figures, were woven into the modern world and the experiences and actions of those who took up arms. Muslims who acted as their predecessors had in the face of adversity embodied the finest generation of believers. The religious storytelling element of this approach further contributed to the pull of Awlaki's message, adding an emotional layer that helped to create agency, define identity, and motivate his followers to act.

Awlaki may not have been the first English-speaking jihadist ideologue to appeal to Western Muslims by framing Salafi-jihadist ideology to appeal to their interests and needs. However, his contributions to the global jihad movement's efforts in the West outstrip those of any of his peers. The widespread respect and devotion he commanded during his early years, exemplified by the senior posts he held at American Islamic institutions, placed him in a unique position compared to other jihadist preachers in the English-speaking world. This meant that his pronouncements carried more weight and, at least when he first began openly calling for jihad, could not be immediately dismissed as the dangerous rantings of a violent preacher, a fact that ensured that he would be able to reach a wider audience.

While much of his ideological work was built around ideas that had previously been formulated by Islamist and Salafi-jihadist scholars and activists, Awlaki also made his own ideological contributions. Most notably, he was the first to provide an in-depth discussion and a religious justification for killing those deemed to have defamed Islam. In addition, his unmistakable strategic contribution continues to influence jihadist activity in the West today. The notion of the "inspired" single-actor attack, which he helped to codify, is now commonplace and is one of the preferred methods pursued by jihadists in Europe and America.[65]

The full impact of Awlaki's contribution to the radicalization and mobilization of Western jihadists is difficult to quantify fully. As previously mentioned, multiple studies have shown that he was a valuable resource for numerous jihadist plotters and attackers in America and Europe. However, precisely how and why he impacted and influenced them has received little attention. As with his own radicalization, the pathways of his followers are the result of a confluence of factors, some identifiable, others less tangible. Awlaki's contribution was likely based upon his ability to appeal to a generation of Western Muslims whose worldview had been so decisively altered by the events of the "War on Terror" era. The people he influenced the most often came across his teachings during turning points in their lives (what the literature refers to as "cognitive openings"[66]), often brought on by a mixture of personal experiences and global events. Their subsequent search for answers was helped along and influenced by Awlaki's outreach. In most cases this connection was indirect and based solely on the consumption of his output. In other situations, Awlaki was able to influence followers through direct contact, either in person or via the internet.

PART TWO

AWLAKI'S DISCIPLES

5

Umar Farouk Abdulmutallab

IN CHRISTMAS DAY 2009, a young, affluent, Western-educated Muslim from Nigeria attempted to detonate a sophisticated explosive device hidden in his underwear on Northwest Airlines Flight 253 over Detroit. The detonation failed, but the event came as a shock to the citizens of the United States—the first jihadist attack on domestic soil during the Obama presidency. Abdulmutallab had been sent on this mission by Anwar al-Awlaki, who by this time was a senior member of AQAP, after initially traveling to Yemen to find the preacher and join the global jihad movement.

Abdulmutallab's introduction to Salafism and political Islam did not begin with Awlaki. His own personal testimonies, which amount to a series of online postings written between 2005 and 2007, reveal a young man who converted to a rigid, yet initially apolitical, version of Salafism. However, these postings reflect the start of a dramatic journey that was born of a web of influences. This chapter will begin with an analysis of these postings, which paint a picture of a strictly religious young man who was concerned with observing the minutiae of Islam and ensuring that he adopted the what he perceived to be the correct Salafi creed.

In the few months after his early internet writings, Abdulmutallab enrolled in a Mechanical Engineering and Business Finance course at University College London (UCL). Already consumed with Salafist religiosity, he encountered a febrile atmosphere created in part by the very active British Islamist milieu that in previous years had embraced Awlaki. He swiftly injected himself into this world after joining the UCL Islamic Society, becoming that group's president before the end of his first year. Abdulmutallab arrived in London during one of the most difficult periods in the history of Islam in Britain; the Iraq War was in full swing, and the July 7, 2005, al-Qaeda attacks contributed to an atmosphere of tension and fear. There was now an increased negative focus in the media and policy circles on young British Muslims and as a result many began to feel persecuted and increasingly alienated from their government and, to a lesser extent, their own society.[1] The organizations and institutions with which Abdulmutallab interacted as a member of the UCL Islamic Society stoked these tensions and promulgated various war-on-Islam frames. At the same time, his intensely literalist yet politically impassive Salafism would soon become more receptive to the activist Islam of the UCL Islamic Society and the wider British Islamist milieu. He would later make a further jump to jihadism. It is therefore important to provide a brief overview and analysis of the milieu that may have inadvertently influenced this change in Abdulmutallab's interpretation of his religion and the framework it provided for responding to the war on Islam.

Although Awlaki had just left the United Kingdom when Abdulmutallab arrived at UCL, his work had a significant impact on British Islamists and the wider Muslim population; in interviews after his arrest, Abdulmutallab stated that the preacher's work was followed by "almost all" of the members of the UCL Islamic Society.[2] Despite the increasingly violent content of his output, Awlaki continued to be sponsored and promoted by the milieu with which Abdulmutallab had become associated.[3] Thus, the end of this chapter will demonstrate precisely how Awlaki came to shape the violent synergy of theory and practice that would be reaped on Christmas Day 2009. It will do so by relying largely on court documents and a series of interviews Abdulmutallab gave to the FBI after his arrest.

Online Writings

In order to understand how Abdulmutallab arrived at this stage, it is necessary to go back a few years to his time as a zealous, yet nonviolent and apolitical, Salafi student in Togo and then Britain and analyze his extensive postings on Islamic forums. Between January 2005 and September 2007, Abdulmutallab regularly contributed to an online Islamic forum, www.gawaher.com, under the moniker "Farouk1986."[4] This period saw his formative journey from the British School of Lomé, Togo, to a survey of Arabic Studies in Sana'a, Yemen, to his presidency of the Islamic Society of the University College London. His comments, which usually offered advice to other forum members but occasionally aired his own personal dilemmas, covered topics ranging from theology and sex to politics and soccer. A careful collective reading of this remarkable stream of consciousness takes us inside the mind of a young man on the path to extremism and violence.

On February 20, 2005, an eighteen-year-old Abdulmutallab responded to a topic on "fantasies": "Alright, I won't go into too much detail about my fantasy, but basically they are *jihad* fantasies. I imagine how the great *jihad* will take place, how the Muslims will win *insha'Allah* [God willing] and rule the whole world, and establish the greatest empire once again!!!"[5] Another topic found Abdulmutallab posting information about his native Nigeria: "So here it is Nigeria. The Muslim Nation. It seems to me that Islam's rise back to power will come from the roots of Nigeria."[6] Elsewhere he argued that "killing is only permitted in *jihad,* retaliation by *Sharia* for murder, etc." and called on Allah to

"unite us all Muslims and give us victory over those who do not believe."[7] On Western foreign policy, Abdulmutallab wrote of the divine
torment that awaited U.S. President George W. Bush and "all the people
who oppress the Muslims" for "invading Muslim lands and killing my
Muslim brothers and sisters."[8]

One of the most striking aspects of Abdulmutallab's writings is how
little such themes featured during his initial involvement online.
Rather, his discourse was dominated by a social, even civilizational, discontent of a notably apolitical kind. In one of his earliest postings, Abdulmutallab provided a monologue in which he appealed to fellow
Muslims for advice on "several dilemmas I want to get out of and [have]
made me lonely."[9] The lament, which dates from his days at the British
School of Lomé, is worth reproducing:

> I have no friend. Not because I do not socialise, etc but because
> either people do not want to get too close to me as they go par-
> tying and stuff while I don't, or they are bad people who be-
> friend me and influence me to do bad things. Hence I am in a
> situation where I do not have a friend, I have no one to speak
> to, no one to consult, no one to support me and I feel depressed
> and lonely.
>
> And then I think this loneliness leads me to other problems.
> As I get lonely, the natural sexual drive awakens and I struggle
> to control it, sometimes leading to minor sinful activities like
> not lowering the gaze. . . .
>
> The last thing I want to talk about is my dilemma between
> liberalism and extremism. The Prophet said religion is easy and
> anyone who tries to overburden themselves will find it hard and
> will not be able to continue. So anytime I relax, I deviate some-
> times and then when I strive hard, I get tired of what I am doing
> i.e. memorising the Quran, etc. How should one put the balance
> right?[10]

Loneliness and sexual frustration are a regular feature of Abdulmu-tallab's writings, both of which he ascribed to the lack of "good Muslims" in Muslim and non-Muslim countries. In May 2005 he debated whether to attend his school prom, only to conclude: "I think it's *haram*. Allah says 'Do not come near *zinah* [temptation]' . . . there's also the extravagance in spending for the prom, drinking usually takes place, music that excites evil desires."[11] He was dismissive of what he saw as a corrupt and debased Western culture centered on "winning girlfriends."[12] For Abdulmutallab, "the biggest obstacle . . . is the *kafir*-imposed school system. These guys are just controlling us around anyhow. We ought to have our own systems that will make our *ummah* do things according to *Quran* and *Sunnah*."[13] He urged his fellow forum users to restrict their activities to the "Islamically good" and "hang around with good Muslims, and students who enjoy studying."[14] All this was set against a strong fixation with the details of religious ritual. In language peppered with classical Arabic terms, Abdulmutallab advised a strict approach to prayer, and from January 2005 he also claimed to be in the process of memorizing the Quran.[15]

On the whole, Abdulmutallab's early musings convey a religious and social outlook strongly analogous to forms of quietist Salafism. There was no evidence yet of specific activist or militant zeal for the creation of an Islamic State or focus on the primacy of jihad. Rather, he emphasized a narrow and socially conservative view of Islam with more interest in *ummah* consciousness and the personal implementation of *sharia* than the political program of Islamist ideology. Above all, he was concerned with the self—religiosity rather than religion—and hence fixated on personal faith (*iman*), dress, speech, and ritual.

This interpretation would seem to be reinforced by the religious scholars and institutions mentioned by Abdulmutallab. He was much taken by the Wahhabi imams of the Grand Mosque in Mecca and singled out the Quranic recitations of Sheikh Saud al-Shuraim and Sheikh Abdul Rahman al-Sudais for special praise.[16] In London, his favored place of worship was the Regent's Park Mosque, which itself was closely linked to and partly funded by the Saudi royal family.[17]

This religious austerity characterizes much of his reflections from the outset; an increasingly strict and literalist approach is evident across his digital footprint. For instance, in his earliest postings, Abdulmutallab discussed soccer with great interest.[18] Yet within days he began to voice doubts: "To be honest football and Islam. . . . they don't blend very well. It's a pity."[19] In the same month he explained that he had stopped wearing clothes by French Connection U.K., because the logo (*fcuk*) alludes to a "foul word."[20] By November 15, 2005, Abdulmutallab, now enrolled at UCL, had definitively turned against soccer: "Let's save our honor and religion and try to stay away from football and do sporting activities that are more Islamically beneficial . . . running, paintball, archery (or any other sport of the like that teaches [how to] target and aim)."[21] Musical instruments were also now considered *haram* and a waste of time.[22]

In December 2005, Abdulmutallab described a sudden crisis over the consumption of non-halal meat, seemingly brought about by a visit from his less observant parents. Appealing for advice from his peers, he explained: "My parents are of the view [that] as foreigners, we are allowed to say *bismallah* [in the name of God] and eat any meat. It occurred to me [that] I should not be eating with my parents as they use meat I consider *haram*." As this was of great concern, Abdulmutallab implored his fellow forum members to "please respond as quickly as possible as my tactic has been to eat outside and not at home 'till I get an answer."[23]

Following his arrival at UCL in September 2005, Abdulmutallab's discourse began to take on a more political tone. There is reason to suspect that this is related to the milieu in which he now found himself, while his first trip to Yemen in the months immediately previous may also have also been a factor. In February 2006, Abdulmutallab wrote at length about the benefits of antiwar demonstrations, arguing that "recruitment into the British Army has hit an all-time low" and "the

British and American governments will at least now hesitate, and not hasten to go to war with Syria or Iran."[24]

In March 2006 the forum discussed *The Road to Guantanamo,* a British film telling the story of the "Tipton Three," three British men who were apprehended in Afghanistan and then held at Guantanamo Bay for three years. When a member questioned the film's version of events, Abdulmutallab referred him to a UCL Islamic Society website containing an interview with Yvonne Ridley, the British journalist and prominent antiwar activist who frequently voiced support for the Taliban and Hamas.[25] Pointing to Ridley's experiences as a captive of the Taliban, he noted "how humane she was treated relative to Guantanamo detainees."[26]

The same month, Abdulmutallab stopped posting on the forum. He resurfaced in January 2007 but offered only a handful of minor contributions. One can only speculate as to the causes of this, but it seems likely that by this time his involvement in the UCL Islamic Society had taken him to a significantly more activist level. His penultimate posting, on January 26, 2007, was a promotion for a major event being held by his UCL Islamic Society, the "War on Terror Week." He wrote of "the death of thousands of innocent lives" and "thousands more detained illegally without trial or judgment."[27] Abdulmutallab was no longer busying himself with online discussions about minor issues of *fiqh.* Salafi Islam was now not only used to explain every aspect of his own life but was also tied in closely with how he began to comprehend the world around him. As he saw it, the situation called for more than just talk—now action was needed.

Abdulmutallab and the British Islamist Milieu

Unlike the two other cases studied in this book, Abdulmutallab lived in a country that at the time had a thriving and influential Islamist scene.[28] Through an analysis of his involvement with various activist

Islamist organizations and adoption of Islamist frames, we can see how his preexisting Salafism was injected with an Islamist influence that was to have an impact on the path his life would take. Indeed, it appears that it was Awlaki's work that helped to inspire this change. A reconstruction of the Islamist milieu in which Abdulmutallab found himself as a young student in London is therefore an important part of understanding how he became a Salafi-jihadist. He arrived on this scene in September 2005 during a storm of Islamist activity in England. Events and campaigns organized by Muslim Brotherhood and Jamaat-e-Islami–inspired groups were taking place on an almost weekly basis, as their influence over British Islam steadily increased.

The wars in Afghanistan and Iraq as well as post-9/11 anti-terror legislation were taken up by British Islamists, who implied that Western governments were engaged in a war on Islam and Muslims, both in the West and in the Middle East. Western Muslims, according to Islamists, were honor bound to stand up for their religion and fight back using nonviolent collective action. Campaigns such as "Stop Police Terror," to which Awlaki lent his support, were in full swing and the Federation of Student Islamic Societies (FOSIS), an organization with which Abdulmutallab was to become associated, also ran its own project in conjunction with this.[29] In an official statement on the issue FOSIS was even more explicit about the war on Islam than the "Stop Police Terror" statement discussed in Chapter 2 while also voicing support for the establishment of a caliphate and the interpretation of Islam as a "political system":

> The persecution of Muslims in Britain began even before 9-11 with the introduction of the Terrorism Act 2000. By the end of April 2005, over 750 Muslims had been arrested under the Terrorism Act. Just over 100 were charged with only three convicted of any terrorism related offence. In the same time, tens of thousands of Muslims have been stopped and searched;

hundreds of homes have been raided, Islamic charities have been shut down, over a dozen Muslim men were interned without charge and are now under control orders, and the community has become demonized and ostracized by elements of the media and the government. Security services are making a concerted effort to recruit informers from the Muslim community particularly on campus.

Whereas previously, it was Muslims themselves under attack, now the agenda to attack Islam, its principles and values as well as its political system of *Shari'ah* and *khilafah* are under attack. New laws making it an offence to associate with "wrongdoers" together with the government's policy of dividing the community into moderates and extremists aim to divide and weaken the Muslim community. The relative concept of "extremism" is being used to condemn Muslims from very diverse political viewpoints.[30]

Abdulmutallab was immersed in an activist environment that helped to lend meaning and direction to his preexisting religious austerity and personal discontent. From his earliest days on the online forum, he had looked forward to the companionship found on campus: "I hope to get over my loneliness when I go to university . . . where there are usually Islamic groups [and] clubs with good Muslims."[31] Once there, Abdulmutallab threw himself into the activities of the UCL Islamic Society. He became the group's president and as such also led the UCL chapter of FOSIS.[32]

FOSIS was established in 1962 to "represent" and "serve" the needs of Muslim students in higher education across Britain and Ireland.[33] According to the memoirs of a former member, in the early 1970s FOSIS events featured regular appearances by Said Ramadan, son-in-law of Hasan al-Banna and a transformational Muslim Brotherhood activist, and Khurshid Ahmad, a leading light of the Jamaat-e-Islami and the party's current vice president. When in 1969 Abul A'la Maududi, founder of the Jamaat, visited London, FOSIS organized a "huge reception" in his honor.[34] FOSIS, which toured Awlaki around British universities just three years before Abdulmutallab's arrival at UCL, remained a vehicle for Islamist activism throughout his time as a student in London.[35]

The UCL Islamic Society also maintained close ties with FOSIS during Abdulmutallab's time there.[36] A week of joint events was organized, and Abdulmutallab's friend and predecessor as president went on to a senior position at FOSIS soon after graduation.[37] More important, the Islamic Society toed the ideological line projected nationally by FOSIS. From the start, Abdulmutallab would have imbibed a culture that privileged almost exclusively Salafist and Islamist preachers and activists. In November 2005, the Islamic Society hosted a number of Salafi and Islamist speakers, notably the previously mentioned British Salafi Abdur Raheem Green as well as Taji Mustafa of the revolutionary Islamist group Hizb ut-Tahrir.[38] Abdulmutallab's presidential tenure followed the same pattern: in December 2007, "Pearls of Wisdom Week" featured American Salafi preachers Abu Usama al-Dhahabi and Murtaza Khan, both of whom had figured in a high-profile exposé that appeared on British television earlier that year.[39] The former was secretly filmed instructing a congregation that "Allah has created the woman deficient" and "take that homosexual man and throw him from the mountain"; the latter described Jews and Christians as "enemies" whom "the wrath of God is upon."[40]

Abdulmutallab was moved by a number of Islam-related causes that had been taken up by activist groups during the time he was in London. In interviews with the FBI he claimed that he had taken part in a number of protests, including anti-Israel marches and a protest against the Muhammad cartoons.[41] He was also moved by the messaging of Cageprisoners and other groups that campaigned for the rights of Muslim prisoners and detainees held in the United Kingdom on terrorism offenses. In addition to taking part in a vigil outside of a British prison in support of Muslim prisoners, he claims to have donated a few hundred pounds to a charity called Helping Households Under Great Stress (HHUGS) that worked with groups like Cageprisoners to highlight the situation of British Muslim prisoners.[42] Like Cageprisoners, HHUGS also presented the charging and imprisonment of Muslims in the United Kingdom for terrorism offenses as part of a right-wing Western desire to subjugate Muslims.

This brings us to War on Terror Week, the climax of Abdulmutallab's presidency of the Islamic Society, which took place in January 2007. According to an eyewitness account of the event, the event began with a video of the World Trade Center collapsing and gun battles between *mujahidin* and NATO soldiers in Afghanistan. Islamic Society members hosting the event reportedly wore the orange jumpsuits of Guantanamo detainees. Speaking to the *New York Times,* the witness stated: "It was quite tense in the theater, because I think lots of people were shocked by how extreme it was. It seemed to me like it was brainwashing, like they were trying to indoctrinate people."[43]

Included in the list of speakers were Asim Qureshi and Moazzam Begg, the senior members of Cageprisoners who at the time were campaigning on Awlaki's behalf during his imprisonment in Yemen. As has already been discussed, Cageprisoners continued to provide favorable coverage of him on their website during this time, including Islamic book reviews taken from his blog, a video message of Awlaki's that had been banned by the British government, and an article describing "Imam Anwar" as an "inspirational figure."[44]

At the time, Cageprisoners typified the British Islamist penchant for the "defensive jihad" of the Taliban in Afghanistan, insurgents in Iraq, and Lebanese, Palestinian, and Kashmiri militants. Writing in 2010, Asim Qureshi provided an account of the talk he gave at the UCL War on Terror Week that was titled "Jihad vs. Terrorism." He explained that his core argument was that modern global jihadist terrorism was distinct from classical, or defensive, jihad: "jihad as the concept of the conduct of hostilities from classical Islamic law is distinct from the modernist actions that have been taken by individuals and how Islam finds no room for terrorism." Unlike the global jihad project, which Qureshi viewed as heretical and a violation of core Islamic teachings, defensive jihad in countries where Muslims were oppressed by foreign powers was a legitimate response: "Many Muslims believe that our brothers and sisters in faith fighting for their survival in various parts of the world have a legitimate right to do so—that policy of self-defence from an Islamic perspective is known as *jihad*."[45] As discussed previously, this is a widely held view among Islamic scholars and analysts of Salafi-jihadism.

Qureshi argued that since this concept was "recognized by the Western world" in 1980s Afghanistan and 1990s Bosnia, the time had come for "public debate" to clarify and refine the "limitations and justifications" of jihad. He hoped that through such discussion violent jihadists in the West could be persuaded, "in light of the grievances mentioned by the 7/7 bombers, Abdulmuttalib and others like him, that the ends can never justify the means." The real problem in his eyes was that Western jihadists did not fully grasp the parameters of a legitimate jihad, and therefore "the discussion on *jihad* is the solution."[46]

Just months before the UCL event, however, Qureshi explained this view of jihad at a Hizb ut-Tahrir rally in central London using a different tone, one that captures the mood of Islamist activism in the United Kingdom during Abdulmutallab's time there: "So when we see the example of our brothers and sisters fighting in Chechnya, Iraq, Palestine, Kashmir, Afghanistan then we know where the example lies. When we see Hezbollah defeating the armies of Israel, we know what the solution is and where the victory lies. We know that it is incumbent upon all of us to support the *jihad* of our brothers and sisters in these countries when they are facing the oppression of the West."[47]

Similarly, Moazzam Begg, director of Cageprisoners, compared contemporary young British Muslims who joined the Taliban insurgency to the *mujahidin* who fought the Soviets in the late 1970s. In a 2008 essay on jihad, he wrote: "By consensus of the Islamic schools of thought, *jihad* becomes an individual obligation, like prayer and fasting, on Muslim men and women when their land is occupied by foreign enemies." Somewhat obliquely, he added: "That obligation extends to neighboring lands until the enemy has been expelled." Further unpacking his theme, Begg continued: "Although in the West *jihad* is often seen as terrorism it is correct to describe it as tourism. Prophet Muhammad said: 'The tourism of my nation is *jihad*.' This is one reason why many Muslims from thousands of miles away traveled to places as far and wide as Palestine, Chechnya, Kashmir and Afghanistan. If resisting the Soviet occupation of Afghanistan was jihad, if the repelling the massacres by the Serbs in Bosnia was *jihad,* then how can resisting the current occupation of these Muslims lands be anything else?" In the same essay, Begg praised the work of Abdullah Azzam, referring to his book *In Defence of Muslim Lands* as a "magisterial discourse."[48] However, Begg did not address the possibility of an ideological overlap between defensive and offensive jihad and did not appear to recognize that Azzam also called for Islam to be spread throughout the world, violently where necessary.[49]

Although Begg did not at any time openly support offensive jihad in the West, fighting in defense of an Islamic land was, for Cageprisoners, a core principle of Islam and an individual duty for Muslims. Such views became increasingly widely espoused in Britain during Abdulmutallab's time at UCL. However, it would be incorrect and misleading to portray Cageprisoners, or any of the other groups and individuals mentioned here, as supporters of al-Qaeda's violent jihad within Western countries. They undoubtedly abhorred Abdulmutallab's attempt to bring down an airliner with over two hundred passengers on board. Nonetheless, it is clear that Abdulmutallab had immersed himself in a British Islamist milieu that saw the act of jihad as legitimate in certain circumstances. The activism of the time had pushed the war on Islam to the forefront of his thinking, and it significantly legitimized the concept of reacting to this supposed aggression with violence. While he still had to make a number of ideological steps in order to condone al-Qaeda's version of jihad, it would be difficult to deny the role that this type of thinking played in his eventual turn to terrorism. Awlaki, who was presented to him as both a legitimate voice and a victim of the War on Terror, had by this time fully endorsed the global jihad movement through his 2005 translation of *Constants on the Path of Jihad,* which Abdulmutallab encountered during his time in Britain.

Mobilization and Awlaki's Influence

During Abdulmutallab's trial, which took place in Detroit, Michigan, in 2011, criminologist Simon Perry undertook the task of assessing the defendant's future threat to the public. In order to properly carry out this assignment, the FBI provided him with the transcripts of all eighteen interviews that they conducted with Abdulmutallab after his arrest. Perry assessed Abdulmutallab's decisions to mobilize as a suicide bomber as a "rational situational choice, based on an evaluation of the cost and the anticipated benefits." This relates to much of the social movement literature discussed earlier, which presents the decision to take part in movement activism as partially the result of a rational cost-benefit analysis. It is up to movement leaders to provide convincing arguments for participation by addressing the benefits of activism as worth the costs that come with it. This rational choice was, according to Perry, based upon Abdulmutallab's adoption of a form of Islam that justified acts of mass murder in response to threats upon the *ummah,* of which Abdulmutallab felt a part due to his adoption of the militant collective identity of the global jihad movement. There is no doubt that Abdulmutallab's radicalization process was guided by deep religious feeling, and Awlaki's work ensured that he "was entirely motivated by his realization of his religious obligation to conduct Jihad."[50] This religious feeling was also guided by Abdulmutallab's Salafism.

The interviews Abdulmutallab gave to the FBI after his arrest have since been released as a result of Freedom of Information Act requests by the *New York Times*. They help to flesh out his experiences in London, Dubai, and Yemen and the process of radicalization he underwent in those places. It was in 2005, upon his arrival in England as a student, that he began to immerse himself Awlaki's lectures after purchasing his CDs at an Islamic bookshop in London. This was not, however, the first time Abdulmutallab had come across him. That summer, just before enrolling at UCL, he attended a lecture of Awlaki's while studying Arabic in Yemen at the Sana'a Institute of Arabic Language (SIAL).[51] He admired Awlaki's style of teaching and religious knowledge, a view that would only be bolstered by his experiences in London. If we consider Awlaki's status among leading British Islamist institutions and groups at the time, Abdulmutallab's interest in him, given his involvement in the British Islamist milieu, is not surprising. These lectures motivated him to consider jihad and martyrdom as a possible mobilization option.[52] However, he did not immediately adopt Salafi-jihadism, opting instead to involve himself in Islamist activism through the UCL Islamic Society.

It was after his time at UCL, while undertaking a postgraduate degree in Business Management at the University of Wollongong in Dubai in 2009, that Abdulmutallab told investigators that God had guided him and that he "saw the doors open" for him to take part in violent jihad, which placed him on the path of seeking out Awlaki in Yemen.[53] Beyond this claim, it is unclear why he made this decision at this time. However, he had now come to regard Awlaki as something beyond a legitimate Islamic scholar. He was now a person from whom he wished to take direct instruction.[54] The sources of Awlaki's legitimacy, in Abdulmutallab's eyes, were both his words and his deeds. He admired the preacher for making what he saw as a *hijrah* from America to Yemen, thus fulfilling his obligation to Islam by being a leader of jihad and helping to plan attacks.[55] He also believed that Awlaki's work provided the most authoritative accounts of the primary Islamic texts available in English. As explained earlier, there was ample justification for this view.

Abdulmutallab's assessment of the legitimacy of carrying out such a mission was strikingly influenced by Awlaki. During one of his post-arrest interviews, Abdulmutallab cited as his inspiration an article from Awlaki's blog titled "Suicide or Martyrdom" in which he addressed the religious legitimacy of suicide bombings.[56] He was also moved by Awlaki's lectures on the lives of Muhammad's companions; despite their lack of direct calls to jihad, he considered these to be influential in his decision to take part in violence due to their use of stories from that era to glorify ancient Islamic battles. *Constants on the Path of Jihad* was also very important to Abdulmutallab, who regarded Awlaki's version of Uyayree's treatise as the clearest explanation of Koranic support for global jihad.[57] He told FBI agents that he saw no need to receive a specific religious ruling, or *fatwa*, from an official Islamic body to pursue jihad, as he saw this as an individual obligation equal to fasting, prayer, and making the hajj pilgrimage. This again demonstrates a direct link with Awlaki's own interpretation and motivational framing of the obligation of jihad as found in *Constants on the Path of Jihad*. He even quoted Awlaki's translation of the work, telling investigators that "fighting has been prescribed for you but you hate it." According to Perry, Abdulmutallab "felt this statement aligned very closely to verses from the Koran, and that it means that at times one needs to participate in bad acts such as 'fighting to achieve the greater good.'"[58]

Awlaki's reputation and credentials were, in Abdulmutallab's eyes, unimpeachable. At one point during his interviews, the agents asked him about the claims of Awlaki's involvement with prostitutes during his time in America, a revelation that might reasonably have ruined his reputation had it become public earlier in his career. It is instructive that, at least in this case, Abdulmutallab's view on Awlaki's legitimacy was not impacted by this. He regarded the claim as either a fabrication invented by the enemies of Islam to discredit a great scholar or, if true, a relatively minor sin that was outweighed by Awlaki's commitment to jihad.[59]

During a two-month break from his course in Dubai in July 2009, Abdulmutallab decided to make the short trip to Yemen and attempt to locate and meet with Awlaki. Other than attending Awlaki's lecture at SIAL in Yemen in 2005, he did not at this point have any previous direct communications with him or any other al-Qaeda members, and he hoped that he could find possible contacts upon arrival in Sana'a. In a likely attempt to avoid the suspicions of his family, who were becoming increasingly concerned about him, he re-enrolled for Arabic lessons at SIAL, where he first met Awlaki in 2005. He soon began taking classes while living in student accommodations nearby, using his free time to seek out Awlaki. He read online that Awlaki was linked to the al-Iman University in Sana'a, which was run by Abdul Majid al-Zindani, and began visiting the campus and asking students for advice on how to make contact.

Abdulmutallab's initial visits were unsuccessful, but then, in early August, a Nigerian he had befriended suggested that they approach Zindani directly at his home in Sana'a to ask for his help. They walked there together and at the front gate were immediately turned away by security guards, who suggested that they try the nearby house of Zindani's son instead. This time Abdulmutallab had more luck. He claims that he was welcomed in and soon found himself sitting with his host and a man who introduced himself as an in-law of Awlaki's. He avoided specific talk of participating in jihad, instead saying that he wished to meet Awlaki and discuss a number of issues, including his views on the conflict involving the jihadist militia Boko Haram in Nigeria. At the end of the meeting he was provided with Awlaki's email address and, in return, gave them his cell phone number in the hope Awlaki would reach out directly.

Abdulmutallab did not expect much from this brief encounter, assuming that it could not possibly be so easy to arrange a meeting. One can only imagine his surprise when, shortly after the meeting, he received a text message from someone claiming to be Awlaki: "This is Anwar. Call me on this number."[60] He immediately called and they had a brief conversation that was likely part of Awlaki's attempt to vet this possible new recruit. Abdulmutallab reports that he told Awlaki he made *hijrah* after listening to his calls to come to the lands of jihad and now wished to participate in the fight. It was then agreed that Abdulmutallab would draft a message for the preacher, explaining his desire to join the movement and give it to the in-law he had met at the house of Zindani's son, who would pass it on to Awlaki. By late August the letter was complete, and Abdulmutallab delivered it as ordered. Sensing that he was about to embark on a journey from which he would not return, Abdulmutallab sent a series of text messages to his mother during the two-week period he spent waiting to hear back from Awlaki. The messages, although cryptic, are the first known revelations of Abdulmutallab's religious motivations to conduct jihad. In one message, he told his mother that:

> Allah knows what is best. . . . I ask you for the sake of Allah to let me stay here and come closer to him. This is *insha allah* [God willing] what is best for me spiritually in my worldly affairs and in the hereafter. . . . don't despair or worry and never lose hope in the mercy of Allah. Read the speech of Allah and its meanings as much as you can. May Allah take care of you wherever you are like you took care of me all my life. May Allah also take care of me wherever I am and I put my full trust in him. I will

be fine wherever I am and nothing will happen to me except
what Allah has written which there is no escape from wherever
I may be. . . . [61]

Awlaki's eventual response was a positive one: Abdulmutallab was
invited to visit Awlaki in his house in Shabwa in southern Yemen.[62]
Shortly afterwards, he made contact with the men who would facilitate the journey from Sana'a. In mid-October, he arrived at Awlaki's
house where they had their first one-on-one meeting. Awlaki told his
new student of the rewards that came with jihad but also warned of
the patience and steadfastness it would require. Over the coming
weeks, he met other AQAP recruits, including Samir Khan and other
English-speaking members of the group who had traveled to join and
help Awlaki. He also received weapons training at a nearby camp
while the AQAP leadership deliberated how best to deploy their latest
asset. Part of this assessment included regular discussions with Awlaki,
who was ultimately to decide what responsibilities would best suit
Abdulmutallab.[63]

During these discussions, Abdulmutallab was directly asked about
his desire to take part in a martyrdom operation, to which he responded
that he had been considering the idea ever since he first listened to *Constants on the Path of Jihad*. He was already primed, and such was his
reverence for Awlaki that all he required were brief face-to-face interactions with the preacher in order to become a fully committed suicide bomber.[64] Abdulmutallab offered himself up to Awlaki unques-
tioningly, believing that he "held all the power" to make a decision
on what his role in global jihad should be.[65] Even the choice of target
was left to Awlaki: Abdulmutallab told FBI interrogators that he was
prepared to carry out jihad in any way, and against any target, of Awlaki's choosing.[66]

By early November, after closely observing Abdulmutallab's level of
piety—specifically his fasting, prayers and commitment to jihad—

Awlaki and other AQAP members had assessed that Abdulmutallab was an ideal candidate for a suicide mission in the United States. Awlaki told him that he was to be sent "somewhere to go learn something," a reference he would later learn was related to the training he would receive from AQAP's expert bomb-maker Ibrahim al-Asiri, who it was revealed in late 2019 was killed by U.S. forces in 2017.[67] After swearing allegiance to AQAP's emir Nasir al-Wuhaishi and to Bin Laden, Abdulmutallab eventually learned from Awlaki that he was to be sent on a martyrdom mission in which he was "going to bring down a plane." Before doing so, they also filmed a martyrdom video, which was scripted by Awlaki and produced by Samir Khan. This was used as part of a video released by AQAP after the attack that also depicted Abdulmutallab's involvement in the AQAP training camp. In the footage, Abdulmutallab gives a brief explanation for his actions, and he later claimed that Awlaki stressed to him the importance of relying upon and citing multiple Koranic verses:

> "Oh ye who believe! Take not the Jews and the Christians for your allies and protectors. They are but allies and protectors to each other, and he amongst you who turns to them is of them. Verily, Allah guides not a wrong doing people." My Muslim brothers in the Arabian Peninsula, you have to answer the call of jihad, because the enemy is in your land; along with the Jewish and Christian armies. Allah the most high says: "Unless you go forth, He will punish you with a grievous penalty and put others in your place, but Him you will not harm in the least."[68]

It was not just the video that Awlaki helped to plan. He was also heavily involved in preparations for the attack, specifying that the target had to be an American-owned airliner bound for the United States and that Abdulmutallab should not expect to survive the operation. He told his student exactly when to detonate the bomb: "Wait until you are in the U.S., then bring down the plane."[69] Awlaki also provided detailed advice on maintaining operational security. He told Abdulmutallab not to take a direct flight from Yemen to America in order to avoid suspicion; instead he should make a stopover in an African country and take a connecting flight to America through Europe. He did not, however, offer specific dates or cities that should be targeted; as long as it took place on American soil, the attack would achieve its objectives.

In interviews, Abdulmutallab stressed the importance he placed on fully grasping the religious legitimacy for such an attack act, and he discussed the issue in detail with Awlaki. One issue on which he required clarification was the permissibility of killing civilians, a debate that continues to divide Salafi-jihadists. Awlaki offered Abdulmutallab guidance on this, explaining that the civilians he was targeting could be considered collateral damage, and therefore it was not a sin to kill them. In lectures Awlaki had already covered this topic, he argued that from a *sharia* perspective, intentionally killing civilians is not allowed unless they can be considered collateral damage. He often relied upon the example of a battle between Muhammad's forces and the Thaqeef tribe in Taif (modern-day Saudi Arabia), during which Muhammad used catapults, which, while not targeting civilians, did lead to unintentional deaths. After Abdulmutallab's failed attack, Awlaki reiterated this point in an interview with al-Malahim Media while also arguing that all Americans are legitimate targets:

> With regard to the issue of "civilians," this term has become prevalent these days, but I prefer to use the terms employed by our jurisprudents. They classify people as either combatants or non-combatants. A combatant is someone who bears arms— even if this is a woman. Non-combatants are people who do not take part in the war. The American people in its entirety

takes part in the war, because they elected this administration, and they finance this war. In the recent elections, and in the previous ones, the American people had other options, and could have elected people who did not want war. Nevertheless, these candidates got nothing but a handful of votes. We should examine this issue from the perspective of Islamic law, and this settles the issue—is it permitted or forbidden? If the heroic mujahid brother Umar Farouk could have targeted hundreds of soldiers, that would have been wonderful. But we are talking about the realities of war.[70]

Armed with both the justification and the motivation to conduct the attack, Abdulmutallab left Awlaki in Shabwa in early December. His next stop was in the Marib governorate, where he met al-Asiri and was provided with the device and instructions on how to use it: This was the now infamous "underwear bomb," designed to catch fire and detonate upon the injection of combustible chemicals sewn into the device. The plastic explosive, a compound called pentaerythritol tetranitrate (PETN) was specially designed by al-Asiri to evade detection at airport security screenings. During the few days he spent in Marib, al-Asiri also showed Abdulmutallab an AQAP propaganda video about the group's attempted assassination of Saudi Prince Muhammad bin Nayef.[71] Months earlier, in late August 2009, al-Asiri's brother, Abdullah al-Asiri, was sent on a suicide mission to kill the Saudi Arabian counterterrorism chief armed with the same type of explosive provided to Abdulmutallab, killing himself but succeeding only in injuring his target.[72]

After leaving Marib around December 5, 2009, Abdulmutallab followed Awlaki's instructions to the letter. Flying through a number of African countries, he eventually booked a flight to Detroit that flew from Lagos, Nigeria, via Amsterdam in the Netherlands. While he was on the final leg of the trip, he kept his eyes trained on the journey map displayed on his in-seat monitor, waiting, just as Awlaki had instructed, until the plane was over American soil before detonating. The moment it was over the Eastern seaboard, he calmly went to the bathroom to make his final preparations to ensure that, according to him, he would "die clean."[73] After washing his face, brushing his teeth, and dabbing on some cologne, he returned to his seat, said a final prayer, and then tried to set off the device.[74]

Of all the case studies analyzed in this book, Abdulmutallab's provides arguably the fullest picture of Awlaki's influence over a Muslim who was radicalized in the West. Not only did Awlaki have an impact upon Abdulmutallab from afar, but the evidence also shows that the preacher had a direct hand in his mobilization. For him, Awlaki was the undoubted leader of the Western global jihad movement; he had spiritual authority to declare jihad and the connections to ensure that he could mobilize in the most effective manner.

Abdulmutallab believed that this movement represented the only legitimate form of Islam, and he was convinced of this in large part due to Awlaki. He adopted the frames that Awlaki constructed and came to see the counterterrorism activities of Western governments as part of multifaceted war on Islam. Abdulmutallab's receptiveness to these frames was likely increased by his involvement in an Islamist milieu in Britain that, while it rejected al-Qaeda, nonetheless revered Awlaki and shared a number of the global jihad movement's diagnostic frames. It also helped ensure that he fused his preexisting Salafist religiosity with the confrontational and revolutionary approach of political Islam. Thus, his time in England also influenced how Abdulmutallab saw himself and his responsibilities as a Muslim in the War on Terror era. A politically passive Salafi before moving to London, he was exposed to activism after enrolling at UCL that soon led him to conclude that his narrow and inward-looking approach would pay no real dividends to Muslims who were suffering. Activism was the only way to ensure change, and the type of activism he chose to pursue only moved toward jihadist violence once he came across Awlaki.

Awlaki presented members of the global jihad movement to him as the only Muslims who were pursuing the correct form of activism, namely fighting jihad, just as Muhammad and the *Sahaba* had done before them. As a result, these frames, along with his own activism, helped reshape Abdulmutallab's identity as a Muslim living in the West. The collective identity constructed by the global jihad movement that Awlaki helped to cultivate among Westerners appealed to him due to the apparent efficacy and religious legitimacy of their actions. Had Abdulmutallab not encountered Awlaki's work at a moment of significant change in his life and circumstances, the self-image he would have had and the type of activism he would have chosen to pursue could have been dramatically different.

6

Nidal Hasan

O N NOVEMBER 5, 2009, Major Nidal Hasan, a psychiatrist in the
U.S. Army, entered his place of work, the Soldier Medical Readiness
Center in Fort Hood, Texas, and opened fire. His attack resulted in the
deaths of twelve American soldiers and one civilian; at the time, it was
the biggest jihadist attack on American soil since 9/11. It was soon revealed that Hasan was an Awlaki follower, had attended the Dar al-
Hijrah mosque while Awlaki was its imam, and had been in contact
with the preacher months before the attack.

Like other mass killers and many jihadists, the catalyst for Hasan's
radicalization appears to be related to a number of personal struggles
he faced over a significant period of time. The most profound of these
was the loss of his parents, which was where he traced the root of his
newfound interest in Islam, until then not an influential factor in his
life.[1] His father died in 1998, and four months after his mother's death
in 2001, nineteen Muslim men carried out the single biggest terrorist
attack in history. The 9/11 attacks, and everything that followed,
opened up a new world, which, combined with his recent trauma,
caused Hasan to question his own identity as an American Muslim soldier, which had defined him since he enlisted in the Army after his

graduation from high school in 1988. These events, according to Hasan, "catalyzed me to learn more about Islam."[2] The new interest in his religion also brought about a gradual shift in his identity, and Hasan soon began questioning his involvement in the military. According to his brother, Anas Hasan, by 2004 he did not want to be involved in "George Bush's war on Islam" and no longer wore his military uniform with the pride he once did.[3]

It was his mother's death that appears to have impacted Hasan most deeply. In the months leading up to it, he moved in with her as she became increasingly sick and watched her deteriorate and eventually die. Hasan claims that he became concerned upon her death that, due to her lack of religious observance, she may not have been guaranteed a place in heaven. In their younger years, his parents had owned a convenience store that sold alcohol, and this too, he believed, may have earned his mother an eternity in hell. This fear for his mother's fate, coupled with a belief that his own pious acts might be able to outweigh her sins and "save" her, led to a period of religious intensification for Hasan that marked the start of his journey to jihadism.[4]

Presiding over his mother's funeral in Virginia was a young charismatic imam, who Hasan would later find out was Anwar al-Awlaki. That he would come across Awlaki at this pivotal moment of religious exploration and spiritual vulnerability demonstrates the oft-overlooked coincidental nature of radicalization. Timing can sometimes be the most important factor of all. After being impressed by Awlaki's command of the religion and his captivating preaching style, he began actively looking for and listening to his recorded sermons. Along with Awlaki's apparent knowledge of the faith, Hasan was also impressed by his combination of Arabic recitations from the Koran and *hadith*, which in his view gave the works an air of authenticity. When asked which of Awlaki's sermons had the biggest impact on him, Nidal Hasan, writing from his cell in the United States Disciplinary Barracks at Fort Leavenworth, cites "The Lives of the Prophets" and

Awlaki's two-lecture series on the life of Muhammad: "He taught the basics of the Quranic teachings in a clear and easy to understand way that was also enjoyable to hear. He had a gift of storytelling. But, these stories weren't made up but from the Quran and reliable tradition of our Prophet. . . . His sermons seemed to be in exact sync with what the Quran was teaching."[5]

As Hasan's religiosity increased over the years, so did both American military involvement in Muslim-majority countries and a general perception that the Muslim world was facing an unprecedented threat. These two factors were to combine and become the source of a major dilemma for Hasan—how to maintain his increasingly *ummah*-centric identity while also serving in the military of a country he was beginning to perceive as the spearhead of a war on Islam. The solution to this dilemma, the beliefs he adopted, and the actions he took in response were to be influenced in part by Awlaki. As with other cases analyzed in this book, Awlaki's outreach to Western Muslims influenced Hasan at a time of transition and vulnerability, offering him a new identity along with explanations for the problems he faced and solutions for fixing them.

Hasan's PowerPoint Presentation on Islam

Before he took up direct contact with Awlaki via email correspondence, Hasan's behavior had already caused concern among his fellow officers at the Walter Reed Army Medical Center, where he was stationed between 2003 and 2009 before moving to Fort Hood.[6] He clashed with colleagues on a number of occasions due to issues related to religious observance, refusing to be pictured alongside women in the Christmas group photos and generally distancing himself in favor of isolated religious study.[7] It was his participation in a weekly presentation series called "Grand Rounds" in June 2007, however, that raised the most concern.

The purpose of the talk, as the host indicated, was to "enlighten us about the Islamic culture and the Islamic tradition and how that relates to being a military member." Beginning with a disclaimer, Hasan stated that his PowerPoint presentation "is just for me" and did not represent the views of the psychiatric department or of the U.S. military as a whole. He described the presentation as part of his ongoing research on "the Koranic world view as it relates to Muslims in the U.S. military." This would show his audience "what the Koran inculcates in the minds of Muslims and what potential implications that may have for the U.S. military and describe the nature of the religious conflicts that Muslims may have with the current wars in Iraq and Afghanistan."[8] Hasan would later admit in his Sanity Board interview, conducted to determine his mental fitness to face trial, that this presentation was in fact autobiographical and described his own thinking and the identity crisis he was facing at the time.[9]

Hasan's main concern in the talk related to a number of "adverse events" involving Muslims in the U.S. military. One of the most important test cases in the presentation was that of Hasan Akbar—a Muslim-American soldier who during the initial phases of the 2003 invasion of Iraq killed two fellow soldiers in an attack on his camp in Kuwait.[10] Nidal Hasan would also consult Awlaki about this case less than two years later. However, at this stage he claimed that he wanted his research to help "identify Muslim soldiers that may be having religious conflicts with the current wars in Iraq and Afghanistan." Hasan argued that Akbar had carried out his attack due to "religious conflicts," quoting the now-imprisoned soldier as justifying his act by claiming that "you guys [fellow soldiers] were going to kill and rape Muslims." Akbar's understanding of his Islamic identity and religion led him to perceive an unbearable hypocrisy and identity clash between being Muslim and serving in the U.S. military. This could only be redressed, as he saw it, through the use of violence. Akbar was in many ways a precursor to

Nidal Hasan himself, and it is notable that he referenced the case repeatedly.[11]

Hasan intended to use his research on Hasan Akbar in order to help the U.S. military "identify a person that might be more predisposed to having conflicts" between being Muslim and serving in the U.S. military. The signs that an American Muslim soldier experiencing such an internal conflict might exhibit, according to Hasan, included the changing of one's name to a more explicitly Islamic one, increased devotion to the Koran and prayer, and increased isolation from one's unit or command structure. He also noted the increasingly persuasive nature of claims that the West was "at war" with Islam, though he avoided giving any personal opinions on the matter.[12]

Hasan expressed a related concern over the lack of reliable Islamic clerics in America and the resultant dearth of sufficient guidance available to Western Muslims. He was especially interested in researching *fatwas* (religious rulings) from respected Islamic scholars on whether or not Muslims could serve in the U.S. military. He acknowledged that in America "there has been a softening" on this position from scholars, many of whom offered vague approval. In the rest of the world *fatwas* "tend to indicate that they don't approve of it, and they feel that Muslims shouldn't be in the United States military." Hasan criticized scholars in America for not being clearer in their rulings on this issue, calling for them to specifically state whether or not it was acceptable for American-Muslim soldiers to fight against the Taliban in Afghanistan and insurgents in Iraq.[13] He did, however, cite U.S.-based scholars who issued *fatwas* in support of Muslim involvement in the military as long as they fight for truth and justice. Nonetheless, he acknowledged the subjective nature of the terms "just" and "unjust," accepting that this argument can be confusing and ambiguous, asking, "How do you define justice?" The question of defining justice is a very important one in this context and relates closely to discussions throughout this book about how Salafi-jihadist ideology redefines these terms so as to portray the situation of Muslims as unjust and linked with the actions of Western countries. It is interesting to observe how, during Hasan's radicalization, his own definitions of justice and injustice were to gradually transform after giving this talk.

Hasan's conclusion on the question of Muslim involvement in the military was that "Muslim soldiers should not serve in any capacity that renders them at risk of hurting or killing believers unjustly." He also suggested a number of other recommendations. These included a proposal that the U.S. Department of Defense should allow Muslim soldiers "the option of being released as conscientious objectors," which may help to decrease the "adverse events" he highlighted earlier in his talk.[14] In yet another indicator that this talk mirrored his own beliefs and experiences, Hasan himself applied for early release from the military as a conscientious objector around 2003, a request that was rejected.[15]

The presentation also offered a discussion of Islamism, with Hasan defining it as a movement that "advocates rule by God's law" and works toward the implementation of *sharia* law while rejecting the separation of church and state. While he was not yet fully radicalized at this point, it is instructive that he understood the implementation of *sharia* and the fusion of church and state as "the ideal in Islam." As part of this discussion, he devoted a slide to the concept of jihad, which he said "spans a spectrum" between the "greater" and "lesser" jihad. At this stage, he accepted the interpretation of the greater jihad as being the inner, spiritual struggle with one's own psyche, while the lesser jihad was related to physical "struggles with outside forces."[16]

Hasan's recognition of the concept of abrogation—whereby later Koranic verses supersede previous ones that contradict them—led him to conclude that violence was an integral part of the practice of Islam. He cited the *hijrah* as the moment when Muslims were first allowed to use violence as part of a "defensive jihad" and argued that all of the peaceful verses in Islam have been supplanted by those that call specifically for both defensive and offensive jihad. He argued that "you'll see sometimes people cherry pick the peaceful verses trying to show Islam in a more peaceful light where, indeed, you could make a great theological argument that those verses were actually abrogated." He too accepted this approach and ended this part of his discussion with a quote from Koran 9:29, which reads: "Fight those who do not believe in Allah, nor in the latter day, nor do they prohibit what Allah and his messenger have prohibited, nor follow the religion of truth, out of those who have been given the Book, until they pay the tax in acknowledgment of superiority and they are in a state of subjection."

While acknowledging that "this is a very uncomfortable verse for Muslims to try to explain," Hasan nonetheless asserted that it is "right out of the Koran" and therefore inherently correct. In his closing slides he offered a few general observations based on the presentation and also provided a glimpse into his future as a jihadist. On the issue of moderate Muslims, whom he referred to as making "compromises" so as to live in the West, Hasan pointed out that "in some cases that [moderation] is really seen as compromising from the Koranic worldview." He may by this time have come across Awlaki's own work on this issue in which the preacher criticized "Rand Muslims" for tailoring or altering their religion so that it suited their Western lifestyles and ignoring injunctions to fight jihad against the enemies of Islam. While Hasan accepted that Muslims could make such compromises, he concluded that "God is not moderate."[17] On the question of using violence to establish an Islamic state, Hasan's interpretation of Islam at this stage led him to believe that this was an act fully supported by the primary texts: "fighting to establish an Islamic state to please God . . . is condoned."

In the question-and-answer session following his talk, one participant asked Hasan how he reconciled being a Muslim and practicing psychiatry, which traditionally rejects the use of religion in therapy.

Another audience member suggested to him that there might be a conflict between "the need for complete submission to the will of Allah
versus that need to keep religion and spirituality separate in your psychiatric practice."[18] Hasan's answer did not betray any sort of extremism, but he was surprised and slightly taken aback by the question, perhaps having not yet identified any conflict between his
religion and his place in Western society.

Another participant wanted Hasan's view on why the numbers of
Muslims worldwide appeared to be rising much more rapidly than any
other religion. In response, he used the same quote used by Awlaki in
his 2002 sermon at Dar al-Hijrah (Hasan's own mosque during that period) regarding efforts to "put out the light of Allah": "God says that
they try to put out the light of Islam, but he won't allow it and he will
increase it despite their attacks." While it cannot be proven that he was
directly inspired by Awlaki's work to use this quote as a response, it
does show that he was adopting and repeating many of the themes
of the movement that Awlaki was helping to convey to a Western
audience. Another audience member pointed out that, on the subject
of how to identify Muslims in the military who may be grappling
with internal dilemmas, his presentation suggested that "anyone
who is a practicing Muslim is someone we should keep an eye on
and be aware of." Hasan failed to provide a convincing response, instead agreeing with this contention and conceding that he was "not
sure how to maneuver over that."[19]

Hasan's Email Exchanges with Awlaki

In 2007, just two years before his attack, we therefore have a man who
was in the midst of his research on Islam and the question of Muslim
servicemen who suffer from internal conflicts about serving in the
military. Yet, Hasan was himself struggling with the question of how

to practice Islam properly and still be a productive member of the U.S. Army. According to his posts on Islamic forums, Hasan had "discovered Islam" at some point in 2003, which suggests that it might have been a reaction to his mother's death in 2001. Having been raised without religion, he was self-educated and turned, as so many do, to the internet. His first known forum post on Islam asked mundane questions about what intoxicants Muslims were allowed to use in order to cure illness. However, even at this stage he was looking for credible, authoritative voices on his religion, writing that an "Islamic leader" should come forward and clarify issues such as what drugs Muslims are allowed to take.[20]

A year and a half after his PowerPoint presentation, he first contacted Awlaki after coming across his blog and signing up for its regular email alerts in mid-2008. By this point, Awlaki's work was making a significant impression on Hasan in terms of how he perceived the war on Islam and the duty of jihad. According to one of his original attorneys, Lt. Col. Kris Poppe, who handled Hasan's appeals after he represented himself at trial, Hasan would listen to Awlaki's CDs "over and over" and accepted the preacher as his sole guide on Islam and how it should be applied. Awlaki was "a major influence in Nidal's life, and his understanding of what his faith required of him, including how best to please God."[21]

Not only, as with so many others, had Awlaki brought Islam to life for Hasan at a time when he was exploring his religion, but he also placed the faith in a modern geopolitical context. According to Hasan, Awlaki's diagnostic framing, which presented an ideological war on Islam, gave this concept a meaning and relevance in his own life. He was inspired by the preacher's claim that the West was attempting to weaken Islam by changing it to suit its own agenda: "His lectures gave me more insight into what it means to be at war with Islam, and how the U.S. / West wanted a castrated form of Islam."[22] Awlaki's work had such a profound impact on him that Hasan took it upon himself to disseminate his CDs among friends and colleagues, keeping multiple copies in the trunk of his car in case an appropriate opportunity arose.[23]

By the time Hasan reached out to Awlaki, the latter was already the subject of an FBI investigation, and all of his communications were being closely monitored. According to an independent investigation into the events leading up to Hasan's attack, which has a specific focus on the actions of the FBI, the Awlaki investigation "served as an occasional 'trip wire' for identifying persons of potential interest" who may have been considering domestic acts of terrorism.[24] On December 17, 2008, Major Hasan snagged that wire when he sent a message to Awlaki via his blog:

> There are . . . Muslims who join the armed forces for a myriad of different reasons. Some appear to have internal conflicts and have even killed or tried to kill other us soldiers in the name of Islam i.e. Hasan Akbar, etc. Others feel that there is no conflict. Previous Fatwas seem vague and not very definitive. Can you make some general comments about Muslims in the U.S. military?
>
> Would you consider someone like Hasan Akbar or other soldiers that have committed such acts with the goal of helping Muslims/Islam . . . fighting Jihad and if they did die would you consider them *shaheeds*. I realize that these are difficult questions but you seem to be one of the only ones that has lived in the U.S. has a good understanding of the Qur'an and *Sunna* and is not afraid of being direct.[25]

It is telling that Hasan's first contact with Awlaki was related to Akbar's attack, and he was clearly wrestling with issues related to it. He remained interested in many of the themes mentioned in his June 2007 presentation, though he had not yet come to any solid conclusions.

While he was still ideologically some way off carrying out his eventual attack, his identity as a Muslim in the U.S. military had been at the forefront of his mind for some time. His consumption of Awlaki's work from this period onwards helped to answer his questions about how he should both come to terms with his situation and also change it.

As Hasan had previously complained, Western Islamic preachers had failed to generate enough clear and concise *fatwas* regarding the question of Muslims serving in the U.S. military. This led him to ask Awlaki—who by this point he viewed as a figure with the authority and legitimacy to pronounce on this issue—to help provide him with further knowledge. Hasan then moved on to address the specific case of Hasan Akbar, who had captured his interest as a striking example of the larger group of American Muslim soldiers with "internal conflicts."[26]

Awlaki did not respond to Hasan's initial email. Weeks later, in early January 2009, Hasan followed this up with a more mundane question about how Iran and Shia Muslims should be perceived by Sunni Muslims; once again, he received no response.[27] Then, in mid-January he sent a further two emails that included questions about indiscriminate killings of Israeli civilians and how the West views the Palestinian terrorist group Hamas. On the former issue, Hasan, appearing to support the idea of Hamas launching rockets that indiscriminately targeted civilians, asked Awlaki for his views: "One may consider the firing of missiles into Israel a transgression in the eye of Allah (SWT) because of its indiscriminate nature. However, it one recalls the verse about the permissibility of transgressing albeit a different scenario I believe it still applies. Verse 2:194 states '. . . Then whoever transgresses the prohibition against you, you transgress likewise against him. And fear Allah (SWT), and know that Allah (SWT) is with Al-Muttaqun [the pious believers].'"[28]

He went on to provide further verses that he saw as legitimizing indiscriminate killing in response to aggression and injustice against

Muslims. Two days after this email, he sent a further lengthy message to the preacher in which he discussed Hamas and Western views toward the group that had been elected into power in the Gaza Strip three years earlier, much to the frustration of Israel and its Western allies. Rather than offering a set of questions, this time he discussed his own views on Hamas and asked Awlaki to give him feedback because "I am a novice at this and would like reassurance."[29] Whereas in his presentation two years earlier, he had been unclear as to where he stood on the subject of the supposed Islamic duty to establish *sharia* law, by this time his mind was made up: "Hamas is a democratically elected Islamic organization that is trying to establish the law of God in their land. That is why they, as well as other Islamic countries are hated by the West."[30]

Hasan's views were now becoming increasingly anti-Western, with his allegiances apparently moving closer toward militant Islamist organizations that were establishing *sharia* law. His identity as an American Muslim serviceman now faced increased pressure as he began to come to new conclusions about the world around him. He also adopted the popular frames of worldwide Western and Israeli aggression and injustice against Muslims, arguing that while Hamas had made mistakes, it deserved the benefit of the doubt because its intentions to establish an Islamic state were pure. America and Israel, he argued, "can get away with so much in the way of the mischief that they create on the earth," while "if any Islamic group makes an error, they are ripped apart by the enemies of Islam." He saw the West as an aggressor due to its objections to the implementation of *sharia* law, either domestically or around the world: "the Western world makes clear that it does not want Islamic rule to prevail . . . not only in their own lands but in the lands of the Muslims as witnessed by their mighty plotting around the world."[31]

The frames he adopted therefore led Hasan to see Hamas as not being afforded any international support due to a prevailing geopolitical system that was centered on oppressing Muslims and preventing them from fully practicing their religion. His opinion on this matter, and support for Hamas against Israel and the West, was also intrinsically linked to his apparent embrace of *al-wala wal-bara*. Writing about his support for Hamas he noted that "the Muslims should know that Hamas and other sprouting Islamic states will make mistakes and is not going to be perfect in the implementation of Shariah. The west will be sure to point these deficiencies out. However, the believers have mercy on the believers and are firm against the non-believers. Not the other way around."[32]

For Hasan, Hamas was a shining example of the implementation of *sharia* law and *al-wala wal-bara*. He praised the group for taking up arms against the enemies of Islam while other Muslims and Muslim-majority states sat idly by. Yet there is no evidence that at this time Hasan had even considered taking part in any violent action to support Awlaki's cause. Nonetheless, he was drawing ever nearer to Awlaki. In February 2009, a juncture when anyone following Awlaki's work would have understood that he was a Salafi-jihadist, Hasan emailed the preacher to inform him of his involvement in a $5,000 scholarship prize to be awarded to the author of the best essay on the topic of "Why is Anwar al-Awlaki a great activist and leader?"[33] In a follow-up email, he also told Awlaki that he would like to offer assistance by sending money to Yemen to contribute to his activities. Despite all of this, Hasan remained interested in finding what he described as a "resolution between Islam and the West," which he began to perceive as locked in a multifaceted battle. It was to Awlaki that he continued to turn in search for solutions.[34]

The content of his emails during this period demonstrate how his religious devotion continued to grow, with the increased inclusion of lengthy tracts about the afterlife and the benefits Muslims will receive if they help the cause of the *ummah*. His messages also reveal a man whose main priority had now become to better understand his duties as a Muslim and to behave in such a way as to please God and guarantee a place in *jannah* (heaven): "In regards to pleasing Allah I, with his mercy, am already involved in giving to the poor. . . . Whether its time or money I truly believe Allah gives it all back and more. My goal is Jannat firdaus [heaven] and I praise and thank Allah for giving me the ability to strive."[35] Hasan also began to criticize specific Muslims he regarded as being too concerned with their lives in the physical, material world (*dunya*), to the detriment of the *ummah*. As an example, in an email about his stuttering efforts to gain funding to run the essay competition in honor of Awlaki, he expressed his frustration that "obstacles have been placed by Muslims in the community that are petrified by potential repercussions. . . . You have a very huge following but even among those there seems to be a large majority that are paralyzed by fear of losing some aspect of dunya. They would prefer to keep their admiration for you in their hearts."[36]

Hasan was unhappy at what he perceived as a witch hunt against Awlaki and began to see the situation through the injustice frames he had by this time adopted. In his view, Muslims who were afraid to pronounce their support for Awlaki were forsaking the most important aspects of the religion, such as standing up for the *ummah*, for the short-term benefits of *dunya*, or their mortal lives in the physical world. Hasan, now seeing himself as a fully-fledged Awlaki acolyte, took on the collective action frames and aspects of the identity required by the movement. As a result he was firmly on the path to violence.

His gradual move toward accepting violence as the only solution to the problems he came to perceive is best demonstrated in a May 2009 email he wrote to Awlaki about suicide bombing as a legitimate act of martyrdom. Voicing his support for the act of suicide bombing as separate from suicide, he provided an example to support his claim that comes chillingly close to his own actions six months later. He wrote of a soldier who entered an enemy camp and detonated a suicide vest on the eve of their attack on his forces. Such an act, according to Hasan, was permissible because "the suicide bomber's intention is to kill numerous soldiers to prevent the attack and save his fellow people." He even concluded that such an attack remained permissible even if it led to the deaths of innocent bystanders, justifying this using Koran 2:190: "Fight in the cause of God against those who fight you, but do not transgress limits." By Hasan's reckoning, the enemies of Islam often speak of "collateral damage" as an acceptable cost of an attack, and this therefore allowed the global jihad movement to respond in kind.[37]

Hasan sent his last message to Awlaki on June 16, 2009, writing to him about a religious lecture he had listened to about the story of Adam and his acceptance of Satan over Allah. This he again tied to *al-wala wal-bara,* claiming that Adam took Satan as his friend just as Muslims now mistakenly take "people of the book," meaning Christians, as their allies. To this end, he wrote that "if we ignore Allah like Adam we will have no excuse if we end up in hell fire because of the advice given by people of the book."[38]

According to several reports, during this time Hasan had business cards made that stated his rank and position as a U.S. Army psychiatrist but also included the additional designation "SoA"—which stood for "Soldier of Allah."[39] This suggests that Hasan was in the midst of a significant identity alteration. For Hasan, the contradiction of being a Muslim and serving in the U.S. Army, combined with his gradual acceptance of Salafi-jihadist ideology, became too much to bear. Just five months later, he killed thirteen people at his base in Fort Hood, Texas, in the name of the global jihad movement.

After Action Report

While Hasan later claimed that he was planning to be "martyred" during his attack, he was arrested after suffering gunshot wounds.[40] Prosecutors charged him with thirteen counts of premeditated murder and thirty-two counts of attempted murder; he eventually stood trial in a court-martial in August 2012. Throughout the legal proceedings, Hasan never denied his guilt and held firm to his ideological commitment to Salafi-jihadism. In a statement he gave on the first day of his trial, he admitted to being the shooter and explained his actions in the following terms: "The evidence will show I was on the wrong side. The evidence will also show that I then switched sides. The evidence will show we Mujahideen are imperfect soldiers trying to establish a perfect religion in the land of the supreme God."[41] Lt. Col. Poppe pointed out in an interview that his client had requested to represent himself in order to avoid receiving a strong defense. Hasan hoped that this would result in him being given the death sentence, allowing him to die as a martyr.[42]

Hasan saw no need to declare himself as a member of any specific organization and became precisely what Awlaki and global jihad strategists had wanted: a self-identified member of the movement, or "soldier of Allah," who took it upon himself to contribute to the struggle in the most effective way at his disposal. He accepted the rigid and simplistic worldwide dichotomy between Muslims and their enemies espoused by the ideology and fully adopted the required militant transnational collective identity.

After his trial and conviction, Hasan engaged in correspondence with journalists at Fox News, answering a number of questions that provide further insight into his influences and mindset. On October 18, 2012, he sent Fox News a handwritten statement renouncing both his U.S. citizenship and his oath of allegiance to the Constitution. The language he used reveals still further the extent of the influence Awlaki and Salafi-jihadist ideology had had over his radicalization. He addressed his rejection of the Constitution in classic Salafi-jihadist terms, stating that he could not support or uphold "any man made Constitution . . . over the commandments mandated in Islam." Hasan also reiterated the importance of recognizing Allah as the sole sovereign and rejected any attempts to "associate partners with the Almighty Allah." In the same correspondence Hasan was also queried about his relationship with Awlaki, to whom he referred as his "teacher, mentor and friend." He praised the preacher for "trying to educate Muslims about their duties to our creator," a process that in Hasan's case had clearly been successful. In a follow-up question from Fox News, Hasan was asked if preferring American democracy over *sharia* law was permissible. His response was based primarily around the *hakimiyya* doctrine, claiming that there is an "irreconcilable conflict" between democracy and Islam, as the former "places sovereignty of man over the sovereignty of Allah."[43] The terms of this answer are highly consonant with, although not exclusive to, the teachings of Awlaki.

Given Hasan's reverence for Awlaki and the preacher's desire to communicate with supporters and encourage violence, it is somewhat surprising that Awlaki barely responded to any of Hasan's ideological queries during the months he was in touch with the Army major. He only replied to the emails regarding Hasan's attempts to set up an essay competition in the preacher's name and his search for a wife, a topic on which he also solicited Awlaki's help. What is clear, however, is that Hasan was desperate for any contact with a man he came to see as his spiritual mentor. He repeatedly asked Awlaki to stay in touch, at one point asking him to "please keep me in your Rolodex in case you find me useful and feel free to call me collect."[44] One can only speculate as to why Awlaki avoided giving Hasan any specific instructions. It may be that at the time Awlaki was still concerned about making himself an obvious target for Western counterterrorism agencies. Perhaps he did not yet wish to risk capture or assassination and wanted to focus first on establishing himself as a leadership figure within AQAP, which he officially joined during the same period that Hasan was in touch with him.

Nonetheless, on November 9, 2009, just four days after Hasan's attack, Awlaki was moved to comment on the incident. His first of a number of reactions to the attack appeared on his blog. Here, he provided various justifications for Hasan's actions, basing them entirely within the framework he had developed over the years by focusing on the war on Islam and the importance of the global jihadist collective identity. Starting with the latter, he claimed that Hasan could no longer "bear living the contradiction of being a Muslim and serving in an army that is fighting against his own people." This was a dilemma that he knew many of his online followers faced in the West, and again he addressed this and reinforced the importance of the *ummah*-centric identity, writing that

> Nidal Hasan is a hero. He is a man of conscience who could not bear living the contradiction of being a Muslim and serving in an army that is fighting against his own people. This is a contradiction that many Muslims brush aside and just pretend that it doesn't exist. Any decent Muslim cannot live, understanding properly his duties towards his Creator and his fellow Muslims, and yet serve as a U.S. soldier. The U.S. is leading the war against terrorism which in reality is a war against Islam. Its army is directly invading two Muslim countries and indirectly occupying the rest through its stooges.[45]

Muslims who chose to ignore the duties of their true identity had, Awlaki argued, "committed treason against the Muslim *ummah*." Here we see further framing of a Muslim's position in the West as untenable, using terminology ("treason") that appealed to Western sentiments. This claim of treason was also intrinsically linked with *al-wala wal-bara*, as Awlaki suggested that to do anything other than attack one's homeland or make *hijrah* from it was to demonstrate loyalty to something other than Islam and the *ummah*. Hasan's act, then, was entirely legitimate in Islamic law, and Awlaki used his standard diagnostic frame to justify this, reminding readers of the global war being waged against

Islam and the Western occupation of Muslim lands. The legitimacy of killing American soldiers on their way to take part in this aggression could, under this frame, not be disputed, and it was the duty of all other Western Muslims to follow in Hasan's footsteps.

Asked if he thought Hasan had betrayed his American homeland, Awlaki argued that "it is more important that he not betray his religion." A far bigger betrayal, according to him, was "serving in the American army in order to kill Muslims." Making the same historical comparisons found in his previous works, he likened America to "the Pharaoh of the past" that was the "the enemy of Islam." For this reason, a Muslim in America "must not serve in the American army, except if he intends to go in the footsteps of our brother Nidal." *Al-wala wal-bara* was crucial for a Western Muslim's understanding of the duties their collective identity demanded. Awlaki alluded to this and the rewards that would come with carrying out these duties when he claimed that "allegiance to Islam means allegiance to Allah, his messengers, and the believers, and not to a piece of soil that they call homeland. The allegiance of the American Muslim [must be] to his Muslim nation, and not to America. Brother Nidal proved that with his blessed operation, and Allah rewarded him the best of rewards."[46]

Awlaki's presentation of Hasan's actions provides further insight into the various processes that the preacher was pursuing in order to create a global jihadist praxis in the West. Not only did he encourage the notion that Hasan identified with the movement due to his adoption of the transnational concept of the *ummah,* but he also claimed that Hasan was acting in accordance with the dicta of his religion, which obligated him to respond to America's war against Islam.

From a strategic perspective, of the three major case studies of Awlaki's followers, Nidal Hasan best fits the description of a lone-actor terrorist. According to the evidence, he was not involved in either online or real-world extremist Islamist or Salafi-jihadist milieus. He never discussed the plotting of his attack with anyone, and he carried it out

entirely on his own. However, yet again, Awlaki's strategic and ideological footprint is unmistakable, as is Hasan's process of moving from
extreme ideas to violent action.

From his earliest available output on the subject of Islam (his Power-
Point presentation), we can see a gradual adoption of the frames and
identity Awlaki helped to formulate. The available evidence also suggests that his vulnerability to Awlaki's framing was brought about by
an identity crisis caused by a search for meaning after his mother's
death and a desire to atone for her sins in the hope of helping her in
the afterlife. After beginning to adopt a new religious identity, he soon
became aware of a supposed plot against him and his fellow believers.
This was a belief brought on, according to him, by Awlaki's diagnostic
framing related to the ideological effort to dismantle Islam. All of these
issues were, in part, addressed by the collective militant identity and
ideology that Awlaki and the wider global jihad movement articulated.
These offered him a way to respond to the threats he believed he and
other Muslims faced while also allowing him to feel that he was pursuing the "correct" Islamic path he had been searching for since his
mother's death.

7

Zachary Adam Chesser

N OCTOBER 2010, a young Virginian named Zachary Adam
Chesser, who had by this time taken on the *nom de guerre* Abu Talhah
al-Amrikee, was convicted of attempting to provide material support
and resources to a designated foreign terrorist organization (namely,
Somalia's al-Shabaab) and communicating threats of murder to two famous American satirists.[1] His case is unique in that his activities in the
online jihadist community were so extensive and self-identifiable that
much of what he wrote and did online is available for research. Although forensic analysis of his online activity does not provide defini-
tive answers about the path he chose, it assists in the analysis of how
and why Chesser adopted the ideology and identity that was constructed by Awlaki and the wider movement, and how this impacted
upon his decision-making.

Chesser considered Awlaki a legitimate leadership figure and admitted after his conviction that, during his period of radicalization, he
was a devoted follower of Awlaki and "did not question [his] theological arguments."[2] Through his work, Awlaki identified and created opportunities and justifications for Chesser to take part in action. While
he also claimed to have been influenced by the work of multiple global

jihadist thinkers and propagandists, he stated that his decision to attempt to join and assist al-Shabaab was heavily influenced by Awlaki. The preacher, according to Chesser, put Somalia "on the map" for him as a global jihad battlefront.[3] Indeed, as we shall see, his first appearance in the online jihadist community was as a prolific commenter on Awlaki's popular blog.

Chesser's gradual adoption of Salafi-jihadism took place between his 2008 conversion to Islam and 2010, although much of his ideological transformation happened in a short space of time within this period. A few weeks after his conversion, Chesser left his job at the video rental chain Blockbuster Video due to his moral objections to films that featured naked women. His parents also later claimed that they began to notice Chesser imposing on himself and others a strict set of rules he believed to be in line with his newfound religion.[4] Despite his increasingly doctrinaire approach to Islam, Chesser nonetheless volunteered for Barack Obama's 2008 presidential campaign but within two months rejected the very notion of elections and democracy as part of his adoption of *hakimiyya*.[5]

It was also during this time that his relationship with his girlfriend broke down, again due to his altering perceptions of his identity, morality, women, and religion. According to the U.S. Senate Committee on Homeland Security, by the fall of 2008 he was "a full-fledged believer in the ideology of violent Islamist extremism and was searching for other like-minded individuals." This search was conducted primarily through the internet, which Chesser later described as "simply the most dynamic and convenient form of media there is."[6] Here he quickly became plugged into the online English-speaking Salafi-jihadi world, which directed his research and shaped his understanding of his religiously mandated duties, as he would later explain: "A Muslim who sincerely investigates their religion will find that it is obligatory to implement Islamic law, that voting is a doubtful matter, that jihad become obligatory in the event that non-Muslims invade Muslim lands. This is what I found [online], and this is what essentially everyone finds."[7]

Unlike the other cases analyzed in this book, Chesser also became a propagandist. By December 2009, Chesser, who was now a true adherent of Salafi-jihadism, had switched his focus from the consumption of propaganda and ideological materials to their creation and dissemination. While becoming very active on a number of jihadist forums, he also made the decision to contribute to the movement by using his technological skills to spread propaganda on various social media and content-sharing sites and create entire blogs dedicated to the movement. By the time he was arrested in late July 2010, Chesser had signed up to approximately six online jihadist forums; had created three YouTube profiles, two Twitter accounts, and a Facebook profile that were used to spread jihadi propaganda; and had built two online blogs calling for a global jihadist revolution.[8] He claims that the strength of the materials online not only convinced him to become part of the movement but also bolstered his extremism during a period when he considered rejecting global jihadism. While he almost changed his views due to the intervention of an acquaintance, the ideological materials he was accessing online were too persuasive: "One person briefly pulled me away, but this was supplemented by online material."[9] As well as using multiple online platforms to disseminate the work of Awlaki and other global jihadist groups and individuals, Chesser also produced original output. A large proportion of this drew heavily from Awlaki's work.

It is important to point out here that "online radicalization" is rare and an exception to the rule.[10] This is based upon the assumption that people radicalize and mobilize based solely on their consumption of propaganda online, without interactions with a wider on- and offline network of like-minded individuals and real-world influences. While Chesser was influenced by the materials he accessed online, he was also constantly engaged in conversation with like-minded Muslims in his community and users of forums, chatrooms, and blogs. According to the FBI investigator who wrote the affidavit for the prosecution, Chesser was not initially part of a wider network but was influenced by a combination of his own online research and discussions with a variety of people: "As Chesser began learning about Islam, he became very 'extremist' in his beliefs. He explained that he was watching online videos, discussions and debates, and over-the-counter CDs almost obsessively. One of the authors and presenters he preferred was Anwar Awlaki."[11] The same investigator also confirmed that Chesser sought specific advice regarding involvement in the movement from Awlaki, contacting him a number of times via email.[12]

In order to better understand Chesser's evolution into a Salafi-jihadist and identify Awlaki's contribution, this chapter will begin with an analysis of his early online involvement, which was largely made up of his writings and interactions on Awlaki's blog. This merits its own section in the chapter because it provides on one single platform a significant amount of detail surrounding his trajectory from new convert to Islam in late 2008 to fully mobilized Salafi-jihadist in mid-2010. Once Chesser's own output is analyzed and contextualized, the chapter will turn to the various official court documents that will corroborate the findings on his online activities. This will then be followed by a short analysis of a selection of his online postings on various forums, most of which were written in 2010.

Chesser and Awlaki's Blog

It is revealing that Chesser chose to play out part of his own intellectual journey to Salafi-jihadism on Awlaki's blog, which also afforded him the opportunity to test-run and discuss various thoughts and ideas with like-minded Awlaki followers. When Chesser converted to Islam in the summer of 2008 after graduating from high school, the speed with which his behavior and beliefs altered was remarkable, and this is evident in the nature of the comments he was posting on the blog.[13]

In early November 2008, when Awlaki posted his article on voting in the U.S. presidential elections in which he decried voting and democracy as an attack on *al-wala wal-bara,* a young reader using the name "Zakariya" posted a comment underneath the article in which he set out his current situation: "I am new to Islam, and my knowledge . . . is still very small. All of my life I have been very thoroughly into politics, even until a month or so ago I was a staunch 'so and so' supporter and was completely intent upon voting. I had even heard that it was *fard* [required by Islamic law] to vote, and I naturally agreed because I was only 2 months into my life as a Muslim and liked anything that was convenient."[14]

It has since been determined that "Zakariya" was in fact Chesser, newly converted to Islam and still navigating his way through the plethora of interpretations of his newfound creed.[15] He was a young, impressionable, and intelligent American teenager, and over the next months the initial stages of his ideological development into a Salafi-jihadist were richly documented on the digital pages of Awlaki's blog. Chesser's contribution to the comments thread in Awlaki's blog help to demonstrate how he began to adopt a new *ummah*-centric identity along with the frames constructed by Awlaki. In some cases, Chesser responded directly to the content of the article he was commenting on, and in others he used the comments thread to air ideas and issues that he was concerned with. It is also in these comment threads that Chesser repeatedly stated his desire to apply *al-wala wal-bara* and eventually make *hijrah* and fight jihad.

In his first posting on the blog, responding to a post in which Awlaki warned Muslims not to become involved in the democratic process, Chesser, still conflicted about being American and Muslim, was trying to find his way and was using Awlaki as his spiritual compass. Yet despite beginning this journey as a more integrationist, mainstream

Muslim, he rapidly became convinced by Salafi-jihadist arguments. Even in his first comment on the blog, mere months after his conversion, he explained how he came to reject democracy after initially embracing it as a Muslim. Chesser's criticism of democracy as a system that assumed a legislative power to be above that of God shows his increasing appreciation for the centrality of *hakimiyya* to Islamic belief. He was also receptive to charismatic preachers, and his first introduction to the concept of rejecting democracy as un-Islamic appears to have been through an unknown acquaintance he referred to as "Muhammad." At this early stage of his development, Chesser was already open to more fringe expressions of Islam but was still far from the man who attempted to travel to Somalia to fight for al-Shabaab:

> one day I was reading Qur'an . . . and I came across an ayat . . . that made me question voting. Then after I was openly "doubtful" on voting, a brother Muhammad, who performed jihad by delivering a controversial hukhbat [sermon] on voting today mashallah, discussed it with me and some brothers from my university after a sporting event with the DC Muslim football organization. . . . I now understand that democracy is a kufr system where you essentially tell a bunch of kufr, "hey! I know that you do not understand the decree of Allah, but I am going to endorse you as the legislator and ruler over Allah."[16]

Chesser chose to introduce himself to the online jihadist community in the comments section of a post that included some of Awlaki's frames directed at Western Muslims and the boundaries he constructed in order to maintain *al-wala wal-bara*. He was already wary of the threat that involvement in American culture and politics presented to his newfound Islamic identity and to his status as a Muslim, and Awlaki's blog heavily reinforced this. His concerns about stepping into the realm of *kufr* (disbelief) were also laid out in this initial post. He wrote of his fear that, through the act of voting for a president, he would be en-dorsing that person to "override Qur'an and hadith" and would there-fore be "in a state of kufr."[17]

In Awlaki's November 5, 2008, follow-up post on this topic, which was critical of Muslims who had voted the day before and warned that all the candidates will be involved in oppressing Muslims abroad, Chesser was again an engaged and active commenter. Following Aw-laki's line, he criticized other commentators who disagreed with the preacher, arguing that the American government would continue to "take advantage of us" as long as Muslims remain either passively or actively involved in the democratic process. Instead, his suggested course of action for Muslims was: "Fight the Jihad. Support the Jihad. Spread the Jihad."[18]

Drawing inspiration from Awlaki's use of stories about the heroic actions of Muhammad, which were juxtaposed with what Awlaki re-garded as the disgraceful passivity of modern-day Muslims in the West, Chesser argued that in the face of pagan aggression in Medina, Mu-hammad did not preach peace but fought back: "Did Muhammad let the Quraish do as they pleased? No. Did Muhammad just say, 'Islam means Peace,' when the *kafr* armies were marching on Madina? No. Muhammad defended his brothers and risked his own life for them." Again echoing Awlaki, Chesser chided his fellow Muslims for not fol-lowing this example, asking, "what of us? What about those of us who do not do our part?"[19]

The global consciousness that Awlaki instilled in his followers was a powerful mobilizing message for Chesser, who was also by now adopting more extreme interpretations of *al-wala wal-bara*. His entire critique of voting for leaders who engage in wars in Muslim-majority lands was based on a strong sense of collective identity that was closely tied to belonging to the *ummah*. Commenting later in the same post, Chesser wrote that a Western Muslim cannot ignore the fact that Amer-ican presidents have "killed MILLIONS [of Muslims] over the last decade" and that he felt compelled to act as "these people are all my brothers and sisters. These people are of the *Ummah*."[20] Describing his experiences at an anti-Israel protest in Washington, D.C., to fellow blog readers, he wrote of his disappointment that most of the pro-testers "were there for Palestine, and not Islam" and were therefore forsaking the ideology that required them to ignore national bor-ders.[21] For Chesser, this was a protest in solidarity with the *ummah* he perceived himself to be part of, and any notion of being specifically pro-Palestinian was beside the point. His understanding of *al-wala wal-bara* also inspired him to organize Muslim-only protests, espe-cially after his experiences in the protest mentioned above. Announcing it to fellow blog readers, he informed them that the protest would only welcome Muslims and that attendees "should not invite *kafir* friends that you should not have."[22]

Chesser still believed, however, in the legitimacy of nonviolent pro-tests in the West as an alternative to violent jihad. From his writings here, it can be argued that he saw his contribution to the jihad as being vocal and active in the West, particularly online, while pursuing a plan to conduct violent jihad abroad in the near future. In response to his account of the protest, one commenter advised Chesser to ignore in-effective protests in the West and make *hijrah* instead: "Brother—this is the reality, I would suggest you *Hijrah*, because Pro-*Mujahideen* people can't last long in a group of Hypocrites. Your Brothers out in Palestine, Iraq, Afghanistan are waiting for you."[23] *Hijrah,* as Chesser put it in his response, "is my number one objective." While he valued learning more about Islam, he was willing to "throw it away and fight until I am shaheed [martyred]."[24] Fighting was still perceived as the pin-nacle of religious duty and observation, and his goal of making *hijrah* was impeded only by his lack of resources to make the journey. Chesser's proposed response to the injustices facing the *ummah* was therefore not to plan or support attacks within the United States but rather the more traditional method of making *hijrah* and fighting jihad in Muslim-majority countries currently "under attack." When explaining his interpretation of jihad in the same comment thread, Chesser did not quote Awlaki but opted instead for more traditional Saudi Salafi scholars, including former Saudi Grand Mufti Sheikh Abdel Aziz bin-Baz and influential quietist Salafi scholar Muhammad ibn al-Uthaymeen.[25]

During these incipient stages of his path to al-Shabaab, Chesser also used the comments thread in Awlaki's blog to publish drafts of lectures or essays he was writing, asking for comments and corrections from his fellow Awlaki fans. In December 2008, under Awlaki's blog post "Finding a Balance," Chesser took the opportunity to post an essay on a number of themes that had been developed by Awlaki, including the "customization" of Islam to suit Western interests, al-wala wal-bara, shirk, and hakimiyya.[26]

As already set out in Awlaki's "Battle of Hearts and Minds" (a lecture that Chesser praised in one of his first comments as "engraved on my heart"), one of the examples Awlaki used to convey the war on Islam was attempts by Western governments, often supported by their Muslim allies, to modify tenets of Islam in order for it to adapt to Western society. Discussing his concerns about Muslims rejecting the implementation of sharia law over democracy and the use of the hijab, Chesser warned that "taking the law of someone else over that of Allah is generally considered shirk. . . . When you say, 'Hijab is not required' . . . when you say, 'Islam needs to adjust to democracy,' you are guilty of shirk. This is not debated. If you choose ANY kufr law over any law of Allah you are committing shirk—the shirk of obeying something over Allah."[27]

This topic was of grave concern to Chesser, who presented it as an emergency within the ummah and particularly in the West. He regarded correction of this mindset as a top priority for the movement in the West. In one of Awlaki's most strident blog posts, in which he provided theological justification for the targeting of Israeli women and children,

Chesser chose to discuss his own take on fighting jihad. Like most other Western Salafi-jihadists, his support for fighting jihad was seen through the various frames articulated by Awlaki. Muslims must fight back because the kuffar "seek to change Islam!" wrote Chesser. He went on:

> They . . . are trying to tell us what Islam really is! This is why we honor the Mujahideen. And this is why we fight. We fight that our fathers can make Hajj. We fight that our children are guided to Jannah. . . . We fight in the *dunya* [physical world] that we may achieve greatness in the *akhira* [afterlife]. We are Muslims. We are the ones on the straight path. . . . we are the ones who listen. The Qur'an does not say, "When you are attacked, and oppressed, and murdered, and raped, and robbed, and forced to leave your homes you lay down and take it." It tells us we fight those who do this us.[28]

For Chesser, like Awlaki, the millions of Muslims he believed had been killed by the United States since 9 / 11 proved beyond any doubt that "it is not a 'War on Terror'. It is a war on Islam." While this war was being waged physically abroad, its ideological component was at work in the West "in a blatant and obvious campaign aimed at . . . changing Islam in its entirety." The Western *kuffar* would not rest until they "eliminate any and all aspects of Islam that challenge their religion of Liberal Western Democracy."[29] While still living in the West, Chesser saw his duty as a supporter of the movement as fighting back against this ideological war through organizing protests and taking part in extensive online activism. Part of this response, in his mind, included warning Western "sell out" sheikhs who "are basically held on strings by the FBI and Western culture" and are therefore willfully ignoring the emergencies within the *ummah*. He was referring specifically to the situation of Palestinians in the Gaza Strip during Israel's Operation Cast Lead in December 2008 and January 2009. How, he asked, can Western Muslims simply ignore this "undeniable attack from the kuffar?"[30]

Chesser's own response to the situation in Gaza was to take part in a march against Israel in Washington, D.C, and he was criticized in the thread by other jihadists. One commenter admonished those who "talk about Jihad until they are blue in the face" but did not take the necessary steps to take part in it, focusing instead on protests.[31] While he agreed with the pro-jihad sentiments, Chesser's measured response was that while "we need jihad," a true *mujahid* could also take part in other activities as long as his "attendance benefits the *ummah*."[32] Echoing the advice found Awlaki's "44 Ways to Support Jihad," Chesser recognized the multifaceted role of the Western *mujahid,* for whom there were a number of options to take part in the global movement that were not limited to taking part in physical jihad or other forms of high-risk activism.

"44 Ways to Support Jihad" was an important document in Chesser's development, as it showed that he too could be a legitimate adherent to the movement despite still living in America. When Awlaki published the document on his blog in early January 2009, Chesser again posted another of his own lengthy essays. Like Awlaki, he wanted to shake Western Muslims out of their apathy about the fate of the *ummah* and called on them to do their part in helping its recovery. As things stood, Muslims remained blind to the state of the worldwide Muslim community and were not fulfilling their obligations to it: "Brothers and sisters your BMW's, your so-called tolerance, your mansions and your wealth mean nothing. . . . We live in the wealthiest country in the world and we feast while our brothers and sisters are starving. What did we do for them? What did we do for our starving brothers and sisters!? For the Ummah that is literally starving!? We left them. . . . Our brothers and sisters are dying and we do nothing! We are more preoccupied with our Western lifestyles than with helping the Ummah."[33]

This was a global struggle that required a global response in which Chesser saw himself and other Westerners as able to offer a unique set of contributions. Listing epicenters of jihad including Palestine, Somalia, Chechnya, Iraq, and Afghanistan, he criticized Western Muslims who "won't even bend over for a second to help" due to their *wahn*, or devotion to the material world and fear of death. This was a pathology that Awlaki repeatedly warned against and was also recognized by Chesser: "instead of making Hijra Feesabililah [in the path of God] we made Hijra for the Dunya. La ilaha ill Allah! [There is no God but Allah] Hear those words and ask yourself, 'What have you done for this Ummah?' Brothers and Sisters what have you done? . . . nothing."[34]

On January 22, 2009, Awlaki posted an article discussing suicide bombing and clarified the distinction between an act of suicide, which is seen as a grave sin in Islam, and an act of martyrdom, the pinnacle of worship for any Salafi-jihadist. In the article, Awlaki provided a noncommittal and vague conclusion, claiming that "if the intentions of the Muslim are good and for the sake of Allah then he is a *shaheed* [martyr] whether he died by the enemy or by his own hands. It is the intention that counts." What was most important for Awlaki was that Muslims displayed "a spirit of strength, sacrifice, hatred of the enemies of Allah and love of the servants of Allah." Awlaki also concluded that, whether or not his readers agreed with the act of suicide bombing, they must "support our Muslim brothers who are in the frontlines. Just like we disagree on many other issues, we should not let our disagreements stand in the way of our solidarity in the face of our adversaries."[35] Awlaki thus urged Western Muslims not to allow differences in opinion to corrupt the purity and maintenance of *al-wala wal-bara*.

Chesser responded with his own take on jihad and martyrdom in the comments thread, and again we can see here his gradual progression toward Salafi-jihadism. Following from Awlaki's own interpretation of suicide bombing as an act of martyrdom rather than suicide, Chesser focused on Israel and Gaza, claiming that jihad there was an individual obligation (*fard al-ayn*) because Muslims were being attacked.

He called on his fellow Western Muslims to fulfill their duty while they were still young and able: "Brothers and sisters jihad belongs to us, the youth." He also wrote, however, of his concerns about the meaning of jihad being distorted by Western values, looking specifically at a *hadith* that described *jihad al-nafs* (struggle within) as being greater and nobler that physical, violent jihad. As Awlaki repeatedly argued, Chesser also regarded this *hadith* as "fabricated, false, or in other words someone simply made it up." He then went on to rely on Awlaki's translation of Ibn Nuhaas's *Book of Jihad* to show that the primary sources all agreed upon jihad being a physical struggle.[36]

Once the primacy of "jihad of the sword" was established, along with the duty of all Muslims to react to the aggression they faced around the world, Chesser moved on to the question of what Western Muslims should do. His belief was that, if they faced no financial obstacles, they were to make *hijrah* to a jihad battlefield as soon as possible, suggesting that a lack of funds was all that was keeping him from becoming "a mujahid tomorrow." At no point, however, did he suggest attacks on the homeland of the United States, claiming instead that "there are wars in Morocco, Algeria, Somalia, Philistine, Sheeshan [Chechnya], Philippines, Iraq, Pakistan, and Afghanistan where you can help."[37]

He was nonetheless motivated by the Awlaki's glorification of the *mujahidin:* "The *Mujahideen* are our protectors," he wrote, "they are a wall surrounding the Kabba as thick as the distance from Indonesia to the United Kingdom. When one of them dies, we cry tears of joy, for this is a man who loved his *ummah.*"[38] Those who feared joining their ranks were, as he had established previously, beholden to *al-wahn* and were not able separate themselves from the material world. In his eyes, these people had not adopted the collective identity and responsibilities to act that accompany it, thus failing in their religious duty. Chesser's view of what he perceived to be a global conflict between the West and Islam was now fully shaped by the collective identity that Awlaki had helped to formulate.

One of Chesser's final contributions to the blog, at the end of January 2009, came in the form of one of his first public claims regarding
his plans to make *hijrah* and fight jihad. He was doing "everything I can
think of to make my way, and as soon as I have the means, I will be
gone." Chesser was under no illusions about what the future may hold,
writing that his fellow commenters might never hear from him again
or would later discover that he was in prison or dead. While it is not
clear precisely when he came to this conclusion, this comment allows
us to approximately date his decision to move from supporter and virtual activist to fully mobilized adherent of the movement. Chesser then
went on to offer specific strategic advice for others wishing to follow
in his footsteps. His suggestions to other potential *muhajireen* (those
who make the *hijrah*) included the destruction of all credit cards and
the closing of all bank accounts. He also listed the various items a *muhajir* would need to take with them, including basics such as toothpaste
and laundry detergent.[39]

Chesser's involvement during 2008 and 2009 in the online network
of Awlaki followers on this blog was merely the beginning of his involvement in the online Western global jihad network. In 2010 Chesser
moved from being mainly a consumer of online Salafi-jihadist propaganda to a prolific producer of it. His propaganda production in 2010
was also heavily influenced by both Awlaki's ideological and strategic
teachings. It may be that he moved to this phase as part of an attempt
to satiate his own guilt for not yet having taken part in any physical
struggle. He would make up for this by fulfilling other repertoires of
action provided to Westerners by Awlaki in "44 Ways to Support Jihad."

Online Writings and Activism

By early 2010, once Awlaki's blog was taken offline, Chesser began to
seek out other opportunities to remain involved in the online move-

ment. He started his own website called *The Mujahid Blog* and soon became acquainted with a group called Revolution Muslim (RM). Inspired by the Western Salafi-jihadist activism of the British based al-Muhajiroun group and its various follow-on organizations, RM, an offshoot of the Islamic Thinkers Society, was founded in 2007 by a group of American jihadist sympathizers led by Samir Khan's close associate Jesse Morton. It was originally created as an online group to promote the work of another popular Western jihadist preacher, Abdullah al-Faisal, but soon evolved beyond that. While its members also had a small physical presence and organized various pro-jihad marches in New York and Washington, D.C., its primary function was as an online Western Salafi-jihadist activist group. Its website ran various articles by its members promoting jihadism, criticizing American domestic and foreign policy related to Muslims and counterterrorism, and promoting the work of other jihadist clerics, including Awlaki and Bin Laden.[40]

According to Morton, RM "facilitated a gateway for Western Jihadists to move from ideas to violence." The site was a magnet for Westerners interested in jihadism, who would often reach out to Morton directly: "We would take them from a level of sympathy to the movement to a level of support and from a level of support to direct engagement." This was a similar approach to that of Awlaki, who lowered the bar for involvement in the hope of creating a larger pool of mobilization potential, some members of which would eventually upgrade to violent action. Morton explained that "first they just contact us out of interest after running into the website, then we would start inundating them with information, online conferences, our YouTube account, things like that." This would be the start of a radicalization and recruitment process. RM would often give tasks to its newest members: "We'd get them to do jobs for us, like cross-posting material on other sites. We would deepen their involvement in the hope this was the start of their pathway to jihadist violence."[41]

RM therefore held an obvious attraction for Chesser, who, having now graduated from Awlaki's blog as a fully-fledged Salafi-jihadist, joined the group in January 2010 and soon became its most prolific member.[42] Morton recalls recruiting Chesser after becoming acquainted with *The Mujahid Blog* and contacting him through a chat function on a popular online forum called *Islamic Awakening*: "I told him I found him bright and articulate and wanted to work more with him." Chesser immediately responded via email. He was enthusiastic about the prospect of joining RM and helping them any way he could: "Just tell me what you want to do, and in sha'a Allah I will do it. I have a lot of free time on my hands, so I can do pretty much whatever needs to be done."[43] He also rejoiced with Morton in Nidal Hasan's attack, which had taken place just two months earlier, and claimed that he had been in contact with the official Taliban website to offer his services, but was turned down.

Awlaki's work continued to be the single biggest influence on Chesser's ideological and strategic thinking and development during his involvement with RM. One of his first posts, in February 2010, was a lengthy piece about the various ways in which Western Muslims could wage war against the West at home. Much of his discussion revolved around low-risk, nonviolent methods such as spreading the call of jihad in the West and countering anti-Islam propaganda through the creation of websites and the organizing of marches that would garner public and media attention. He also recommended that fellow Western jihadists help spread the works of Awlaki as part of this effort, with the "Battle of Hearts and Minds" lecture featuring prominently: "a good introductory lecture for anyone even people far from the 'aqīda . . . is 'Battle of Hearts and Minds' by Shaykh Anwar Al-Awlaki. I advise you get a blank CD and burn at least one copy of this lecture and think of someone to give it to. . . ."[44]

Chesser's thinking at this time was also impacted by Awlaki's call for individual jihad, and he began to become more open to the legitimacy of domestic terrorist attacks. In fact, Chesser had used the phrase "open source jihad" in his writing before it appeared in the first issue of *Inspire*. This suggests that, as a leading figure in the online milieu of American Salafi-jihadist propagandists, he was sharing ideas with Samir Khan and others involved with the production of the magazine. In March 2010, three months before *Inspire* was first released, Chesser wrote about this concept for RM, displaying a very similar understanding of the movement to that which Awlaki and Khan were beginning to develop at the time. The global jihad was "a single message" behind which all Muslims could now rally and "find their own way to act upon." Chesser celebrated that this new approach would inspire "amazing creativity and ingenuity" among Western jihadists and ensure that "the jihad movement has moved from the mountains and caves to the bedrooms of every major city around the world."[45]

Chesser also recognized that open source jihad had helped to both remove barriers to participation in the movement faced by many Westerners and also created and identified multiple opportunities to become involved—both highlighted earlier as important components of Awlaki's work. The movement's effective strategic use of the internet now ensured that propaganda and recruitment materials were easy to access. A Western Muslim no longer needed to spend time researching and inventing justifications for taking part in the movement. This meant that "today the support for jihad is so great that someone who simply wants to please Allah, but has done little studying, can be easily motivated to go and fight." Apart from physical jihad, Western Muslims now had numerous options available to them should they wish to participate in the movement. Chesser directed readers to Awlaki's "44 Ways to Support Jihad," writing that "the first westerner to pioneer the concept of open source jihad was Shaykh Anwar Al-Awlaki. . . . [he] encouraged others to take part in whatever they could to further the message in many articles and lectures."[46]

While much of Chesser's writings by this stage were focused on Awlaki-inspired strategies related to spreading jihadism in the West, he also continued to display a close ideological affinity to the preacher. This is best demonstrated by two major interests of his found in his online writings. The first was his increasing obsession with al-Shabaab in Somalia and the idea of making *hijrah* to fight for them. As he would later admit, it was Awlaki's work that "put Somalia on the map" for him and enlightened him about the duty of *hijrah* in Islam.[47] In an April 2010 article on *The Mujahid Blog,* he called upon Western Muslims to join the jihad in Somalia and, as a motivational example, referred to reports of twenty Somali-Americans traveling from Minnesota to Somalia to fulfill their duties in this regard.[48] Having now become well informed of the situation for Muslims in Somalia and elsewhere thanks to the work of the online jihadi media community, Chesser wrote, "It is time for those [Western Muslims] learning the truth to act." He praised those who made *hijrah,* including U.S.-born Abu Mansour al-Amriki (also known as Omar Hammami, who had by this time built a reputation among Western jihadists), writing, "will you be like . . . Brother Abu Mansour and answer the call to Jihad?" In the same post, Chesser also described the practicalities of leaving for jihad, such as raising funds for travel, obtaining the necessary documentation, and changing one's appearance.[49]

Along with his eventual decision to attempt to join al-Shabaab, there is no better example of Awlaki's impact on Chesser than his endorsement of the preacher's call to kill people deemed to have insulted Muhammad. While in Europe much of the controversy regarding depictions of Muhammad originated with a collection of newspaper cartoons, America's inevitable "Muhammad cartoons moment" came after the airing of an episode of American TV series *South Park* in which Muhammad and the controversy surrounding his depiction were given the usual satirical treatment by the show's producers, Trey Parker and Matt Stone. On the morning of April 15, 2010, one day after the episode was aired, Chesser posted on his Twitter feed, "May Allah kill Matt

Stone and Trey Parker and burn them in Hell for all eternity. They insult our prophets Muhammad, Jesus, and Moses."[50] This was then followed up by a post on *The Mujahid Blog* and RM in which Chesser, taking his cue from *Inspire*'s similarly named crusade, called on readers to join him in "the defense of the Prophet campaign." In the post, he used Awlaki's "The Dust Will Never Settle Down" lecture to threaten Parker and Stone, writing that, "We have to warn Matt and Trey that what they are doing is stupid and they will probably wind up like Theo Van Gogh [the Dutch film director who was murdered after making a film criticizing Islam] if they do air this show. . . . join us in this campaign to let Matt Stone & Trey Parker know that . . . the dust will never settle down."[51] The post ended with the details of various home addresses registered to the two satirists. He also included a video he created titled, "South Park: The Dust Will Never Settle Down," in which pictures of other famous targets—including Ayaan Hirsi Ali and Salman Rushdie—were accompanied by the audio of Awlaki's description of the demise of Kaab ibn al-Ashraf, the poet who had insulted Muhammad.[52]

The post garnered much media attention and led to the shutting down of the RM site. However, Chesser used one of his other online outlets, *The Mujahid Blog,* to issue a lengthy response. The piece drew on a number of themes developed by Awlaki, including the war on Islam as manifested by the cartoons and efforts to change Islam along with the threat to the *ummah*-centric collective identity from Western culture. Chesser decried the immorality and hypocrisy of Western culture as a "cancer which bites at the root of global injustice . . . and drives to dehumanize the intrinsic morality of the rest of the world." *South Park* was merely a product of this, and their insulting depiction of Muhammad showed a desire to "degrade and mock a man who is held in the highest regard by Muslims." America and the West were responsible for the deaths of countless Muslims and, referring to the RAND Corporation reports criticized by Awlaki in the past, "openly say it is in a 'battle of hearts and minds'" to change Islam. Yet this

culture expected Muslims to champion its cherished values, including freedom of speech. Asking Muslims to accept such values and
stay silent about the cartoons was yet another example of efforts to
change Islam as part of "the destruction of the Islamic identity."[53]

This identity that Awlaki so adeptly constructed for Westerners
therefore allowed Chesser to define himself and the entire *ummah*
against the values of the West. While free speech "may be an American value . . . this is not a value that the Muslims share with America."
Freedom in the West led to moral corruption and decay and was "interpreted as the right to promote pornography, homosexuality, slander,
and libel against that which is considered sacred." The values of the
ummah must instead be formulated based upon a strict reading of the
texts and the works of scholars such as Ibn Taymiyya, whose writings
from the late 1200s continue to influence modern Salafism. Chesser argued that there was widespread consensus among the "legitimate"
scholars that no one is free to mock religion. To back this up, he quoted
Ibn Taymiyya's sanctioning of the murder of "whoever curses the Messenger of Allah," which Awlaki also referenced. Not only is murder
called for, he argued, but it is obligatory for all Muslims. With the help
of Awlaki's work, he also used the story of Kaab ibn Al-Ashraf as further evidence of Muhammad's support for violence against those who
defame him. Chesser argued that killing those who insult Muhammad,
based on a "correct" reading of Islam, was an article of any Muslim's
faith and could not be criticized or changed—any effort to do so was
an attack on Islam.[54]

Mobilization and Aftermath

Chesser's online activity soon gained the attention of the FBI, and he
was questioned and interviewed by FBI agents on a number of occasions prior to his eventual arrest. In an affidavit submitted to the court,

one FBI agent explained what the FBI had been able to piece together about his radicalization and path to al-Shabaab. These materials included intercepted phone calls, in-person communications, various FBI interviews with Chesser, and information obtained by other government agencies.[55]

According to the affidavit, in the course of the investigation agents found Chesser to be a highly active online jihadist. He later confirmed to the FBI that he owned *The Mujahid Blog,* on which he posted materials and wrote short posts in line with his ideological worldview.[56] The blog was described by Chesser as "primarily devoted to spreading knowledge regarding Jihad and the Mujahideen in keeping with the laws of whatever country in which it is being published. It is not intended to encourage any specific acts of violence. Rather, it is only intended to encourage general and ambiguous acts of violence. So, to this I say, 'Go Fight Jihad!'"[57]

One of the blog postings on this site that most concerned agents was his April 2010 claim of support for joining al-Shabaab's jihad in Somalia in which he explained how one could go about becoming a recruit to the group. The FBI found that this post was surprisingly accurate, and Chesser would go on to carry out every measure for planning the journey to Somalia he set out in the post, with the FBI affidavit confirming that "the information provided by Chesser . . . is nearly identical to his own recent activities." In an interview with FBI agents Chesser also confirmed that, by July 2010, he had taken over the primary administrative and blogging duties at RM and was also active on the English-language version of the popular Salafi-jihadist web forums *Ansar al-Mujahideen* and *al-Qimmah,* the official online forum for al-Shabaab. His activities on *al-Qimmah* also included creating and posting videos and other propaganda on behalf of al-Shabaab members in Somalia.[58]

The first agent to interview Chesser did so in May and June 2009, before his arrest. In these interviews Chesser claimed that he became interested in Islam in July 2008 and developed extremist beliefs as he began to learn more. His development into the man who tried to join al-Shabaab was, according to the information he gave in these initial interviews, greatly influenced by his participation in online discussions and debates, particularly watching online videos and listening to "over-the-counter CDs almost obsessively."[59] Chesser also confirmed that one of the authors and speakers he had been most influenced by was Awlaki and that he had communicated via email with the preacher on several occasions, receiving two replies.[60] During these initial interviews in Spring 2009, which were undertaken when Chesser was a person of interest to the FBI rather than a suspect in any specific terrorist activity, Chesser claimed that he no longer consumed jihad propaganda and that his views "had moderated over time."[61] Although he admitted that he understood jihad as a physical struggle, he also claimed to reject acts of terrorism and simply wanted to see the failure of American military efforts abroad.

On July 10, 2010, Chesser attempted to board a Uganda-bound flight from New York's Kennedy Airport with his infant son and was stopped by U.S. Customs and Border Protection, who then passed him on for interview by the Secret Service. His intention was to travel from Uganda to Kenya and then on to Somalia, where he would join up with al-Shabaab, but he did not disclose this during his interview with the Secret Service agent. Chesser did, however, reveal more details about himself. He confirmed that, despite his 2009 interviews with the FBI, he continued to favorably post lectures and other material related to Awlaki and continued to support and admire the preacher's work. Although he was turned away from the flight, Chesser was released after the interview and allowed to return home.[62]

Shortly after, however, Chesser contacted the FBI informing them that he wanted to provide them with information. Speaking again to agents on July 14, 2010, he confirmed that he had planned to travel to Somalia to join al-Shabaab just days earlier but then experienced a last-minute change of heart after hearing of a July 11 bombing carried out by al-Shabaab in Uganda that killed seventy-four people. While he was put off by this act of mass murder, Chesser still believed in Salafi-jihadist interpretations of jihad, contrary to what he told the FBI in spring 2009 about having revised these beliefs. It was during this interview that he first admitted trying to join al-Shabaab when he was stopped from flying to Uganda in July 2010, and he also confirmed that he was in contact with the organization. Chesser was informed by his contacts of the ease with which people could cross from Kenya into Somalia and join al-Shabaab and so planned to take this route until he was stopped at Kennedy Airport. This was his second attempt to join al-Shabaab, having also tried to do so with his pregnant wife in November 2009; in that instance he was stopped by his mother-in-law, who refused to hand over her daughter's passport.[63] This attempt to take his family to a region under the governance of Islamic law would later become common practice for Westerners joining or attempting to join the Islamic State in Syria and Iraq, many of whom took their wives and children to live in the utopia of the Caliphate.[64]

As Chesser understood it (and later explained to FBI agents), al-Shabaab was operating in a highly decentralized manner in Somalia, with what were essentially autonomous units carrying out their work independently of one another. His contact in al-Shabaab advised him that Westerners could be very useful to the group given their access to laptops, cameras, and other multimedia equipment, which they could then bring with them and use to produce propaganda for the militia. Chesser told the FBI agent that all new trainees would be given a six-week basic training course and would then move on to a specialist field. Most of the foreign fighters, including many Westerners, were placed in the al-Shabaab media branch, located in Mogadishu.[65] His hope was to assist with propaganda creation while also being able to take part in front-line fighting.

Some weeks after his final July 14 interview with the FBI, Chesser was arrested and charged with a number of terrorism-related offenses. In October 2010, he was sentenced to twenty-five years in prison for, among other things, communicating threats to Trey Parker and Matt Stone and providing material support to al-Shabaab, a designated terrorist group. In prison, he engaged in correspondence with staff from the U.S. Senate Committee on Homeland Security and Governmental Affairs. In his letters to committee staff, he revealed more about his initial motivations to become an online jihadist activist and eventually attempt to join al-Shabaab. When asked why he began to post his own, original global jihadist propaganda online, he claimed that it was "a means to an end." He also explained how Awlaki's open source jihad concept allowed Muslims in the West, for whom opportunities for involvement in the movement were more limited, to pursue means other than physical fighting. Through his online activism, which he refers to in Awlaki's own terms as "jihad of the tongue," Chesser was given the opportunity to feel part of the movement, which eventually led to him on to other means of expressing his support.[66]

An analysis of Chesser's own explanations to staffers about how and why he became radicalized also reveals the level of his religious devotion. In his letters he identified the two main factors that influenced his decisions: "religion and the state of the world." According to him, "I saw a nasty situation in the world, and I turned to my religion for a solution," or, as he put it in a separate letter, "I simply plugged the global situation into my religion and saw no other path forward." This is precisely what Awlaki's work urged followers to do. In Chesser's case, after converting to Islam he turned to it for explanations of, and solutions to, geopolitical issues and perceived injustices. In this search, he found Awlaki's interpretation of Islam to be the "most accurate" in this regard. He explained that his investigations into Islam led him to discover that "it is obligatory to implement Islamic law, that voting is a doubtful matter and that jihad becomes obligatory in the event that non-Muslims invade Islamic lands."[67]

This research into his religion eventually led Chesser to conclude that the best way to practice Islam was to make *hijrah* to Somalia, and his letters offer more details as to why this was his preferred destination. Once he accepted that violent jihad was an obligation, he "started to look for places to fight it" while also pursuing jihad through propaganda creation. He claimed that he was first interested in joining the jihad in Chechnya against the Russian state but was put off by a number of factors, including the Chechen militant attack on a school in the town of Beslan in 2004 that resulted in the deaths of 385 people. For him, this act was "Islamically unacceptable," and it is worth noting here how important Islamic jurisprudence was to Chesser, who was very eager to ensure that, through his actions, he was following Islamic law to the letter.[68]

As he began to turn away from the Chechen jihadists, Somalia "popped up on Awlaqi's website." By his reckoning, the situation there "had all of the same pros as Chechnya, but none of its cons."[69] Not only, as Awlaki's blog explained, was al-Shabaab a shining example of the successful pursuit of the Salafi-jihadist methodology, but it was also a destination to which Western jihadists had a realistic chance of traveling without being caught. It was therefore a combination of ideology and practical concerns that led Chesser to decide upon al-Shabaab as the most appropriate destination for his violent mobilization.

When analyzing Chesser's path to jihad, a number of factors must be taken into account. It is undeniable that he was heavily influenced by Awlaki's work, both ideologically and strategically. He came across Awlaki's writings shortly after his conversion to Islam, at a stage when he was engaging in research to find the most persuasive interpretations of the religion that were also relevant to his interests in geopolitical events related to Muslims. Swiftly convinced by Awlaki's framing, he adopted a very similar approach to Islam as a political ideology that called for violence in defense of Muslims. Chesser also took on the type of collective identity that Awlaki helped to formulate for Western Muslims, after which he saw the plight of Muslims around the world as an urgent issue that concerned him directly and one that he was obligated to react to, first through online activism and later through violent jihad in Somalia.

There is also a clear link between Chesser's ideas, as influenced by Awlaki, and his mobilization, both online and in the physical world. In fact, his path is precisely the one that Awlaki hoped his followers would take when he wrote "44 Ways to Support Jihad." The text offered various options for low-risk activism in the hope it would be the catalyst for readers to eventually become more deeply involved in the global jihad movement. Chesser began with low-risk activism, which for him was a gateway toward increased support for the movement and involvement in more direct, high-risk activism in the form of traveling to fight jihad.

Once he adopted the ideology and made the decision to become part of the movement, Chesser began what he understood to be "jihad of the tongue" through his extensive online activism. He took this upon himself after consuming Awlaki's work, which explained to him that, while violent jihad was the pinnacle of movement activism, other actions related to spreading propaganda were also vitally important. However, the lure of a more robust, physical mobilization soon led Chesser to seek out other opportunities. As seen in his writings, the concept of making *hijrah* for the purpose of fighting jihad was a powerful one for Chesser, and he discussed it often. His decision to travel to Somalia was heavily influenced by Awlaki's work, which identified the conflict there as an ideal opportunity to fight for the *ummah*.

For Western Salafi-jihadists like Chesser, the hypocrisy of preaching jihad online while living peacefully in the West can become too much to bear, and this helps to explain why some choose physical mobilization. That this was an issue for Chesser is demonstrated in a posting that admonished fellow Western Muslims who do not make *hijrah* and who "talk but do not act." He complained that he came across numerous people who "watch jihad nasheeds . . . and talk about fighting Kuffar all day long" but do little else. Chesser also recognized this in his own conduct, admitting that "I was one of such people" and calling for the end of "blog-only Mujahideen."[70]

Chesser is a classic example of a person for whom the dissonance between his online persona and his physical self became increasingly unbearable. As jihadism analysts Jarret Brachman and Alix Levine have explained, many Salafi-jihadists in the West whose contribution to the movement amounts to internet activity are often painfully aware of the vast discrepancy between their online persona and their real-world physical persona. They went on to argue that "online al-Qaeda supporters eventually want to become their avatar because it embodies all of the hopes, dreams, and goals that they are unable to actualize in the physical world."[71] The pressure to act brought to bear on Chesser was formulated by the global jihad movement and transmitted by Awlaki. The collective and global *ummah*-centric identity he adopted made it impossible for him to simply air his grievances online and organize small protests about the suffering of the *ummah*. He had to act, and the shape his activism took was directly influenced by the ideas and values articulated by Awlaki.

8

Awlaki and the Islamic
State in the West

SINCE AWLAKI'S DEATH, the global jihad movement has continued
to evolve. Most notably, the Islamic State has overtaken al-Qaeda
as its principal spearhead. The group's popularity has surpassed that
of its rival among Western Salafi-jihadists, many of whom have either
joined its ranks in Iraq and Syria as foreign fighters or have acted on its
behalf in their home countries. A number of English-speaking ideologues have emerged as influential figures and mainly engage with
their audiences through social media.[1] However, Awlaki's fingerprints
can still be found in IS ideology and propaganda aimed at Westerners
and the international terrorism strategies it pursues. When he was
alive, Awlaki recognized that the creation of wider jihadist mobilization potential in the West was useful not just for the conflicts taking
place at the time but also for future conflicts in which he foresaw the
involvement of Western Muslims. With this in mind, he ideologically
primed and prepared Western jihadists for the arrival of a group like
IS, and as a result he continues to serve as a reference point for those
who either join the group abroad or plot domestic terrorist attacks in
its name.

The success of the Islamic State added a new dimension to the appeal of Salafi-jihadism. While al-Qaeda has been able to maintain some level of support, it was never able to attract the numbers that IS has seen in a relatively short time. In terms of recruiting Western foreign fighters and plotting or inspiring attacks in the West, IS has been markedly more successful than al-Qaeda.[2] This new threat came as something of a shock to Western leaders and some terrorism analysts. Part of the reason for this is that, from around 2005 until the Arab uprisings in late 2010, an era that was also Awlaki's peak as the leading English-speaking voice of jihad, the global jihad movement faced its most difficult period of the post-9/11 era. The safe havens the movement cultivated in Afghanistan and Pakistan were severely reduced after years of military pressure. Domestically, Western intelligence and security agencies refined their methods, and governments developed new counterterrorism laws. The Arab uprisings had yet to offer Salafi-jihadists a second chance by giving them the opportunity to exploit new vacuums of power, and IS was but a twinkle in the eye of a struggling leadership of the Islamic State of Iraq (ISI—the precursor group to IS).[3] In May 2008, CIA director Michael Hayden summed up the thinking of the time when he announced that al-Qaeda was facing "near strategic defeat" in Iraq and Saudi Arabia and "significant setbacks . . . globally." It had "overplayed its hand," and its leaders, Osama bin Laden and Ayman al-Zawahiri, were losing the battle for the hearts and minds of Muslims.[4]

Meanwhile, in the West, where the numbers of jihadist attacks and thwarted plots were dropping, this confidence appeared to be merited.[5] The global jihad movement was struggling to maintain a relevant presence anywhere in the world, let alone in relatively stable and secure Western nations. However, Hayden's comments also allude to a misunderstanding about how the threat had evolved, morphed, and metastasized into something far beyond a single, hierarchical group with identifiable members who could be systematically killed off. For the new generation of jihadists in the West, it was much more than just al-Qaeda they were now fighting for, it was a global countercultural movement of which Awlaki was one of the leaders, and he was winning over their hearts and minds to an extent that few had yet fully realized.

Awlaki's work throughout this time ensured that he was able to keep the pot boiling for the global jihad movement during the lull it was experiencing, ideologically priming his audience for the next chance to take part. When IS was at its peak between 2014 and 2016, this meant that it was reaching out to an audience in the West that had already been prepared by Awlaki and the strategy he helped cultivate. The ideas it espoused—from the centrality in Islam of fighting jihad for the recreation of the Islamic state to the end times prophecy related to its establishment—were already mainstreamed for Western jihadists. Without Awlaki, IS would almost have had to start from scratch in the West. Thanks to his efforts, it was instead able to draw upon a generation of jihadists who are already primed to understand and accept the group's presentation of Islam and the terrorist strategy it is pursuing in the West.

It is no coincidence that when it began its outreach to Westerners, IS turned almost immediately to Awlaki's most popular lectures in order to grab their attention. In the first installment of the "Establishment of the Islamic State," one of its earliest English-language video series, al-Hayat, the IS media wing, made extensive use of audio extracts from Awlaki's 2008 lecture "Battle of Hearts and Minds." While the four subsequent volumes of the series used audio lectures of other famous jihadi figures, including Osama bin Laden and Abu Bakr al-Baghdadi, Awlaki was the figure IS propagandists chose to start with. His picture features prominently on the bottom of the screen as he celebrates the 2006 establishment of the ISI as a significant leap forward for the global jihad project: "A recent event is the announcement of the establishment of an Islamic State in Iraq, in Baghdad—the capital of

Figure 8.1   Screenshot from the Islamic State's "Establishment of the Islamic State" video series featuring Anwar al-Awlaki's "Battle of Hearts and Minds" lecture (*Source:* al-Hayat / LiveLeak)

the longest-serving Islamic Khilafah. . . . I believe this to be a monumental event."[6] Not only was this state's emergence to be celebrated, but it also "represents a move of the idea, from the theoretical realm to the real world." It provided that all-important link between ideas and action that defined Awlaki's mission, and ISI derived its legitimacy through the fullest possible implementation of Salafi-jihadist ideology.

While direct mention of Awlaki in IS propaganda is relatively scarce due to the bitter rivalry between it and al-Qaeda and the group's reticence over acknowledging the contribution of al-Qaeda to its own success, it nevertheless owes much to Awlaki's ideological groundwork in the West.[7] His sole mention in the IS digital magazine *Dabiq* comes in the fourth issue, in which he is presented as a figure to be revered and is given the epithet *rahimullah* (Allah have mercy upon him), often used by Salafi-jihadists as a mark of respect. He is also quoted alongside other major ideologues such as Osama bin Laden and Abdullah Azzam. Notably, the editors refrain from referring to Zawahiri, the current leader

of al-Qaeda, in such terms. Well aware of Awlaki's enduring importance to many in its Western audience, IS sees no benefit in doing
away with the value of his brand.

Ideological Groundwork

There are two interrelated themes found in IS messaging that, for a
Western audience, had already been introduced and popularized by
Awlaki. The first is what Shiraz Maher refers to as the "simple, binary
choices between two dichotomous and caricatured positions" that IS
offers its audience.[8] Namely, the fight Muslims must undertake between
haqq (truth) and *batil* (falsehood). More so than al-Qaeda, IS welcomes
any developments that encourage the separation of the world into these
two warring camps. It uses this division in order to help define the
movement's collective identity and to pressure Western Muslims into
choosing sides.

This approach feeds into the claim made by IS and other jihadist
groups that emerged during the Syrian Civil War that the conflict between Islam and unbelief is the very same that God proclaimed would
presage the coming of Judgment Day and the Apocalypse. IS sees its
fight in Syria as one of the final steps in the realization of this prophecy.
It bases this belief on an Islamic eschatology that focuses on the
prophecy of *al-yaum al-qiyama* (the day of resurrection).[9] There are
various signs listed in both the Koran and *hadith* of the impending apocalypse, and IS is particularly interested in *al-Malhama al-Kubra*, or the
great battle between the forces of Islam and the Romans, who represent unbelief. It is prophesied in the *hadith* to take place in the town of
Dabiq, which is in modern Syria.[10] As explained in the group's online
magazine *Dabiq*: "As for the name of the magazine, . . . it is taken from
the area named Dabiq in the northern countryside of Halab (Aleppo)
in Sham. This place was mentioned in a hadith describing some of the

events of the Malahim (what is sometimes referred to as Armageddon in English). One of the greatest battles between the Muslims and the crusaders will take place near Dabiq."[11] According to the texts, this event will also coincide with the arrival of the Mahdi, a redeemer of Islam who will descend from heaven, reestablish the faith, and lead the Muslims in this final showdown. IS uses language throughout its propaganda that tries to link this prophecy with occurrences in modern times and has been credited with making this an important component of Salafi-jihadist ideology.[12]

In the past, the al-Qaeda leadership rarely relied upon the end-times prophecies, and little was said by its leaders about the imminent arrival of the Mahdi.[13] One of the few exceptions to this is Awlaki, who, as a soon-to-be member of al-Qaeda, used the *haqq / batil* frame and the apocalyptic prophecies to define collective identity and mobilize Western jihadists. In a 2006 lecture called "Allah Is Preparing Us for Victory," he presented this conflict in terms that his audience at the time would relate to:

> So now the *Ummah* needs to be separated in to *Mu'min* [Muslim] and *Munaafiq*. And Allah has destined that [U.S. President George W.] Bush will be part of this test; he is the one putting people to the test. Bush is putting the *Ummah* through the test on one side and the *Mujahideen* are putting the *Ummah* to the test on the other side. So you have *Mujahideen* on one side and Bush on the other and they are attracting people towards their camps and that is what the Americans call "the battle of the mind and heart." It is really the battle between *al-Haqq* and *al-Baatil.*[14]

We have already seen in his translation of *Constants on the Path of Jihad* Awlaki's "promise to the believers" that Allah prophesied a final and ultimate victory to *al-taifa al-mansura,* but Awlaki also provided details of how this would take shape, in ways that mirror those IS now relies upon. IS propagandists, well acquainted with Awlaki's "Allah is Preparing us for Victory," also used clips from this lecture in addition to drawing from his "Battle of Hearts and Minds" lecture for the first volume of their "Establishment of the Islamic State" series.[15] The establishment of ISI in 2006, Awlaki suggested, was the first sign that *al-Malhama* was taking place; that it happened so quickly should provide further motivation for Muslims to take part:

> What was the situation of these areas twenty years ago? Al-Iraq was a *Baath* government that was officially secular, officially against religion and the Iraqi people were the furthest away from the religion amongst the Arab people. . . . So within a short period of time . . . all of this is happening. Does this not tell us that victory is soon? Does it not show us that these areas that *Rasoolullah* emphasized and talked about in the *hadith* are being prepared by Allah for the next stage? Al-Iraq, Khurasaan, Yemen and *al-Shaam* are being prepared for what is coming next. And what is coming next is *al-Malhama* because *Rasoolullah* talks about these places in reference to al-Mahdi and *al-Malhama* . . . and that will be followed by the global *Khilafah*.[16]

The establishment of ISI, however, was not the end of the story for Awlaki. Muslims now had to ensure its survival and expansion by attacking America because they were "living in a global village" and not a "local *khilafa*." They could not just take over a region and be left alone, as "the long arm of American injustice will get you wherever you are." He went further, pointing out a number of other "indications" that the apocalypse was imminent that Western Muslims could relate to. One of these was that "fundamentalists in the West are on the rise and religion getting into state affairs is also on the rise." He drew again on the George W. Bush quote about his "mission from God," insisting that the forces of Christianity were gaining power in America to help fight the final battle. Meanwhile, famous evangelical Christian leaders in America like Pat Robertson and Franklin Graham were making apocalyptic statements about a fight against Islam and helping contribute to a "psychological preparation" for *al-Malhama*. Even Denmark—"one of the most secular European countries"—was engaging in religious warfare though its cartoonists' attacks on Muhammad. For the enemies of Islam to take part in *al-Malhama*, "there needs to be motivation in the hearts first, and this motivation is starting to formulate in the West."[17]

During its peak 2014–2016 period, the claim that the *yaum al-qiyamah* prophecy was supposedly being fulfilled was one of the most powerful components of the IS message; it continues to hold weight in the present day despite the current struggles facing the group. IS links this to the concept of *hijrah* and refers regularly to *al-taifa al-mansura,* claiming that "the bulk of at-Tā'ifatul-Mansūrah [the victorious group] will be in Shām [Syria] near the end of times, because the Khilafah will be there."[18] Readers of *Dabiq* are told that "the best of the people on the earth in the end of times" are those who make the *hijrah* to the Caliphate and leave behind "the apes and swine" who choose to remain outside of it.[19] Modern-day Muslims are fortunate to be living at a time when this is taking place and must not miss their opportunity to take part. The train is leaving the station, as it were, and this might be one's last chance to fulfill their obligations to Islam and the *ummah,* thereby guaranteeing a place in paradise before Judgment Day.

As with the deployment of the prophecies, however, IS was not the first group to use this type of messaging to attract Westerners. Rather, it owes much to Awlaki's preparation of Western Muslim minds over in the last decade. When ISI was founded, Awlaki argued that Muslims were witnessing the most important moment in the history of Islam since its establishment, and many people of previous centuries spent their lives "wishing they were there." "It's not going to last forever," he warned, "if you sit behind, if you hesitate, if you are reluctant, then you will miss out because the chance only comes once." We are living in a "golden era" and "don't want to be sitting on the sidelines and lose out on all of this *ajr* [rewards from Allah]." The practice and implementation of *al-wala wal-bara* and jihad would ensure the establishment of the Islamic State, and that project needed to be pursued before one could enter paradise:

> These are two stations you have to pass through before you enter into *Jannah* and before you are established on earth: *Jihad fe Sabeelillah* and *al-Walaa wal Baraa*. So before these two issues become clear there cannot be establishment on earth. The *Ummah* has to fight *Jihad fe Sabeelillah* and the *Ummah* has to make it clear that their *Walaa* belongs to Allah, His Messenger, and the Believers and that they are disavowing; they are distancing themselves from *shaytan* and *al-Kuffar*. . . . So this party of Allah cannot be victorious until this issue of *al-Walaa* is cleared—the *Walaa* to the believers.[20]

Western Muslims, therefore, had to act immediately, and this helped to further bolster Awlaki's claim that they could no longer peacefully live in their home nations, "sitting on the sidelines" while a critical moment in Islam was playing out in front of their eyes. IS propaganda relies heavily on this type of messaging, and in issue 7 of *Dabiq*, readers were warned: "As the world progresses towards al-Malhamah al-Kubrā, the option to stand on the sidelines as a mere observer is being lost. As those with hearts diseased by hypocrisy and bid'ah are driven towards the camp of kufr, those with a mustard seed of sincerity and Sunnah are driven towards the camp of īmān. . . . Muslims in the lands ruled by the apostate tawāghīt will find themselves driven to the wilāyāt [province] of the Islamic State."[21]

Reminiscent of a topic mentioned in Chapter 3, IS uses a concept called "the gray zone" as a way of describing the space occupied by peaceful Muslims living in the West who refuse to join the group and fight jihad. An outcrop of the *al-wala wal-bara* doctrine, it describes the space between *haqq* and *batil*. According to IS, the gray zone is shrinking, and Muslims now must make a choice about which side to choose. Its propaganda is replete with references to this, arguing that since the establishment of the Caliphate by IS there was no longer any excuse for Muslims not to make *hijrah* and fight jihad. Whereas in the past they could claim there was nowhere to turn in order to live under *sharia* law, this was no longer the case. Further, by conducting terrorist operations in the West that further strain communal relations between Muslims and non-Muslims, IS aims to "compel the crusaders to actively destroy the gray zone themselves" by turning against Western Muslims.[22] The gray zone was now critically endangered and soon to be eliminated, in the process creating more space for Muslims to join either the IS project or the forces of falsehood and *kufr*.

One of the most revealing episodes in the Islamic State's pursuit to destroy the gray zone was seen in Western IS supporters' reactions during the aftermath of the November 2016 election of Donald J. Trump as president of the United States. A man who, in his election campaign, was perceived as targeting Muslims and who even threatened to ban all Muslim immigration to the United States had just been chosen by the American people to lead the nation. What more, asked IS supporters, did Western Muslims need in order to be convinced that the war on Islam was real and that it was time to pick a side? They flooded Twitter with comments such as: "I'm happy because of Trump. . . . he will also kick out coconuts from the gray line of hypocrisy like IS did";[23] and "Donald Trump's victory is just one more step towards 'the extinction of the gray zone' so consider it a blessing in disguise."[24]

Many have understandably—but mistakenly—attributed the development of the concept of the gray zone and the coining of this phrase to IS propagandists, but in fact it was first formulated by Awlaki. One of the first times that IS propaganda mentions this concept was in volume 6 of the "Establishment of the Islamic State" video series. The reference came in the form of an audio clip from Awlaki's "Allah Is Preparing Us for Victory" in which he used the term "gray area" as a way to explain the importance of *al-wala wal-bara* in the West: "You are either with us or against us; you have to make a choice—you can't be standing on both sides of the fence; now you have to make a choice. . . . You can't play both roles; you have to make it clear who you are with. So that grey area is disappearing. That's why *Rasoolullah* said this test will carry on until the two camps are completely separate; a camp with *iman* and no *Nifaaq* [hypocrisy] and a camp with *kufr* and no *iman*."[25]

Over half a decade before IS came to prominence and began attracting Westerners to its cause, Awlaki was one of the first preachers to identify the mobilizing power of the stories of the early history of Islam and the end times prophecies within the wider global jihad movement. He communicated in English the ideas IS now bases much of its ideology upon, offering motivation to his followers to both take on the *taifa al-mansura* identity and accept the dangers of the jihad program. The success of Islam and the Caliphate, as Awlaki told his followers, was written in the stars long ago, and IS now presents itself as the body that Awlaki assured them would soon appear, despite the movement facing overwhelming odds during his own time. Similarly, the gray zone was identified and defined by him long before IS propagandists tried to create this sense of tension and urgency for Western Muslims in the hope of convincing them to make *hijrah* or fight jihad at home.

Posthumous Inspiration

As the jihadist elements of the insurgency against the Bashar al-Assad regime in Syria began to gain momentum in 2012, it had a dual effect on the movement in the West. In the first instance, it was the catalyst for the biggest foreign jihadist mobilization in history. While the numbers of foreign fighters reduced drastically since IS began losing large parts of its territory in 2017, estimates for the total number of people who traveled to fight for it or other jihadist groups in Syria or Iraq range from 27,000 to 31,000, over 5,000 of which are from Western countries.[26] The allure of fighting jihad, however, was not the only motivation for many of these travelers. Some of them were attracted to the utopian promises of IS, wishing to contribute in any way they could to the group's state-building project.[27] Aside from fighting, they fulfilled multiple roles and offered their services as, among other things, technology experts, doctors, and teachers.

During the initial stages of this mobilization, it was not clear how intent the jihadists were on continuing al-Qaeda's global terrorist campaign. While some harbored a hope that this new wave of jihadists would focus solely on local conflicts and consolidation of their gains, others saw it as only a matter of time until the fight became global. These fears were eventually realized after the leader of ISI Abu Bakr al-Baghdadi announced the creation the Islamic State of Iraq and al-Sham in April 2013. In September 2014, the group's spokesman, Abu Muhammad al-Adnani, made his infamous announcement calling for supporters to attack targets in their own countries. The message differed little from what had already been produced by Awlaki and *Inspire*. Al-Adnani also drew on *al-wala wal-bara* while attempting to shame Western Muslims into acting after a lifetime of standing by as their *ummah* was systematically destroyed. Strategically and tactically, it also mirrored the lone-actor jihad championed by AQAP years earlier:

> If you can kill a . . . disbeliever . . . including the citizens of the countries that entered into a coalition against the Islamic State, then rely upon Allah, and kill him in any manner or way however it may be. . . . O you who believes in walā' and barā' . . .

will you leave the American, the Frenchman, or any of their allies to walk safely upon the earth while the armies of the crusaders strike the lands of the Muslims. . . . How can you enjoy
life and sleep while not aiding your brothers, not casting fear
into the hearts of the cross worshippers, and not responding to
their strikes with multitudes more?[28]

Al-Adnani's speech was soon followed up with IS propaganda that
built upon this call to arms. In issue 12 of *Dabiq*, released shortly after
the November 14, 2015, Paris attacks in which seven IS members killed
130 people in a series of shootings and suicide bombings, the magazine
heralded the start of the "just terror" era.[29] This term, defined by IS as
"operations in Dar al-Kufr executed by mujahidin with bay'ah [alle-
giance] to the Khalifah," was used "instead of using the term 'lone
wolf'" and mainly referred to IS-related attacks in the West. It underlined both the religious legitimacy and strategic expediency of terrorism in the West, and is the IS version of AQAP's "open source
jihad." Similar to *Inspire,* the IS online magazines *Dabiq* and *Rumiyah*
presented these attacks primarily as acts of revenge, emphasizing a
small-scale, "low-tech" approach including the use of knives and ve-
hicles: "one need not be a military expert or a martial arts master, or
even own a gun or rifle in order to carry out a massacre or to kill and
injure several disbelievers and terrorize an entire nation. A hardened
resolve, some basic planning, and reliance on Allah for success are
enough for a single mujahid to bring untold misery to the enemies of
Allah."[30]

As Awlaki had done years earlier, IS propagandists recognized the
power of propaganda of the deed when developing a strategy for
striking the West. Any act, from a stabbing to a mass shooting, carried
a message for both the enemies of Islam and Muslims living in the West.
For the former, jihadist attacks demonstrated the futility of Western
efforts to stop the movement—"and let the crusaders know that the

Islamic State will remain despite all their military arsenal"—and the price they must pay for fighting against the establishment of God's law on earth: "So when will the crusaders end their hostilities towards Islam and the Muslims? When will they realize that the Khilāfah is here to stay? When will they recognize that the solution to their pathetic turmoil is right before their blinded eyes? For until then, the just terror will continue to strike them to the core of their deadened hearts."[31]

For Muslims living in the West, acts of "just terror" were designed to inspire action, further reduce the gray zone, and define the core elements of a militant collective identity. Each attack therefore "demonstrated what the bond of faith and the loyalty of brotherhood can achieve" to those who remained unsure about taking part. The attackers embodied the aims of the movement and resisted the influences of deviant Muslims and infidels alike. They were "an example of those who dutifully bore their responsibilities of jihad, who sought honor through Allah alone, and who shunned the deviant calls to degradation."[32]

Abu Muhammad al-Adnani's call to arms, backed up by the "just terror" campaign of *Dabiq* and *Rumiyah,* has been heeded around the world, and the nature of attacks conducted by IS supporters in the West have taken on various forms.[33] Some of them are "inspired" attacks carried out by individuals or small groups with no connection to IS. Other plots are planned and conducted by groups or individuals who are part of an IS network with connections to its international operations section.[34] These approaches differ little from the al-Qaeda threat, but a more recent innovation represents a hybrid of the lone-actor strategy and the more traditional networked plots. Since 2014, around thirty attacks in Europe and North America have been plotted or carried out by individuals who acted alone, planning a small-scale attack while in online contact with an IS facilitator based in the group's territory.[35] These facilitators—who are referred to as "virtual entrepreneurs" or "virtual plotters"—use social media and encrypted messenger applications to establish relationships with, motivate, and guide jihadist sympathizers based in the West, many of whom have no other connections to jihadist networks.[36]

The extent of this new approach became clear in late 2016 after two separate revelations. The first came in October, shortly after three separate attacks in France, including the beheading of a Catholic priest during Mass. Originally assumed to be the work of unconnected lone actors, investigators discovered that a French IS member named Rachid Kassim had coordinated them. From his base in IS-held territory, Kassim used the encrypted messaging and social media application Telegram to contact and direct the young men involved in the attacks. On his private Telegram channel, he imparted his terrorist expertise, advising followers on anything from how to make a bomb to counter-surveillance techniques.[37]

During the same period, four IS-related terrorism trials took place in America that revealed the involvement of a group of around a dozen Western members of IS that the FBI dubbed "The Legion."[38] From their base in Raqqa in northern Syria, they made contact with American and other Western IS sympathizers and instructed them on when, where, and how to act. In the court documents relating to each of these four cases, there was one thread that connected them. Junaid Hussain, the leader of the Legion, was a twenty-one-year-old former hacker from Birmingham, England, who joined IS in Syria in mid-2014 and soon rose to prominence as one of the most popular Western foreign fighters. His activities were deemed such a threat by the British and American governments that he was killed in the summer of 2015 by an American drone.[39]

One of the U.S. terrorism cases in which Junaid Hussain acted as a virtual entrepreneur was that of Ohio resident Munir Abdulkader, who pleaded guilty to attempting to murder government employees and officials, possessing a firearm, and attempting to provide material support to IS.[40] In court documents relating to his trial, it was claimed that Abdulkader "was in electronic communication with . . . Junaid Hussain, and placed himself under the direction of ISIL and its overseas leadership." In their communications, Hussein "ultimately laid out . . . an overall terrorist attack plan for Abdulkader . . . to implement."[41] More specifically, Hussein instructed Abdulkader to kidnap a U.S. soldier and record his killing on camera; later he suggested that he attack a police station in Cincinnati.

Hussain, like many others who traveled to Syria from Britain and America, was also motivated and inspired by Awlaki. During the height of his fame, he gave an interview to British Muslim news website *5Pillars* from his base in Syria in which he demonstrated his own reverence for the preacher. Quoting at some length from one of Awlaki's most famous talks, he told his interviewer:

> And as Sheikh Anwar al Awlaki said: "Victory is on our side because there is a difference between us and you. We are fighting for a noble cause. We are fighting for God and you are fighting for worldly gain. We are fighting for justice because we are defending ourselves and our families and you are fighting for imperialistic goals. We are fighting for truth and justice and you are fighting for oppression. You have your B52's, your Apaches, your Abrahams, and your cruise missiles and we have small arms and simple IED's but we have men who are dedicated and sincere with hearts of lions and blessed are the meek for they shall inherit the world."[42]

Hussain was also active on Twitter before his death and would often refer to and quote Awlaki on his feed, posting messages such as: "'I specially invite the youth to either fight in the West or join their brothers in the fronts of jihad'—Sheikh Anwar Al Awlaki rahimuAllah"; and "'you have two choices: either hijrah or jihad'—Sheikh Anwar Al Awlaki (RahimuAllah)."[43]

Not only did Awlaki posthumously inspire planners like Junaid Hussain, but for domestic attackers and foreign fighters linked to IS, Awlaki remains a favored source for both Islamic learning and strategic direction, despite his connections to al-Qaeda. He is regularly cited by them, and their words signal the influence of his lectures. Of all 161 IS-related terrorism cases in the United States until May 2018, for example, Awlaki is directly mentioned as an inspiration for 37 (23 percent) different American jihadists.[44] A study by the author of two of the largest and most authoritative databases on Western IS supporters online also demonstrates Awlaki's enduring popularity.[45] An analysis of the largest single database of pro-IS English language social media accounts, which contains all of the tweets of 2,543 accounts from January to December 2016, finds that Awlaki is favorably referenced in one out of every ten accounts.[46] A similar study of the social media activity of 104 British citizens and residents who traveled to Syria and Iraq to fight jihad finds that he is mentioned favorably by 24 of them (23 percent).[47] One of the most influential of the British citizens to join IS, Ifthekar Jaman, who was killed in Syria in December 2013, cited Awlaki regularly.[48] When asked on the online question-and-answer platform *Ask.fm* who his favorite Islamic speaker was, he wrote: "Anwar al-Awlaki, May allah have mercy on his soul." Other British IS members used social media to praise Awlaki with comments such as: "All the english speaking mujahideen know and listened to Anwar Al Awlaki. . . . he invited and participated jihad may Allah accept him" and "my shaikh is Awlaki."[49]

Telegram, the encrypted social media platform currently preferred by IS, contains numerous pro-IS channels with thousands of followers that are dedicated to reproducing transcripts of Awlaki's work. Users are also provided links to download his audio and video lectures and are regularly reminded of the ongoing relevance of his words. In one channel, members are given specific directions for how to send funds to IS without being detected, and the message is accompanied by a quote from Awlaki's "44 Ways to Support Jihad" in which he presents giving money to the *mujahidin* as equal to fighting: "Whoever sponsors a fighter in the cause of Allah has fought."[50] Awlaki has also become the subject of many internet memes shared by jihadists across various social media platforms. They usually consist of his picture alongside one of his many famous quotes about jihad, *hijrah, al-wala wal-bara,* martyrdom, and the importance of establishing Islamic law.

Beyond his popularity in the world of online jihadism, one of the most enduring features of Awlaki's work is his call to assassinate anyone who insults Islam and the honor of Muhammad. Two separate IS-linked plots in America, for example, revolved around a desire to kill individuals who were involved in drawing of cartoons of Muhammad. One of these took place in early May 2015, when Elton Simpson and his accomplice, Nadir Soofi, traveled to Garland, Texas, as part of a plot to use assault rifles to kill the attendees of an event celebrating the cartoons. In the months preceding the attack, which ended in the deaths of both men before they could reach the venue, Simpson was in direct contact with Junaid Hussein. They chatted online using either direct messages on Twitter—Simpson's profile picture was a headshot of Awlaki—or the encrypted messenger app Surespot.[51] Shortly before Simpson mobilized, he logged on to Twitter and urged users to follow Hussain's Twitter account. An hour before the attack Hussain tweeted a number of messages suggesting that he was aware of the impending shooting, including, "the knives have been sharpened, soon we will come to your streets with death and slaughter!"[52] Two days later, IS released a statement taking credit for the attack in what was their first of a number of such claims for operations in America.

Both Soofi and Simpson had previously expressed support for Awlaki. Soofi was in possession of DVDs of Awlaki's lectures, and his mother later told reporters that the preacher's assassination "instigated a deeper passion for his teachings."[53] Simpson was a longtime follower of Awlaki's work and adopted the ideas of the global jihad movement before the emergence of IS. In 2009 he tried to join al-Shabaab in

Somalia, a country that preceded Syria as the prime destination for Westerners wishing to make *hijrah*.[54] His interest in al-Shabaab also led him, in the months before his attack, to reach out to another influential online jihadist operative named Muhammad Abdullahi Hassan, also known by his online moniker Mujahid Miski. A Somali-American, he traveled to Somalia in 2008 to join al-Shabaab and in 2014 began communicating with various American IS sympathizers, encouraging them to carry out lone-actor attacks.[55]

In December 2014, Miski engaged with Simpson via Twitter's direct message service. Their discussions included their support for the January 2015 attacks in Paris and their shared admiration for Awlaki. Simpson was wary of discussing his violent plans with Miski via Twitter, once lightheartedly chiding him for his lax protocols: "I expect a higher level of security from you my brother, :)." He did, however, discuss his dreams, and in January 2015 asked Miski, "I wonder what it means when one sees imam Anwar [al-Awlaki] in a dream," to which Miski ominously replied, "maybe he's telling you what he told nidal," a clear reference to Nidal Hasan's attack on Fort Hood.[56]

Simpson's previous involvement with jihadism before the emergence of IS and his subsequent actions on behalf of the group point to another of Awlaki's ongoing contributions to the movement. Simpson is one of a number of Western jihadists who can be described as Awlaki "graduates"—individuals who were introduced to Salafi-jihadist ideology by Awlaki before the rise of IS but acted in the name of the group by the time they mobilized. Perhaps the deadliest of these graduates was Syed Rizwan Farook. From as far back as 2007, Farook used Awlaki's lectures to help convince his friend, Enrique Marquez, to convert to Salafi-jihadism. Between 2007 and 2012, while stockpiling weapons and explosives as part of various terrorist plots they were planning, they both relied heavily on Awlaki's work, including *Inspire* magazine and his series on Umar bin Khattab.[57] During their discussions, Farook told Marquez of his desire to join AQAP and of his

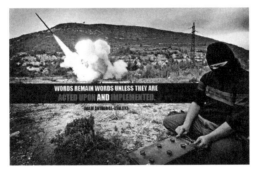

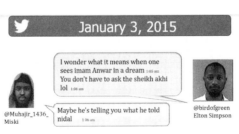

Figure 8.2   From top to bottom: Two examples of popular memes circulating on social media featuring memorable Anwar al-Awlaki quotes; extract of January 2015 Twitter direct message conversation between Muhammad Abdullahi Hassan (Mujahid Miski) and Nadir Soofi in which they discuss Awlaki (*Sources:* Telegram; Twitter)

interest in enlisting in the U.S. military, most likely as part of a plan to follow in the footsteps of Nidal Hasan.[58] While their plans never came to fruition, Farook, accompanied by his wife Tashfeen Malik, conducted an attack some years later in the form of a shooting spree on in December 2015 in San Bernardino, California, killing fourteen people after pledging allegiance to the leader of IS.

Awlaki's work has also continued to influence and cause internal conflicts for Muslim members of the American armed forces, as it had done for Nidal Hasan. Mohamed Bailor Jalloh was a member of the United States National Guard until he came across Awlaki's lectures. At some point between June 2015 and January 2016, he traveled to Nigeria and met IS operatives while seeking advice on attack planning before returning to the United States. Following this, he caught the attention of the FBI, who engaged him in a sting operation through the use of an informant. During conversations with the informant, Jalloh claimed that Awlaki's work had helped him "understand" his duty to defend Muslims in Iraq and Afghanistan against Western aggression.[59] This prompted him to leave the National Guard, while the establishment of the Islamic State spurred him to research other opportunities to do his part as a Muslim. At first, he considered following in the footsteps of Hasan, explicitly telling the informant during their conversations about jihad that he was thinking about doing "Nidal Hasan type of things." He, too, seems to have been exercised by the Muhammad cartoon event in Garland, Texas, at one point insinuating to the informant that the organizer of that event was one of his targets. Drawing from Awlaki's warnings about Western Muslims "sitting on the sidelines" as the most historic moment in Islam passed them by, he told the informant of the sense of urgency he had felt since the establishment of the Caliphate: "Sometimes you just have to take action . . . you can't be thinking too much . . . you have to pick a action and take it cuz time is not on your side . . . since Khilafah was announced, what, June, 2014? It's nearly two years now . . . time flies. Before you know it, it's three, four, five years, and you're still stuck in dunya or in dar ul kufar . . . find yourself not, on the side lines still, which is the problem."[60]

These Awlaki graduates also demonstrate how little the divisions between different jihadist groups matter to Western sympathizers. While most jihadist activity in the West since 2014 has ostensibly been carried out in the name of IS, this has had more to do with the group's ascendency since 2014 than any specific devotion to its leadership.[61] This focus on the ideology and goals of the wider global jihad movement over the importance of specific groups would have been welcomed by Awlaki, who believed that such a trend was crucial to the movement's survival in the West. When, for example, Chérif and Saïd Kouachi attacked the offices of *Charlie Hebdo* in Paris, they declared allegiance to al-Qaeda and Awlaki. However, their accomplice and friend Amedy Koulibaly, who on the same day carried out an attack on a Jewish supermarket in which he killed five people, pledged his allegiance to Abu Bakr al-Baghdadi and IS.[62] The rivalry between the two groups was scarcely relevant to them; it was the movement, or in their eyes simply Islam, that they were fighting and killing for.

In other cases, lone attackers have cited both Awlaki and IS as inspirations. After the Afghan-born American citizen Ahmad Khan Rahimi detonated homemade bombs in New York and New Jersey and was arrested following a shootout with police in September 2016, sections of his blood-soaked journal were released to the public. In it, he had written that "he looked for guidance and guidance came," followed by references to Awlaki and al-Adnani and praise for IS and al-Qaeda.[63] Two months later, in Ohio, Abdul Razak Artan drove his car into crowd of people on the Ohio State University campus and then attacked them with a knife before being killed by a nearby police officer. Soon after, posts from his Facebook account were released in which he described "how sick and tired I am of seeing my fellow Muslim Brothers and Sisters being killed and tortured EVERYWHERE." He urged America to "make peace with Dawla in al-Sham [the Islamic State]" and warned of "lone wolf attacks" if the oppression of Muslims continued. He urged his Facebook followers to ignore American Muslim scholars and institutions and "listen instead to our hero Imam, Anwar Al-Awlaki."[64] Ten days later, as has now become routine, IS claimed Artan as one of its own in *Rumiyah*. Referring to him as a "soldier of the Islamic State," it asserted that "the attack was carried out in response to the Islamic State's call to target the citizens of the nations involved in the Crusader coalition."[65] No other details or claims of IS involvement were included, suggesting that he was acting without direct IS command and control. The group was only too happy, however, to reap the propaganda benefits of Artan's actions, and those of the many others who have been inspired by the global jihad movement. Despite having no direct connection to IS, attacks like these are presented in the group's propaganda

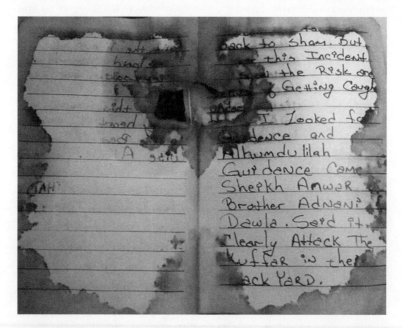

Figure 8.3 Pages from Ahmad Khan Rahimi's journal in which he cites Anwar al-Awlaki and Abu Muhammad al-Adnani *(Source: The Long War Journal)*

in a section called "Operations," often with surprisingly little fanfare, and listed alongside other attacks the group had undertaken around the world, including Syria and Iraq.

Awlaki's work has therefore proved useful during both of the main phases of IS activity in the West, beginning with its initial calls for Westerners to make *hijrah* and its current preference that they conduct attacks at home. His enduring popularity among Western jihadists prompts the question of what his perceptions of the group would be if he were still alive today. Would he have switched allegiances when it announced its establishment in Syria in 2013 as the Islamic State of Iraq and al-Sham, or in Yemen in November 2014 as the Islamic State in Yemen (ISY), or would he have remained with al-Qaeda? Awlaki would certainly have found himself in an awkward position, having lavished praise upon its predecessor ISI in previous years, while also speaking in the same apocalyptic terms now so closely associated with IS. His Western followers, many of whom are now enamored with al-Baghdadi and his cohort, might also have placed him under great pressure to do so.

However, Awlaki was also a senior member of AQAP, a group that has remained loyal to al-Qaeda and its current leader Ayman al-Zawahiri despite pressure from IS to swear allegiance to its leadership. Since July 2018, the two organizations have also been involved in a bitter conflict in Yemen in which AQAP retains the upper hand. Further, ISY's presence in Yemen is limited, and its members do not yet appear to possess the resources or tribal connections required to replace AQAP as the dominant jihadist force in the country.[66] Records show that while Awlaki was in Yemen, he spent his time in parts of the al-Marib, al-Jawf, and Shabwah governorates. These are areas where AQAP were present at the time and retain influence to this day.[67] Had he chosen to switch allegiances while remaining in Yemen, he would have risked causing trouble not just for himself but also his tribe, the Awalik, who are engaged in a complex relationship with AQAP.[68] Additionally, Awlaki was wary of applying an unbending version of *takfir* and seldom relied on sectarianism in his work, preferring instead to stress the importance of unity among Muslims. While both groups can be described as *takfiri*, IS, unlike al-Qaeda, pursued a brutally anti-Shiite sectarian program in Iraq that was influenced by the ideology of Abu Musab al-Zarqawi and has resulted in the killing of countless Shiite and other related Islamic sects. Finally, at the time of writing, no other senior al-Qaeda figure has joined IS, and were Awlaki to have turned his back on the group, he would have represented a very rare exception. Indeed, current research suggests that, of the jihadist defections in Yemen, most are ISY fighters choosing to join AQAP, seeing the group as more powerful and representative of the needs and concerns of locals.[69]

Much of this, however, is pure speculation that also takes it as a given that Awlaki would be in the same position today that he was when he was killed in 2011. If we were to consider the fact that he was held in such high regard by AQAP head Nasir al-Wuhaishi that he wanted Awlaki to replace him, then it is not beyond the realm of possibility that, by the time IS rose to prominence, Awlaki would have been in a position to act as more of a peacemaker and a link between the two groups. This is, admittedly, perhaps the most speculative of all the suggestions related to the Awlaki / IS question. However, were he still alive today, there is reason to believe that the terrain of the global jihad movement would have looked rather different.

Conclusion

THE STORY OF Anwar al-Awlaki, his intellectual progression to Salafi-jihadism, and the impact he had on his audience and the wider global jihad movement provide unique and revealing insights into jihadism in the West. This movement is no longer confined to Muslim-majority countries, and through his efforts and those of a cohort of like-minded preachers and activists, its message now resonates with a small portion of Western Muslims. It achieved this through a process that includes the appropriation of contemporary Western political discourse about human rights, injustice, and foreign policy interwoven with the history of Islam and the fostering of a global, *ummah*-centric collective identity that demands violent action in order for the movement to survive and expand.

Awlaki's transformation, the focus of the first half of the book, can be understood as the result of a confluence of ideas, global events, and personal experiences. This book has argued that, when combined, these factors turned Awlaki into a leading advocate for global jihad among Western jihadists. The emphasis has, however, been on the evolution of Awlaki's intellectual journey and the influence and impact that long-standing ideas he held and preached had on his decision to embrace

Salafi-jihadism. This is because, in the view of this author, Awlaki's reaction to both global events and personal experiences was fundamen-
tally shaped by his preexisting ideological outlook.

We have seen how, during the early stages of his career, Awlaki's
output loosely fell into the activist Salafi category. In his lectures, he
fused modern geopolitics with Salafi theology, while his references to
modern-day *jahiliyyah* and the importance of *tawhid al-hakimiyya* often
betrayed the influence of key Islamist ideologues. However, it must be
said that many activist Salafis have adopted similar approaches and expressed analogous beliefs without ever turning to jihadism. In Awlaki's case there were also early signs of a sympathy toward more violent forms of Salafi activism. While he did not begin by openly and
unequivocally endorsing violence as a solution, he always held a roman-
ticized view of jihad and was open to changing his position on the
correct methodology for achieving change. His early endorsement for
suicide bombing, a conclusion he reached by relying on the story of the
King and the Boy, set him apart from most other Salafis operating in
America at the time. This, along with his description of jihad as a constant and unchanging form of worship, suggests that he was drawn to
the work of Yusuf al-Uyayree years before he openly endorsed the jihadist ideologue in his 2005 translation of *Constants on the Path of Jihad*.
Even before 2005, while living in England, his decision to highlight for
a Western audience Ibn Nuhaas's contribution to justifying violent jihad
was questionable at best. Of the numerous more relevant works he
could have spent his time translating and discussing, he chose *The Book
of Jihad* at a time of heightened tension and increased jihadist activity
in the West.

The ideological and methodological flexibility that was to define
Awlaki's journey may also have been the result of his lack of scholarly
credentials. His activist Salafi outlook, unmoored from the direct guidance of any specific sheikhs or scholars, meant that he was far less re-
stricted in how he viewed jihad and its implementation and he did not

have to answer to anyone for his views and interpretations. This lack of a powerful scholarly influence along with the Islamist ideological component of his Salafi theology meant that his beliefs were volatile and subject to significant transformation. A gradual change is distinctly noticeable in his judgment of specific Salafi doctrines. His interpretation of these became more extreme in reaction to geopolitical shifts that in Awlaki's perception were causing increasing levels of harm to the *ummah*.

The most important of these doctrines is of course jihad. A component of any strand of Salafi belief, it was always uppermost in Awlaki's thoughts. From a historic perspective, he regularly glorified the military exploits of Muhammad and the Salaf in his early work. At the same time, the activist component of his ideology as well as his engagement with contemporary geopolitics led him to support the defensive cause of pre-9/11 classical jihad campaigns in places like Afghanistan, Chechnya, and Bosnia. When on 9/11 al-Qaeda announced to the world its brand of global jihadism—defined by the mass killing of civilians in Western countries—it is likely that Awlaki did not embrace this new development fully. This helps in part to explain his initial condemnations of al-Qaeda in the months following the attacks. At this early stage of global jihadism, Awlaki may not yet have come to terms with the fact that this was the future of the movement. 9/11 announced to the world that acts of indiscriminate international terrorism were now the new face of Salafi-jihadism, and while Awlaki had yet to catch up with this development, his ideological flexibility coupled with a preexisting sympathy for modern-day jihad meant that it would not take him long to do so. As jihadism evolved, so did he, and within four years of 9/11 he was an open supporter of al-Qaeda.

Not only did 9/11 show Awlaki the future of jihad, but it was also the catalyst for a number of major global events and domestic developments that were to influence his evolution from activist to jihadi Salafism. The most important of these were U.S. military engagements

that came to characterize the early years of the War on Terror era. In
Awlaki's eyes, the U.S. invasion and occupation of Muslim-majority
countries was more than just a response to the al-Qaeda threat; it was
the next stage of a war on Islam that stretched back to the moment the
Koran was revealed to Muhammad in the seventh century. Inside the
United States, Awlaki also believed that this war was being stepped up
through government action such as the passing of the PATRIOT Act,
the aggressive pursuit by federal authorities of Islamic organizations,
and cultural efforts to redefine the very meaning of Islam and the use
of satire to ridicule its prophet.

On the occasions that Awlaki reflected on his own intellectual
pathway, he rarely cited any negative personal experiences in order to
explain his support for jihad. His explanations instead focused on his
abandoning of nonviolent activism after observing a relentless wave of
anti-Muslim activity in the West. This, he claimed, eventually convinced him that violence was the only way to save the *ummah* and to
do away with man-made law. By allowing his beliefs and methodology
to become beholden to global affairs, he became open to adopting
and endorsing violence. That his initial beliefs had been influenced by
Islamist and jihadist activists, thinkers, and scholars made it all the
more likely that he would change his approach.

Despite this, Awlaki's 2006 imprisonment in Yemen is often regarded
as a turning point in his career. His mistreatment at the hands of authorities acting on behalf of America, according to this reasoning,
pushed him to violence and influenced his decision to join and recruit
for al-Qaeda. While it may have had some impact on him, it is important not to overstate the significance of this episode. By the time of his
arrest, Awlaki had already produced his translations of Ibn Nuhaas's
Book of Jihad and Yusuf al-Uyayree's *Constants on the Path of Jihad*.

The argument that Awlaki's transformation can be traced back to
the FBI's apparent threat to expose his involvement with prostitutes is
equally unconvincing and based on little more than speculation. Some

of those who knew him at the time believe that this is the only way to explain why he left such a promising career as an American Islamic preacher. However, similar to the prison claims, this is not something Awlaki ever publicly addressed. While it may explain his reasons for leaving America and certainly can be considered one of a number of factors, it alone does not account for why he then chose the path of jihadism. Claims that Awlaki simply had "nowhere else to turn" and became radicalized as a result of "blocked ambition" are not sufficient. Even if one was to rely upon personal experiences (or "push factors") as the main reason for his radicalization, it would have to be with the concession that other factors were at play.

What emerges from the analysis of Awlaki's output over the span of roughly fifteen years is that no radical or sudden transformation ever did take place. Among the most striking elements of his evolution is how little he changed his diagnostic framing and the sources he relied upon. Between the late 1990s and 2010, when he officially aligned with al-Qaeda, the only discernible changes in his message were his solutions to the problems facing Islam and Muslims in the West. Patient and long-term Islamic activism was discarded in favor of the instant gratification and apparent results of violence. What brought about this prognostic modification is a question that may never be fully answered, but the evidence suggests that Awlaki took both Salafist and Islamist teachings to conclusions that had already been made intellectually available by the more violent incarnations of both of these movements. One of the main features of this analysis is a demonstration of how Awlaki simply needed a slight adjustment in emphasis, making minor changes in the language and tone he used, in order to justify jihadist violence. It is a testament to the nature of his earlier work that much of it remains popular with Western Salafi-jihadists to this day, and almost none of it contradicts his later support for the global jihad movement.

It is therefore possible to observe a gradual move toward greater support for violence, which itself followed a well-worn path from activist

Salafism to Salafi-jihadism. This path was one that his contemporary and close associate, Ali al-Timimi, forged immediately after 9/11. Unlike Awlaki, however, al-Timimi was more constrained in his approach because of his connections to, and respect for, scholarly authority. Al-Timimi's main criticism of 9/11, for example, was that the perpetrators did not consult with or receive permission from a recognized Salafi scholar before the attack. He embraced a form of classical jihad, which has a much stronger basis in *sharia* law than its global, mass casualty–centered alternative preferred by his less learned friend.

It is not just a coincidence that Awlaki, a Salafi preacher influenced by Islamist trends, became a Salafi-jihadist. The hazy and permeable boundaries that exist between different forms of Salafism and Islamism demonstrate that we cannot ignore the impact of both of these sets of ideas, be they violent or not. Awlaki's own journey to jihadism was the result of a volatile fusion between Salafi theology and Islamist ideology, and he was able to move painlessly along the spectrums of both of these movements until he openly joined al-Qaeda.

That Awlaki underwent an evident ideological evolution goes some way toward explaining his popularity. Because of his established reputation as one of the most reliable sources of Islamic teaching in the English language—a reputation that landed him a senior position at one of the most influential mosques in America—when he began preaching jihad he was better placed than any other English-speaking jihadist ideologue to legitimately argue that Salafi-jihadism represented "true" Islam. Violent jihad, while central to his thought, was presented as merely a part of a grand project to establishing the sovereignty of God on earth. Islam, as he saw it, was the cure to the ills of humanity and provided the blueprint for a utopia based on the vision of God. As much as many would like to dismiss them as such, Awlaki and his followers (and indeed many other Salafi-jihadists) are not simply mindless, bloodthirsty killers. Many are thoughtful individuals driven by a warped sense of altruism; they sincerely see the jihad project as one aimed at improving humanity. The adoption of terrorism is therefore regarded as a means to an end, rather than violence for its own sake. Awlaki's work assisted in ensuring that the global jihad movement came to be perceived by his followers as the purest representation of Islam, rather than as the sole preserve of any specific individual or group. It would, he hoped, survive the collapse of any organization and the death of any leader. Thus far, the evidence suggests that he was correct.

One of the most powerful features of Awlaki's messaging was his mastery of encouraging violent activism while rarely needing to be explicit. Through his storytelling, which provided a skewed version of history, Islam, Western society, and geopolitics, he was able to take people to the edge of violence. Listeners were made to feel as if their final decision to support or commit an act of terror was the result of a process of rational, fact-based thinking couched in proper religious knowledge. He allowed them to feel a sense of personal agency in their decision-making. One of the numerous examples of this tactic was his justification for killing Western cartoonists and satirists who dared to turn their attention to Islam and its prophet. His lecture on the topic, one of the most detailed of its kind, was given in the context of the Muhammad cartoon controversy and purported to present listeners with the "facts" about how the prophet, whose behavior his followers are told to emulate, dealt with similar matters in his time. Awlaki's conclusion, that Muhammad and his followers responded to similar threats with violence, served as a subtle call to arms while also avoiding accusations of direct incitement to murder from all but the most eagle-eyed observers. This call to violence was so subtle, in fact, that clips from his "Dust Will Never Settle Down" lecture remained openly available on YouTube until the end of 2017 despite the removal of the vast majority of his videos, as it seemingly did not meet the criteria for violating the company's terms of service due to its lack of direct incitement to violence or hatred.[1]

For a generation of Western Muslim youth looking for easy answers to complex questions (often via the internet), Awlaki helped find a way for the global jihad movement to appeal to many who may otherwise have been beyond its ideological reach. Through cleverly designed and easily understood collective action frames, Awlaki's work succeeded in convincing a significant number of Western Muslims that jihad is not a foreign concept practiced in faraway lands by highly trained operatives. Rather, it is a duty that can be carried out anywhere and at any time, with little to no religious sanction required. Similarly, the mission to destroy the *ummah* was no longer confined to Muslim-majority countries but is evident within Western nations. Across the Western world, the ancient conspiracy to destroy Islam and Muslims was expanding, and Western Muslims were to take their cue from the most violent periods of Islamic history and resist this attack.

Whether he knew it or not, Awlaki successfully fulfilled many of the requirements of a social movement leader. Through his framing efforts, he was able to construct a convincing new reality—a way to understand global and local events—and to provide a blueprint for how to change it for the better. This new reality was, at times, brought to life through storytelling. Awlaki did not always create new stories, but he used this medium to draw upon and highlight a shared narrative for his Muslim audience while presenting their struggles as the continuation of a story that dates back to the glorious era of the *salaf al-salih*.

Awlaki's creation of this new reality depended upon the construction of clear and relevant diagnostic frames that both exploited preexisting grievances and highlighted new ones. Relying primarily on the war on Islam trope, Awlaki used this type of framing as part of an effort to convince his audience not only that was there a war being waged on their faith by their own country but also that they would soon find themselves a direct target if they did not fight back.

The war on Islam was used by Awlaki to frame and connect a multitude of events and ideas in order to claim the emergence of an existential threat brought on by a wide-ranging conspiracy that, without Awlaki's intervention, his followers may never have perceived. Developments as disparate as the War on Terror, the Muhammad cartoon controversy in Europe, and attempts by Western think tanks to define a moderate Islam, which may have been ignored or regarded by his audience as isolated incidents irrelevant to their lives, were now seen as indelibly connected and a direct threat. Using his unique storytelling style, he connected and interwove history, religion, and feelings of injustice into a convincing narrative and in the process created a platform for Salafi-jihadist praxis in the West.

Not only did Awlaki create the frames through which his followers came to understand their situation as Muslims in the West, but through his various prognostic frames, he also identified different opportunities for them to take part in the movement depending on their capabilities. For some, the call was to use their positions to plan and conduct acts of terrorism at home, while others with the means and skills were informed of the benefits of *hijrah* so that they could join and fight for an overseas jihadist militia. The ways Western Muslims could support and pursue jihad were also expanded beyond these two choices, as Awlaki worked to add as many adherents as he could to the movement by lowering the bar for involvement. In this way, approaches such as "jihad of the tongue" became perceived as almost equal to taking part in terrorism and insurgency for those not yet ready to take the leap into violence. Many other "ways to support jihad" were also offered as entry-level tasks for Western Muslims, with the hope that once they felt part of the movement, they would become incrementally more involved.

Awlaki's prognostic frames calling for violence relied upon operationalizing core Salafi doctrines and concepts, including jihad, *hijrah,* and *al-wala wal-bara.* Jihad was presented primarily as a defensive and retaliatory measure, no matter where it was carried out. Abdulmutallab's actions on Christmas Day 2009, for example, though attempted over

American soil, were described by Awlaki as an act of defense and revenge. Jihad was, he argued, a form of worship that ensured the protection of the *ummah* and was the only effective and legitimate method
through which Western Muslims could respond to the increasing
physical and ideological threats they faced.

Like any good social movement leader, Awlaki also recognized that
collective identity was a critical component of collective action. The
preservation and cultivation of a collective Islamic identity for Western
Muslims as a response to the war on Islam was therefore always uppermost in his thoughts throughout his career. He also knew that his
frames would only be effective if they were presented to an audience
that possessed a sense of shared purpose and experience, common
grievances, and a desire to work together to achieve change.

As Awlaki turned toward jihadism, this issue became increasingly
urgent, and the cultivation of a militant *ummah*-centric identity formed
one his most important prognostic frames. *Al-wala wal-bara* went
from a tool to protect identity to, as Awlaki defined it, "a central element of our military creed." It allowed for a clear delineation of two
important identity boundaries couched in the language of Salafism,
and formed a building block for the justification of violence. The
first boundary allowed Awlaki to cleave the most important social
division for Western Muslims, that between them and the majority
non-Muslim population. Awlaki identified *all* non-Muslims as the
cause of the ills of the *ummah* and the future executioners of Muslims in the West. He put forward convincing arguments that made
his audience view their apparently friendly and harmless non-Muslim
friends, neighbors, and colleagues in a new, terrible light. In this
way, he helped begin a process of creating both an in-group of Muslims under siege and an out-group of non-Muslim society and governments engaged in the persecution of Muslims. Presented in this
way, violence against the latter came to be justified as the only way
to ensure safety and future prosperity.

The second boundary that Awlaki helped to define was that between the "true" Muslims—those who implement Salafi-jihadism and represent the current manifestation of *al-taifa al-mansura*—and those who refused to take part in the communal defense of their people. By identifying those who were on the correct path, Awlaki was able to create a sense of urgency and the forming of a critical mass, either encouraging or shaming the inactive into taking part before it was too late. Awlaki deployed this in direct response to one of the biggest dilemmas facing his Western Muslim audience: what is the "correct" Islam, and which of the many Islamic groups are practicing it? The significance of these questions cannot be overstated. Young Western Muslims, often unable to relate to their parents' often culturally infused and apolitical Islam but retaining a desire to find a more compatible expression of their religion were prime targets for figures like Awlaki. He preyed on the "religious seeker," offering an Islam that formed the basis of their identity and addressed modern political and social issues that concerned them and made up part of their day-to-day lives and conversations.[2] Awlaki's description of the true Islam is simplistic yet convincing to the seeker: follow the practices of Muhammad and his followers and react to threats as they did. For those who have not studied Islam and its many scholarly interpretations, his knowledge of the religion's history and perceived scholarly credentials placed him in a position of authority and permitted listeners to take his word at face value.

Finally, through his motivational framing, Awlaki pursued the final requirement for mobilization. In the context of faith-based ideologies like Salafi-jihadism, motivational frames are often reliant upon religious obligation. By presenting violent action through the lens of religious principles and the historic actions of Muhammad and his followers, Awlaki argued that Salafi-jihadism was the most authentic expression of Islam. Through this approach, he also provided a cost-benefit analysis for his audience in favor of participation in violent activism. Fighting jihad, while dangerous, offered not only the individual benefit of pleasing God and guaranteeing heaven but would also help the cause of the collective *ummah*.[3] Practical examples of the rewards of violence were evident for all to see, from al-Shabaab's success in taking over much of Somalia in 2008 to the economic and societal impact of operations conducted by followers like Umar Farouk Abdulmutallab. As is evident in his reaction to Abdulmutallab's failed attack and his endorsement of a form of jihadist propaganda of the deed, Awlaki also recognized the motivational power of violence itself, and the force-multiplier effect that even small-scale or unsuccessful terrorist attacks can have.

In all three case studies of Awlaki followers presented in this book, it is possible to observe how his approach affected individuals experiencing some form of identity change, offering them a new sense of self, a coherent explanation for the global suffering of Muslims such as themselves, and a blueprint for action. In each case, they happened upon his work during critical junctures in their lives, when they were arguably at their most vulnerable. For Nidal Hasan, Awlaki was indirectly able to present Islam and involvement jihadist activism as form of redemption both for his parents' supposed failure to follow Islam (as he understood it), and his own involvement in the United States Army, an institution that was, as he came to see it, at the forefront of the war-on-Islam conspiracy. Thus, his act of mass murder helped Hasan to reconcile the apparent hypocrisy within his own identity which Awlaki's work helped him to identify and address.

In Umar Farouk Abdulmutallab's case, he came across Awlaki's work during his time as a student in London while undergoing a significant transformation of his own. A zealous convert to an initially apolitical form of Salafism, his engagement with the Islamist student activist scene in London led him to begin researching the most effective ways to use activism to save the *ummah*. Awlaki, a very popular figure among members of Abdulmutallab's milieu, was at the same time just beginning to produce his most openly jihadist lectures and translations.

Finally, for Zachary Chesser, who discovered and became deeply engaged in Awlaki's blog shortly after converting to Islam, the preacher's work acted as a moral and ideological compass. During his early search for answers about his newfound faith, Awlaki offered him a revolutionary vision of Islam that resonated with his experiences and requirements. As he engaged with Awlaki's lectures and writings, he discovered a way to understand what he could do to help the *ummah,* initially through online activism and eventually in the form of his attempt to join and assist al-Shabaab with its own propaganda efforts. Inspired by Awlaki's praise of "jihad of the tongue," he is a prime example of someone whose involvement in the movement began with low-level online engagement that acted as a gateway to more direct activism.

Beyond Awlaki's ideological contribution, his strategic thinking has had an observable impact on the form taken by jihadist operations since the first issue of *Inspire* was released. Jihadist activity in West has evolved in precisely the way Awlaki and his propaganda team at *Inspire* envisioned. The attack planning phase is, on the whole, less formal and less reliant upon the command and control of hierarchical groups. Attacks carried out by individuals or small cells acting alone while retaining a loose (often virtual) connection to jihadist groups or like-minded individuals has become one of the most common expressions of jihadism in the West. This has, in part, been made possible by the establishment of an accessible and dynamic social movement. In contrast to any kind of formal group, this movement is driven primarily by the power and resonance of its ideas and has so far been able to survive traditional counterterrorism measures.

Awlaki influenced not just the form that jihadist attacks would take but also the way that the global jihad movement came to view acts of violence. He contributed significantly to a change in how the al-Qaeda leadership, and global jihadists more generally, approached attacking the West. Many became more willing to loosen their control over recruitment and attack planning and came to see any act of violence committed in the name of global jihad as beneficial to the movement, no matter how small or ineffective it was. The jihadist propaganda of the deed approach first codified in *Inspire* was seen as so effective at ensuring that the movement maintained a presence in the West and motivated followers that it was adopted and refined by IS after it rose to prominence and replaced al-Qaeda as the driving force of the global jihad movement. This form of terrorism has become so pervasive to everyday life in the West that even random traffic accidents and acts of violence in major cities that have no connection to terrorism oblige law enforcement, politicians, and the media to question publicly if there is a jihadist motive. This has resulted in groups like IS reaping propaganda advantages even from events they have nothing to do with. Their propaganda work, in other words, is now being done for them, and this is a significant strategic success for the wider movement.

Since his death in 2011, Awlaki has therefore continued to influence not just the strategic but also the ideological trajectory of jihadism in the West. When IS turned its attentions to Western Muslims in 2011, it was able to draw upon a milieu of jihadist sympathizers already ideologically primed, in part, by his outreach during the previous decade. This is seen in both IS English-language propagandists' reliance on his work during their initial outreach and the many examples of Awlaki followers who went on to act on behalf of IS after his death. His assassination undoubtedly robbed the global jihad movement of one of its most important Western assets, but it also earned him a place alongside its other renowned martyrs. Like the efforts of those who came before him, his work will live on and continue to influence the direction of the global jihad movement in the West for years to come.

GLOSSARY

NOTES

ACKNOWLEDGMENTS

INDEX

Glossary

ajr   A reward from God.

aqidah   Creed, specifically referring to the core and undeniable components of the Islamic belief system. *Aqidah* is a crucial concept for Salafis, who place much emphasis on ensuring that Muslims follow the correct religious path. While Salafis broadly follow the same creed, interpretation of methods is what differentiates the various strands.

wali (pl. *auliya*)   Friend, protector, or helper. Often used in reference to those who are closest to God due to following the correct Islamic belief and practice.

batil   Falsehood (relates to the false beliefs that go against Islam and the *sharia*).

bida   *Bida* or "innovation" refers to heretical innovations in Islam. Salafis believe that any practice that developed in Islam that is not directly based on the ways that the first believers practiced Islam is *bida* and therefore not authentic. *Tabdi*, a term rooted in the word *bida*, refers to the declaration of a Muslim as an innovator (*mubtadi*).

dar al-Islam / dar al-harb / dar al-ahd   The terms *dar al-Islam*, or "territory of Islam," and *dar al-harb*, or "territory of War," refer to the main geographical distinctions in Islam. Although their exact limits and borders vary across time and interpretation, *dar al-Islam* is the territory where Muslims rule according to Islam, and *dar al-harb* is the territory where non-Muslims rule and Islamic law is not enforced. *Dar al-ahd*, or land of covenant, refers to a non-Muslim area which is engaged in some form of treaty with Islam.

dawah   To make an invitation. Refers to proselytization and public outreach and represents the act of convincing others to accept Islam.

dunya   The material, physical world. As opposed to the afterlife.

emir   A leader, ruler, or Islamic authority figure.

fard al-ayn / *fard al-kifaya*   *Fard al-ayn,* translated as "individual duty," and *fard al-kifaya,* literally "sufficient duty," represent the two forms of duty recognized as religious obligations by Muslims. Duties that every individual Muslim is required to complete are considered *fard al-ayn;* duties that only a certain number of community members are required to complete are *fard al-kifaya.*

fatwa (pl. *fatawa*)   Ruling on Islamic law provided by a recognized scholarly authority.

fiqh   Islamic jurisprudence.

hadith (pl. *ahadith*)   Collections of teachings, sayings, actions, and traditions of the Prophet Muhammad. The *hadith* are collected and presented in volumes, including Bukhari, Daud, Muslim, Tirmidhi, Majah, and Nasa'i.

hakimiyya   The rule of Allah as the sole sovereign. Also known as *tawhid al-hakimiyya,* it is a concept developed by a number of Islamists and activist Salafis. According to this concept, the only legitimate sovereign and lawmaker is Allah. Democracy, where the population lives under manmade laws and decides who should govern, associates individual humans with powers that only Allah should have and is therefore seen as a form of idol worship, or *shirk.* Based on this concept, many Salafis encourage their followers to refrain from participating in democratic elections and rejecting the legitimacy of democratically elected governments. In the most extreme interpretation, Muslims are called upon to fight against and remove governments that implement democracy and manmade law.

halal   Permissible.

haram   Forbidden.

haqq   Truth (relates to the truth and righteousness of Koranic message).

hijrah   Flight or departure. Refers to migration. In its original context, it refers to the journey undertaken by the original followers of the prophet Muhammad from Mecca to Medina from A.D. 615–620. In the Salafi interpretation, *hijrah* refers to the act of Muslims departing from Muslim-minority countries to Muslim-majority countries or areas being governed under Islamic law.

ibadah   Worship.

ijazah Permission. Refers to a certificate of authority granted to a scholar to teach and interpret Islamic scripture.

ijtihad Independent juristic reasoning by a qualified scholar who uses scripture to deduce a legal ruling.

iman Belief in Islam.

jahiliyyah Ignorance. Refers either to the historical period before Islam was revealed to Muhammad or, for Islamists, to any society that has not fully embraced the law of God over man-made laws.

jihad To struggle. Also has a legal meaning related to combat and fighting. The method by which this struggle should take place is disputed. A person who engages in jihad (usually in the context of violent resistance) is called *mujahid* (pl. *mujahidin*).

kafir (pl. *kuffar*) A non-Muslim unbeliever.

khilafah Caliphate.

madhhab Refers to one of the four schools of jurisprudential thought in Sunni Islam: Hanafi, Hanbali, Maliki, and Shafi.

manhaj Method. Refers to the specific method of applying the creed (*aqidah*) that Salafis follow regarding subjects such as worship. While Salafis broadly follow the same creed, interpretation of methods is what differentiates the various strands.

muhajir (pl. *muhajireen*) One who makes *hijrah*.

mujahid (pl. *mujahideen*) One who engages in jihad.

munafiq (pl. *munafiqeen*) A hypocrite, or someone who outwardly expresses to be a Muslim but secretly acts against the interests of Muslims and Islam.

mushrik (pl. *mushrikin*) A polytheist.

nasiha Advice promoting reform, usually in the form of a respectfully worded letter.

Sahaba Companions of the Prophet Muhammad.

Sahwa Awakening. Refers to Salafi revivalist movements in the Arab world.

al-salaf al-salih The "pious predecessors" of the Prophet Muhammad. Refers to the first three generations of Muslims.

sharia The Islamic legal system.

shirk Polytheism or idolatry. It comes in major and minor forms, with major *shirk* being an unforgivable sin. The association of mortal figures with Allah is considered major *shirk*. Those who practice *shirk* are referred to as *mushrikin* and are considered enemies of Islam.

Sunnah   Verbally transmitted records of the teachings, sayings, actions, experiences, and omissions of the Prophet Muhammad found in the *hadith* and used to develop sharia law alongside the Koran.

Tabiun   The generation directly following the *Sahaba,* and one of the generations that make up the *salaf al-salah.*

Taba Tabiun   The generation directly following the *Tabiun,* and the last of the generations that make up the *salaf al-salih.*

taghut (pl. **tawaghit**)   One who exceeds their limits. It refers to those who actively rebel against God. *Taghut* is used by certain strains of Salafis to refer either to secular leaders of Muslim-majority countries or to conquering empires that wage war against Muslims. It is also frequently used to refer to leaders of America, Western European countries, and Russia.

al-taifa al-mansura   The victorious group. The implication is usually that this is the group of Muslims that will ascend to heaven.

takfir   Excommunication of Muslims, banishment from the faith. *Takfir* is derived from the root *kafir* and is best translated as "the act of declaring someone to be a non-believer."

tawhid   The oneness of God as the sole deity worthy of worship, the core component of Islam and the most important factor of Salafi creed. For Salafi Muslims, *tawhid* is more than the concept that "there is only one God—Allah," including also the premise that nothing external to Allah should be associated with Allah. Salafis incorporate three interrelated forms of *tawhid: tawhid al-rububiyya* (the affirmation of the oneness of God), *tawhid al-asma' wa-al-sifat* (God as one in his names and attributes), and *tawhid al-uluhiyya* (God as the sole deity worthy of worship).

ummah   The global community of Muslims.

al-wala wal-bara   To love and to hate for the sake of Allah, the twin poles of loyalty and disavowal. According to the Salafi interpretation of this concept, Muslims should live their lives completely under the rules of Islam and reject anything that has any basis outside the confines of the faith.

Notes

Introduction

1. This is based on data gathered from court documents, written and oral testimonies of American jihadists, and media reporting.
2. This data covers the period between January 2007 and January 2015. New America Foundation, available at http://securitydata.newamerica.net /extremists/analysis.
3. "Case by Case: ISIS Prosecutions in the USA," Center on National Security, Fordham Law School, 2016.
4. Donald Holbrook, "The Spread of its Message: Studying the Prominence of al-Qaida Materials in UK Terrorism Investigations," *Perspectives on Terrorism* 11, no. 6 (2017): 3.
5. The first reference to this is in issue 1 of *Inspire*, released January 2010. "Just terror" was first used in order to describe rudimentary lone-actor attacks in the West in issue 12 of the IS online magazine *Rumiyah*, released November 2015.
6. See Cole Bunzel, *From Paper State to Caliphate* (Washington: Brookings Institute, March 2015).
7. See Peter Neumann, "The Trouble with Radicalization," *International Affairs* 89, no. 4 (2012).
8. Clark McCauley and Sophia Moskalenko, "Individual and Group Mechanisms of Radicalization," in *Protecting the Homeland from International and Domestic Security Threats: Current Multidisciplinary Perspectives on Root*

Causes, the Role of Ideology, and Programs for Counter-Radicalization and Disengagement, ed. Laurie Fenstermacher, Larry Kuznar, Tom Rieger, and Anne Speckhard, white paper, Washington, D.C., 2011, 82.

9. Haroro Ingram, *The Charismatic Leadership Phenomenon in Radical and Militant Islamism* (Surrey, U.K.: Ashgate, 2013); Quintan Wiktorowicz, *Radical Islam Rising* (Lanham, MD: Rowman and Littlefield, 2005); Fathali M. Moghaddam, "The Staircase to Terrorism," *American Psychologist* 60, no. 2 (2005); John Lofland and Rodney Stark, "Becoming a World-Saver: A Theory of Conversion to a Deviant Perspective," *American Sociological Review* 30, no. 6 (1965).

10. Wiktorowicz, *Radical Islam Rising,* 21.

11. Andrew Silke, "Holy Warriors: Exploring the Psychological Processes of Jihadi Radicalization," *European Journal of Criminology* 5, no. 1 (2008); Wiktorowicz, *Radical Islam Rising;* John Venhaus, "Why Youth Join Al-Qaeda," United States Institute of Peace, May 2010; Tomas Precht, "Home-Grown Terrorism and Islamist Radicalization in Europe," Danish Ministry of Justice, 2008.

12. Marc Sageman, *Understanding Terror Networks* (Philadelphia: University of Pennsylvania Press, 2011); Moghaddam, "Staircase to Terrorism"; Clark McCauley and Sophia Moskalenko, "Mechanisms of Political Radicalization: Pathways Toward Terrorism," *Terrorism and Political Violence* 20, no. 3 (2008).

13. Ingram, *Charismatic Leadership Phenomenon,* 49.

14. Jeroen Gunning, "Social Movement Theory and the Study of Terrorism," in *Critical Terrorism Studies: A New Research Agenda,* ed. Richard Jackson, Marie Breen Smyth, and Jeroen Gunning (Abingdon, U.K.: Routledge, 2009), 157.

15. Mario Diani, "The Concept of Social Movement," *Sociological Review* 40, no. 1 (1992): 8.

16. Charles Tilly and Sidney Tarrow, *Contentious Politics* (Boulder, CO: Paradigm, 2007), 4–12.

17. See Marc Sageman, *Leaderless Jihad* (Philadelphia: University of Pennsylvania Press, 2008); Jarret Brachman, *Global Jihadism: Theory and Practice* (Abingdon, U.K.: Routledge, 2009); David Snow and Scott Byrd, "Ideology, Framing Processes, and Islamic Terrorist Movements," *Mobilization* 12, no. 2 (2007).

18. Wiktorowicz, *Radical Islam Rising,* 210.

19. Quintan Wiktorowicz, "Islamic Activism and Social Movement Theory: A New Direction for Research," *Mediterranean Politics* 7, no. 3 (2007): 190.

20. Wiktorowicz, "Islamic Activism," 190.

21. Gunning, "Social Movement Theory," 157. The works Gunning refers to are: Andrew Silke, "The Road Less Travelled," in *Research on Terrorism: Trends, Achievements and Failures*, ed. Andrew Silke (London: Frank Cass, 2004), 186–213; Donatella della Porta, *Social Movements, Political Violence, and the State: A Comparative Analysis of Italy and Germany* (Cambridge: Cambridge University Press, 1995); Magnus Ranstorp, "Mapping Terrorism Research: Challenges and Priorities," in *Mapping Terrorism Research: State of the Art, Gaps and Future Direction*, ed. Magnus Ranstorp (London: Routledge, 2006), 2–24.

22. Gunning, "Social Movement Theory," 157.

23. Sydney Tarrow, *Power in Movement: Social Movements and Contentious Politics* (Cambridge, U.K.: Cambridge University Press, 1994), 4.

24. Erving Goffman, *Frame Analysis: An Essay on the Organization of Experience* (Cambridge, MA: Harvard University Press, 1974); Martha Crenshaw, "Decisions to Use Terrorism: Psychological Constraints on Instrumental Reasoning," in *Social Movements and Violence: Participation in Underground Organizations*, ed. Donatella della Porta (Greenwich, CT: JAI Press, 1992), 31.

25. Snow and Benford define collective action frames as "interpretive schemata that simplifies and condenses the 'world out there' by selectively punctuating and encoding objects, situations, events, experiences and sequences of actions within one's present or past environments." David A. Snow and Robert D. Benford, "Ideology, Frame Resonance, and Participant Mobilization," in *International Social Movements from Structure to Action, Comparing Social Movement Research Across Cultures*, ed. Bert Klandermans, Hanspeter Kriesi, and Sydney Tarrow (Greenwich, CT: JAI Press, 1988), 137.

26. Snow and Byrd, "Ideology, Framing Processes, and Islamic Terrorist Movements," 124.

27. Robert Benford, "'You Could Be the Hundredth Monkey': Collective Action Frames and Vocabularies of Motive within the Nuclear Disarmament Movement," *Sociological Quarterly* 34, no. 2 (1993).

28. Snow and Byrd, "Ideology, Framing Processes," 128.

29. David A. Snow and Robert D. Benford, "Framing Processes and Social Movements: An Overview and Assessment," *Annual Review of Sociology* 26 (2000): 624.

30. Wiktorowicz, *Radical Islam Rising*, 135–61; Snow and Benford, "Framing Processes," 619.

31. See Alaine Touraine, *The Voice and the Eye: An Analysis of Social Movements* (Cambridge, U.K.: Cambridge University Press, 1981); Randy Stoecker, "Community, Movement, Organization: The Problem of Identity Convergence in Collective Action," *Sociological Quarterly* 36, no. 1 (1995); Alberto Melucci, *Nomads of the Present: Social Movements and Individual Needs in*

Contemporary Society (Philadelphia: Temple University Press, 1989), 34; Enrique Larana, Hank Johnston, and Joseph R. Gusfield, "Introduction," in *New Social Movements: From Ideology to Identity,* ed. Enrique Larana, Hank Johnston, and Joseph R. Gusfield (Philadelphia: Temple University Press, 1994), 5.

32. Eric Hoffer, *The True Believer: Thoughts on the Nature of Mass Movements* (New York: Harper Perennial, 2010), 12.

33. Hoffer, *True Believer,* 13.

34. David A. Snow, "Collective Identity and Expressive Forms," Center for the Study of Democracy, 2001, available at http://repositories.cdlib.org/csd/01-07.

35. Scott Hunt and Robert Benford, "Collective Identity, Solidarity, and Commitment," in *The Blackwell Companion to Social Movements,* ed. David A. Snow, Sarah Soule, and Hanspeter Kriesi (Oxford, U.K.: Blackwell, 2007), 433–60.

36. Francesca Polletta and Pang Ching Bobby Chen, "Narrative and Social Movements," in *The Oxford Handbook of Cultural Sociology,* ed. Jeffrey C. Alexander, Ronald N. Jacobs, and Philip Smith (Oxford, U.K.: Oxford University Press, 2012); Francesca Polletta, Pang Ching Bobby Chen, Beth Gharrity Gardner, and Alice Motes, "The Sociology of Storytelling," *Annual Review of Sociology* 37 (2011).

37. Benford, "'You Could Be the Hundredth Monkey'"; William Gamson, "How Storytelling Can Be Empowering," in *Culture in Mind: Toward a Sociology of Culture and Cognition,* ed. Karen A. Cerulo (Abingdon, U.K.: Routledge, 2001); Thomas Hegghammer, ed., *Jihadi Culture: The Art and Social Practices of Militant Islamists* (Cambridge, U.K.: Cambridge University Press, 2017).

38. James M. Jasper, "The Emotions of Protest: Affective and Reactive Emotions in and around Social Movements," *Sociological Forum* 13, no. 3 (1998); Marshall Ganz, "The Power of Story in Social Movements," paper presented at the annual meeting of the American Sociological Association, Anaheim, California, August 2001; Joseph E. Davis, "Narrative in Social Movements: The Power of Stories," in *Stories of Change: Narrative and Social Movements,* ed. Joseph E. Davis (Albany: State University of New York Press, 2002).

39. Marshall Ganz, "Power of Story."

40. Polletta and Chen, "Narrative and Social Movements," 4.

41. Anwar al-Awlaki, "44 Ways to Support Jihad," Victorious Media, 2009. For more on the motivational power of *anashid,* see Nelly Lahoud, "A Capella Songs (*anashid*) in Jihadi Culture," in *Jihadi Culture,* ed. Hegghammer, 42–62.

42. Needless to say, while the global jihad movement can be understood as a modern social movement, this is not to say that it is a monolith. Within it (as with many other transnational social movements) differences exist between various groups and individuals. The movement is so diverse,

transnational, and polycephalic that any study attempting to analyze it must take into account the geographical differentiations that exist among its numerous variants. It is important, therefore, to divide study of this movement along geographical lines that take into account the specific contexts that are at play; a global jihadist in Iraq, for example, who may share a similar ideology with their Western counterpart, will nonetheless likely differ in their reasons for joining, in their backgrounds, and in their strategies and tactics. In a similar vein to Egerton, this study has identified a specifically Western version of the movement. Frazer Egerton, *Jihad in the West: The Rise of Militant Salafism* (Cambridge: Cambridge University Press, 2011), 6–7.

43. For an in-depth discussion of Salafism, see *Global Salafism: Islam's New Religious Movement,* ed. Roel Meijer (London: Hurst, 2009); Joas Wagemakers, *A Quietist Jihadi: The Ideology of Abu Muhammad al-Maqdisi* (Cambridge, U.K.: Cambridge University Press, 2012), 3–4.

44. Mehdi Mozaffari, "What Is Islamism? History and Definition of a Concept," *Totalitarian Movements and Political Religions* 8, no. 1 (2007): 22–23.

45. Roxanne L. Euben and Muhammad Qasim Zaman, "Introduction," in *Princeton Readings in Islamist Thought: Texts and Contexts from al-Banna to Bin Laden,* ed. Roxanne L. Euben and Muhammad Qasim Zaman (Princeton, NJ: Princeton University Press, 2009), 4.

46. Euben and Zaman, "Introduction," 4.

47. Gilles Kepel, *The Roots of Radical Islam* (London: Saqi, 2005), 20.

48. Notable exceptions include Ingram, *Charismatic Leadership Phenomenon;* Daurius Figueira, *Salafi Jihadi Discourse of Sunni Islam in the 21st Century: The Discourse of Abu Muhammad al-Maqdisi and Anwar al-Awlaki* (Bloomington, IN: iUniverse, 2011); Scott Shane, *Objective Troy: A Terrorist, a President, and the Rise of the Drone* (New York: Tim Duggan Books, 2015); Richard A. Nielsen, *Deadly Clerics* (Cambridge, U.K.: Cambridge University Press, 2017).

49. For a detailed look at Awlaki's life, see Shane, *Objective Troy.*

1. From America to Yemen

1. For more on this relationship, see Stephane Lacroix, *Awakening Islam* (Cambridge, MA: Harvard University Press, 2011).

2. Chris Heffelfinger, *Radical Islam in America: Salafism's Journey from Arabia to the West* (Washington, DC: Potomac Books, 2011), 34.

3. Heffelfinger, *Radical Islam in America,* 34.

4. Scott Shane, *Objective Troy: A Terrorist, a President, and the Rise of the Drone* (New York: Tim Duggan Books, 2015), 54–56.

5. Jarret Brachman, "Anwar al-Awlaki," *Encyclopaedia Britannica*, September 10, 2014, available at www.britannica.com/EBchecked/topic /1736723/Anwar-al-Awlaki.

6. Shane, *Objective Troy*, 59–60.

7. Shane, *Objective Troy*, 60.

8. Article of amendment for "Al-Basheer Company for Publications and Translations, LLC," Office of the Colorado Secretary of State, March 23, 1999; Statement of intent to dissolve "Al-Basheer Media Group LLC," Office of the Colorado Secretary of State, July 7, 1997. This account comes from the previous owner of al-Basheer, Jamaal Zarabozo, who was al-Turki's business partner for a brief time before he sold the company to him.

9. These are: "The Hereafter"; "Lives of the Prophets" (2001); "Abu Bakr al-Siddiq: His Life and Times"; "Ummar Ibn Al-Khataab—His Life and Times"; and "Dreams and Dream Interpretations." Four out of the five are difficult to date with certainty but can be placed between the late 1990s and 2003.

10. Tariq Nelson, interview with the author, Falls Church, Virginia, May 15, 2017.

11. Thomas H. Kean and Lee Hamilton, "The 9/11 Commission Report: Final Report of the National Commission on Terrorist Attacks upon the United States," Washington, D.C., 2004, 517.

12. The United States House of Representatives Permanent Select Committee on Intelligence and the Select Senate Committee on Intelligence, "Report of the Joint Inquiry into the Terrorist Attacks of September 11, 2001," December 2002, 178–79.

13. "Report of the Joint Inquiry," 178.

14. Tom Hays, "FBI Eyes NYC 'Charity' in Terror Probe," Associated Press, February 26, 2004.

15. United States Treasury Department, "United States Designates bin Laden Loyalist," February 24, 2004, available at www.treasury.gov/press-center /press-releases/Pages/js1190.aspx.

16. "Report of the Joint Inquiry," 179.

17. Kean and Hamilton, "9/11 Commission," 221.

18. "Report of the Joint Inquiry," 178.

19. Shane, *Objective Troy*, 63.

20. Anwar al-Awlaki's academic transcript, 2001, issued by George Washington University.

21. Shadee Elmasry, "The Salafis in America: The Rise, Decline, and Prospects for a Sunni Muslim Movement among African-Americans," *Journal of Muslim Minority Affairs* 30, no. 2 (2010): 224.

22. Kean and Hamilton, "9/11 Commission," 230.

23. Kean and Hamilton, "9/11 Commission," 221.

24. Shane, *Objective Troy*, 83.

25. Laurie Goodstein, "A Nation Challenged: The American Muslims; Influential American Muslims Temper Their Tone," *New York Times*, October 19, 2001.

26. "Muslim Students Are Wary of the War," *Washington Times*, October 11, 2001.

27. Awlaki sermon at Dar al-Hijrah, recorded by *PBS Newshour*, October 30, 2001, available at www.pbs.org/newshour/updates/religion-july-dec09 -alawlaki_11-11/.

28. Awlaki sermon at Dar al-Hijrah, October 30, 2001.

29. See Fawaz Gerges, *The Far Enemy: Why Jihad Went Global* (Cambridge, U.K.: Cambridge University Press, 2009).

30. Awlaki sermon at Dar al-Hijrah, October 30, 2001.

31. "Live Dialogue with Anwar al-Awlaki," *IslamOnline*, September 17, 2001. This page is no longer accessible, but a saved version is in the author's possession.

32. "Live Dialogue with Anwar al-Awlaki."

33. Internal Department of Defense email, February 1, 2002. This email was uncovered as part of a Fox News investigation and was made available via a Freedom of Information Act request.

34. Susan Schmidt, "Imam From Va. Mosque Now Thought to Have Aided al-Qaeda," *Washington Post*, February 27, 2008.

35. Anwar al-Awlaki, "Message to the American People," Global Islamic Media Front, 2010.

36. Johari Abdul Malik, interview with the author, Falls Church, Virginia, June 24, 2011.

37. See Scott Shane, "Born in U.S., a Radical Cleric Inspires Terror," *New York Times*, November 18, 2008; Scott Shane and Souad Mekhennet, "Imam's Path from Condemning Terror to Preaching Jihad," *New York Times*, May 8, 2010; Shane, *Objective Troy*, 62–63.

38. Shane, *Objective Troy*, 119.

39. Johari Abdul Malik, interview with the author.

40. Yasir Qadhi, interview with the author, Maryland, April 1, 2017.

41. Richard A. Nielsen, *Deadly Clerics* (Cambridge, U.K.: Cambridge University Press, 2017), 51–52.

42. The first report confirming Awlaki's involvement with prostitutes was in July 2013. See Catherine Herridge, "Terror Leader Awlaki Paid Thousands for Prostitutes in DC Area, Documents Show," *Fox News*, July 2, 2013, available at www.foxnews.com/politics/2013/07/02/terror-leader-awlaki -paid-thousands-for-prostitutes-in-dc-area-documents-show.html.

43. JIMAS is an acronym of Arabic words that translate to "The Association to Revive the Way of the Messenger." See Sadek Hamid, "The Attraction of 'Authentic' Islam: Salafism and British Muslim Youth," in *Global Salafism*, ed. Roel Meijer (New York: Columbia University Press, 2009), 386.

44. Abu Muntasir, interview with the author, Ipswich, U.K., February 22, 2011.

45. Abu Muntasir, interview with the author, London, U.K., August 1, 2016. This transformation, according to Abu Muntasir, took place for him and much of JIMAS before 9/11, as they moved closer to interpretations influenced by Muhammad Nasiruddin al-Albani, an influential quietist Salafi sheikh.

46. Abu Muntasir, interview with the author, Ipswich.

47. Abu Muntasir, interview with the author, Ipswich.

48. On Islamist and Salafi activism in the United Kingdom, see Innes Bowen, *Medina in Birmingham, Najaf in Brent: Inside British Islam* (London: Hurst, 2014).

49. Abu Muntasir, interview with the author, London.

50. Peter Bergen and Paul Cruickshank describe the MAB as a "Muslim Brotherhood group." Peter Bergen and Paul Cruickshank, "The Unravelling: The Jihadist Revolt Against bin Laden," *New Republic*, June 11, 2008.

51. An April 2009 report published by the British Government's Department for Communities and Local Government notes that "the Jamaat-e-Islami (JI) along with the Muslim Brotherhood were pioneers in developing student activism through the Federation of Student Islamic Societies (FOSIS)," U.K. Government Department for Communities and Local Government, "The Pakistani Muslim Community in England: Understanding Muslim Ethnic Communities in England," London, April 17, 2009, 40.

52. *Inspire*, Muslim Association of Britain, September 28, 2002.

53. *Inspire*, Muslim Association of Britain.

54. These were: the School of Oriental and African Studies; Imperial College; the London School of Economics; and King's College London.

55. MAB literature advertising all of Awlaki's British appearances in author's possession.

56. The East London Mosque and its sister organization, the Islamic Forum of Europe, were revealed to be taking their ideological line from Maududi's work in a *Channel 4 Dispatches* investigation, "Britain's Islamic Republic," first aired on Channel 4 (U.K.), March 1, 2010. See also Andrew Gilligan, "Inextricably Linked to Controversial Mosque: The Secret World of IFE," *Daily Telegraph*, February 28, 2010.

57. "ELM Trust Statement on Anwar Al-Awlaki," November 6, 2010, available at http://archive.eastlondonmosque.org.uk/uploadedImage/pdf/2010_11

_07_15_44_46_Awlaki%20Statement%206%20Nov10%20-%20Full%20
Statement.pdf.

58. Rashad Ali, interview with the author, London, U.K., August 7, 2016.

59. Rashad Ali, interview with the author.

60. This roughly translates to "The correct path for those who seek the battle-field." The book is more commonly known as *Kitab al-Jihad* [Book of jihad].

61. Aimen Dean, interview with the author, London, U.K., May 20, 2016.

62. Aimen Dean, interview with the author.

63. For more on the jihadist associations of the July 7 plotters, see "Could 7/7 Have Been Prevented? Review of the Intelligence on the London Terrorist Attacks on 7 July 2005," United Kingdom Intelligence and Security Committee, May 2009.

64. Usama Hasan, interview with the author, London, U.K., May 9, 2011.

65. Usama Hasan, interview with the author.

66. FBI interview with Umar Farouk Abdulmutallab at Milan Federal Correctional Institution, January 2010.

67. United States Treasury Department, "Treasury Designates Anwar Al-Aulaqi, Key Leader of Al-Qa'ida in the Arabian Peninsula," July 16, 2010, available at www.treasury.gov/press-center/press-releases/Pages/tg779.aspx.

68. Usama Hasan, interview with the author.

69. Intoodeep comment on "Imam anwar-al-awlaki imprisoned," *Islamic Awakening,* November 4, 2006, available at http://forums.islamicawakening .com/threads/imam-anwar-al-awlaki-imprisoned.2157/.

70. The group has now changed its name to "CAGE."

71. "Imam Anwar Al Awlaki: Urgent Appeal: Imam Anwar Al Awlaki—A Leader in Need," Cageprisoners, November 8, 2006, available at www .islamicity.org/forum/forum_posts.asp?TID=9876.

72. "Moazzam Begg Interviews Imam Anwar al-Awlaki," December 31, 2007, available at www.cage.ngo/moazzam-begg-interviews-imam-anwar-al -awlaki.

73. Charles E. Allen, keynote address, GEOINT Conference, October 28, 2008, available at www.dhs.gov/xnews/speeches/sp_1225377634961.shtm.

74. Charles E. Allen, interview with the author, Washington, D.C., June 8, 2011.

75. William H. Webster et al., "Final Report of the William H. Webster Commission on the Federal Bureau of Investigation, Counterterrorism Intelligence, at the Events at Fort Hood, Texas, on November 5, 2009," Washington, D.C., August 1, 2012, 34.

76. "Reflections on the Cageprisoners Fundraiser: Another Ramadan 2008," September 10, 2008, available at https://web.archive.org/web /20120306000554/http://old.cageprisoners.com/articles.php?id=26116.

77. "Reflections on the Cageprisoners Fundraiser."
78. Anwar al-Awlaki, "Another Ramadan," speech at Cageprisoners annual Ramadan Iftar event, September 2008.
79. Awlaki, "Another Ramadan."
80. "ELM Trust Statement on Anwar Al-Awlaki."
81. Al Wasatiyyah Foundation advertisement for "Virtues of the Sahaba" course, available at https://web.archive.org/web/20090425100811 /http://www.alwasatiyyah.com/courses.php?courseID=5.
82. Tom Whitehead, "Calls to Ban Extremist Video Message," *Daily Telegraph,* April 10, 2009.
83. Whitehead, "Calls to Ban."
84. Michael Keating, interview with the author, London, U.K., April 11, 2019. On Prevent during this time, see "Preventing Violent Extremism Path-finder Fund: Mapping of project activities 2007/2008," United Kingdom Department for Communities and Local Government, December 2008.
85. Michael Keating, interview with the author.
86. "Statement regarding Kensington Town Hall ban on Imam Anwar al-Awlaki," Cageprisoners, August 26, 2009, available at https://web .archive.org/web/20120108043506/http://old.cageprisoners.com/articles .php?id=30185.
87. "Statement regarding Kensington Town Hall ban."
88. Fahad Ansari, "Beyond Guantanamo—Review of Cageprisoners Fund-raising Dinner," October 2, 2009, available at https://web.archive.org/web /20160402141228/http://old.cageprisoners.com/articles.php?id=30493.
89. Jason Lewis, "Top Charities Give £200,000 to Group Which Supported al-Qaeda Cleric," *Daily Telegraph,* November 6, 2010.
90. Cageprisoners YouTube page, www.youtube.com/user/cageprisoners, accessed August 12, 2016. The audio was taken off the site in 2017, shortly after the author emailed Cageprisoners in December 2016 to confirm whether it was aware of its presence and to inquire if the organization wished to provide any comment on it. By the time it was removed, the video had received nearly three thousand views.
91. Anwar al-Awlaki, "A Message to the Prisoners from the Prisoners," banned Awlaki speech intended for broadcast at April 2009 Cageprisoners event in Kensington and Chelsea Town Hall.
92. The author followed this incident closely at the time. See also Pakinam Amer, "Islamic Radicalization on UK Campuses: Who Is Anwar al-Awlaki?" *Egypt Independent,* August 2, 2010, available at www .egyptindependent.com/islamic-radicalization-uk-campuses-who-anwar-al -awlaki.

93. Nasser al-Aulaqi (on behalf of Anwar al-Aulaqi) v. Barack H. Obama, Robert M. Gates, and Leon E. Panetta, No. 1:10-cv-01469-JDB, Document 15-2: James R. Clapper's Unclassified Declaration in Support of Formal Claim of State Secrets Privilege, 8 (United States District Court for the District of Columbia, September 25, 2010).

94. Anwar al-Awlaki, "Nidal Hassan Did the Right Thing," www.anwar -alawlaki.com, November 9, 2009.

95. United States v. Barry Bujol, No. 4:10-mj-00486, Application for Search Warrant, 4–5 (United States District Court for the Southern District of Texas, May 28, 2010).

96. United States v. Zachary Adam Chesser, No. 1:10 mj-504, Affidavit, 10 (United States District Court for the Eastern District of Virginia, July 2, 2010).

97. United States v. Umar Farouk Abdulmutallab, No. 2:10-cr-20005, Government Sentencing Memorandum, 12–14 (United States District Court for the Eastern District of Michigan Southern Division, February 10, 2012).

98. Scott Shane, Mark Mazzetti, and Charlie Savage, "How a U.S. Citizen Came to Be in America's Cross Hairs," New York Times, March 9, 2013.

99. Vikram Dodd, "British Airways Worker Rajib Kareem Convicted of Terrorist Plot," The Guardian, February 28, 2011.

100. Scott Shane, "U.S. Approves Targeted Killing of American Cleric," New York Times, April 6, 2010.

101. United States Treasury Department, "Treasury Designates Anwar Al-Aulaqi."

102. Abu Bashir Nasir al-Wuhaishi, "In Defence of Anwar al-Awlaki," al-Malahim, June 2010.

103. Letter from Osama bin Laden to Atiyah Abdul Rahman, August 27, 2010. This was among a trove of papers recovered from bin Laden's hideout in Abbotobad, Pakistan, after he was killed. It is categorized as SOCOM-2012-0000003.

2. Awlaki and Activist Salafism

1. The most convincing and well-researched claim of Awlaki's early moderation is provided by New York Times journalist Scott Shane, who correctly points out that it would be "egregious" to conclude that "listening to Awlaki's CDs caused terrorism." He also argues that "by most accounts, Awlaki's preaching in the early years was unobjectionable" and that it would be a "mistake" to mix these up with his later work, which endorsed

violence. Scott Shane, *Objective Troy: A Terrorist, a President, and the Rise of the Drone* (New York: Tim Duggan Books, 2015), 100, 178.

2. These include: *Global Salafism: Islam's New Religious Movement*, ed. Roel Meijer (London: Hurst, 2009); Shiraz Maher, *Salafi-Jihadism: The History of an Idea* (London: Hurst, 2016); Henri Lauzière, *The Making of Salafism: Islamic Reform in the Twentieth Century* (New York: Columbia University Press, 2015); Robert Rabil, *Salafism in Lebanon: From Apoliticism to Transnational Jihadism* (Washington, DC: Georgetown University Press, 2014); Zoltan Pall, *Salafism in Lebanon: Local and Transnational Movements* (Cambridge, U.K.: Cambridge University Press, 2018); Francesco Cavatorta, *Salafism After the Arab Awakening: Contending with People's Power* (Oxford, U.K.: Oxford University Press, 2017); Alexander Thurston, *Salafism in Nigeria: Islam, Preaching, and Politics* (Cambridge, U.K.: Cambridge University Press, 2016); Laurent Bonnefoy, *Salafism in Yemen: Transnationalism and Religious Identity* (Oxford, U.K.: Oxford University Press, 2012).

3. Translated by Bernard Haykel in Bernard Haykel, "On the Nature of Salafi Thought and Action," in Meijer, ed., *Global Salafism*, 38.

4. One of the best examples of this development is the emergence of the rationalist Mu'tazila school of thought in the eighth century. See Albert Hourani, *Arabic Thought in the Liberal Age, 1798–1939* (Cambridge, U.K.: Cambridge University Press, 1983), 142.

5. As Ibn Taymiyya wrote: "One is not to state that the meaning of 'hand' is power or that of 'hearing' is knowledge." Translated by Bernard Haykel in Haykel, "On the Nature of Salafi Thought and Action," 38.

6. Haykel, "On the Nature of Salafi Thought and Action," 38.

7. Madawi al-Rasheed, *A History of Saudi Arabia* (Cambridge, U.K.: Cambridge University Press, 2010), 15–19.

8. Stephane Lacroix, *Awakening Islam* (Cambridge, MA: Harvard University Press, 2011), 11. As a result of al-Wahhab's influence on Salafism, the term is often (incorrectly) used interchangeably with Wahhabi. Some Salafis see the term as derogatory. While all Wahhabis can be described as Salafi, not all Salafis follow or support the Saudi Royal Family or the Wahhabi scholars of the country's religious establishment. In addition, unlike Wahhabis who follow the Hanbali school of *fiqh*, Salafis reject the four *madhhabs*. Part of the appeal of Salafism lies in its refusal to be beholden to any of the four schools and its rejection of *taqlid* (conforming to one school of thought) in favor of individual interpretation (*ijtihad*). Not only do Salafis see the *madhhabs* as a form of sinful division among Muslims, but the existence of these schools go against the Salafi belief that there is only one correct approach, that outlined by Allah in the primary sources of Islam.

See Quintan Wiktorowicz, "The New Global Threat: Transnational Salafis and Jihad," *Middle East Policy* 8, no. 4 (2001): 21; Roel Meijer, "Introduction," in *Global Salafism,* ed. Meijer, 4.

9. This is a thumbnail history of Saudi Arabia. For a more in-depth treatment, see David Commins, *The Wahhabi Mission in Saudi Arabia* (London, U.K.: I.B. Tauris, 2009).

10. Quintan Wiktorowicz, "Anatomy of the Salafi Movement," *Studies in Conflict and Terrorism* 29, no. 3 (2006): 208.

11. Wiktorowicz, "Anatomy of the Salafi Movement," 208; Haykel, "On the Nature of Salafi Thought and Action," in *Global Salafism,* ed. Meijer, 47–50.

12. Joas Wagemakers, "Revisiting Wiktorowicz: Categorising and Defining the Branches of Salafism," in *Salafism After the Arab Awakening: Contending with People's Power,* ed. Francesco Cavatorta and Fabio Merone (Oxford, U.K.: Oxford University Press, 2016), 7–10.

13. The leading quietist scholar Muhammad Nasiruddin al-Albani, for example, supported the political notion of an Islamic State, but only after the purification of society through a *manhaj* based on *dawah* and *tarbiyah.* On the teachings of al-Albani, see Stephane Lacroix, "Between Revolution and Apoliticism: Nasir al-Din al-Albani and his Impact on the Shaping of Contemporary Salafism," in *Global Salafism,* ed. Meijer, 58–81.

14. Wagemakers, "Revisiting Wiktorowicz." In this paper, Wagemakers also offers a further three subcategories of quietist Salafis: "Aloofists" inspired by Muhammad Nasiruddin al-Albani; "Loyalists" influenced by Sheikh Abd al-Aziz ibn Baz, the former Grand Mufti of Saudi Arabia, and Sheikh Muhammad ibn al-Uthaymeen; and "propagandists," also referred to by other Salafis as "Madkalis," who take their line from Sheikh Rabee al-Madkhali and define supporting the Saudi regime almost as an article of faith.

15. Roel Meijer, "Politicising *al-jarḥ wa-l-taʿdīl,*" in *The Transmission and Dynamics of the Textual Sources of Islam Essays in Honour of Harald Motzki,* ed. Nicolet Boekhoff-van der Voort, Kees Versteegh, and Joas Wagemakers (Leiden, the Netherlands: Brill, 2011), 387–88.

16. Zoltan Pall, "Kuwaiti Salafism and Its Growing Influence in the Levant," Carnegie Endowment for International Peace, May 2014, 23; Madawi al-Rasheed, *Muted Modernists: The Struggle over Divine Politics in Saudi Arabia* (Oxford, U.K.: Oxford University Press, 2015), 12, 77.

17. Wagemakers, "Revisiting Wiktorowicz." It is also worth noting that activist Salafi currents differ from country to country, although in most cases they are associated with Salafi political parties or prominent movements in their area of operation. One of the key early figures

associated with this current, the Egyptian Abdul Rahman Abdul Khaliq, broke new ground in 1981 when he encouraged Salafis in Kuwait to run for office. See Samuel Tadros, "Mapping Egyptian Islamism," Hudson Institute, December 2014, 32; Pall, "Kuwaiti Salafism."

18. On Hizb al-Nour in Egypt, see Stephane Lacroix, "Egypt's Pragmatic Salafis: The Politics of Hizb al-Nour," Carnegie Endowment for International Peace, November 1, 2016.

19. Lacroix, *Awakening Islam*, 52.

20. Lacroix, *Awakening Islam*, 17.

21. Originally a member of the Syrian Muslim Brotherhood in the 1960s, Surur moved to Saudi Arabia, where he was influenced by Salafist theology. Haykel describes how the Surur's followers "blended the organizational methods and political worldview of the Muslim Brotherhood with the theological puritanism of Salafism." See Bernard Haykel, "Al-Qaeda and Shi'ism," in *Fault Lines in the Global Jihad*, ed. Assaf Moghaddam and Brian Fishman (New York: Routledge, 2011), 187.

22. Sayed Khatab, *The Power of Sovereignty: The Political and Ideological Philosophy of Sayyid Qutb* (Abingdon, U.K.: Routledge, 2006).

23. Lacroix, *Awakening Islam*, 53.

24. Hegghammer refers to the *Sahwa* as the Islamist mainstream Saudi Arabia. Thomas Hegghammer, *Jihad in Saudi Arabia: Violence and Pan-Islamism Since 1979* (Cambridge, U.K.: Cambridge University Press, 2010), 83.

25. Meijer argues that the third and final category of Salafism, the Salafi-jihadis, emerged as a result of the fusion of these two strands. Meijer, "Politicising al-jarh wa-l-ta'dīl," 387. Similarly, Rabil traces the roots of the Salafi-jihadi movement to a hybridization of the Muslim Brotherhood's political approach and the Salafi creed, claiming that "the foundation of the Salafi jihadists can be traced to that of the *Sahwa* . . . [and] the ideology of the Salafi jihadist is an extension to the ideology of politicized Salafists." Rabil, *Salafism in Lebanon*, 44. Madawi al-Rasheed notes that, after 9/11, "Saudi Islamism was destined to split into multiple trajectories," one of the most popular of which was the jihadi path, with many activists leaving the country to "engage in jihad abroad." al-Rasheed, *Muted Modernists*, 31.

26. Hegghammer, *Jihad in Saudi Arabia*, 83.

27. Joas Wagemakers, *A Quietist Jihadi: The Ideology of Abu Muhammad al-Maqdisi* (Cambridge, U.K.: Cambridge University Press, 2012), 12; Wagemakers, "Revisiting Wiktorowicz"; Jarret Brachman, *Global Jihadism: Theory and Practice* (Abingdon, U.K.: Routledge, 2009), 23–25.

28. Wiktorowicz, "Anatomy of the Salafi Movement," 225–28. To further complicate matters, Wagemakers also notes that the assumption that

jihadists are radicalized politicos is erroneous since "the relative political isolationism of purists can lead (and in some cases has led) to radicalization as well. In practice, this means that Jihadi-Salafis can just as easily have a purist background as a political one. Moreover, purists and jihadis share a certain rejection of party politics that politicos, who are more sophisticated and politically savvy in their world view, do not agree with." Wagemakers, "Revisiting Wiktorowicz," 13.

29. For a fuller account of Salman al-Awdah's transformation, see al-Rasheed, *Muted Modernists*, 77–93.

30. Meijer, "Politicising *al-jarḥ wa-l-taʿdīl*," 387–88. On al-Shuaybi in particular and the emergence of the al-Shuaybi school, Hegghammer writes that they were among the first Saudi religious scholars to "endorse mass-casualty terrorism against the West." Hegghammer, *Jihad in Saudi Arabia*, 83. However, none of these individuals were ever actual members of the *Sahwa,* and the movement itself did not create any violent offshoots.

31. Roel Meijer, "Re-Reading al-Qaeda: Writings of Yusuf al-Ayiri," *ISIM Review* 18 (Autumn 2006): 16. For the links between the *Sahwa* ideology and Uyayree's Saudi jihadi movement, see Roel Meijer, "Yusuf al-Uyairi and the Making of a Revolutionary Salafi-Jihadi Praxis," *Die Welt des Islams* 47, no. 3–4 (2007).

32. Meijer, "Re-Reading al-Qaeda," 17.

33. Hegghammer, *Jihad in Saudi Arabia*, 7.

34. Haykel, "On the Nature of Salafi Thought and Action," in *Global Salafism,* ed. Meijer, 48. These diverging views of jihad are partly due to the different historical experiences of members of each strand. The Salafi-jihadis emerged and gained prominence after the Afghan war, and as a result they regard fighting as the only legitimate method for establishing an Islamic society. Thus, whereas the politicos adopted political activism through study and education, jihadis received their political training on the battlefields, seeing politics solely through the lens of warfare. See Wagemakers, "Revisiting Wiktorowicz."

35. One of the most recent contributions to the discussion of Salafi-Jihadism comes from Maher, who defines Salafi-jihadism through five key doctrinal pillars: jihad, *al-wala wal-bara, takfir, tawhid,* and *hakimiyya.* Maher, *Salafi-Jihadism,* 15.

36. Meijer, "Introduction," 18.

37. To back up their claims, these Salafis refer to a handful of Koranic verses, including 3:28: "Let not believers take disbelievers as allies rather than believers. And whoever [of you] does that has nothing with Allah, except

when taking precaution against them in prudence. And Allah warns you of Himself, and to Allah is the [final] destination."

38. Joas Wagemakers, "Framing the 'Threat to Islam': *al wala' wal bara'* in Salafi Discourse," *Arab Studies Quarterly* 30, no. 4 (2008): 4.

39. Abdur Raheem Green, "Surviving the West," undated, available at www.youtube.com/watch?v=5FkRVz7456I.

40. Gilles Kepel, *The Roots of Radical Islam* (London: Saqi, 2005), 45–59. Before disavowing IS in 2014, al-Maqdisi was a mentor to Abu Musab al-Zarqawi, the founder of its predecessor, al-Qaida in Iraq.

41. Wagemakers, *A Quietist Jihadi*, 166–68.

42. Wagemakers, *A Quietist Jihadi*, 172.

43. For more on al-Maqdisi's interpretation of *al-wala wal-bara*, see Joas Wagemakers, "A Purist Jihadi-Salafi: The Ideology of Abu Muhammad al-Maqdisi," *British Journal of Middle Eastern Studies* 36, no. 2 (2009): 286–88.

44. Abu Muhammad al-Maqdisi, *Millat Ibrahim* (At-Tibyan Publications), 9.

45. Meijer, "Introduction," 18.

46. Thomas Hegghammer, "Jihadi Salafis or Revolutionaries?," in *Global Salafism*, ed. Meijer, 263.

47. Hegghammer, *Jihad in Saudi Arabia*, 234.

48. Jacob Olidort, "The Politics of 'Quietist' Salafism," Brookings Center for Middle East Policy, February 2015, 5.

49. Abdin Chande, "Islam in the African American Community: Negotiating between Black Nationalism and Historical Islam," *Islamic Studies* 47, no. 2 (2008), 230–231.

50. Quran and Sunnah Society Certificate of Incorporation, Office of the Secretary of State for Ohio, Document No. 9511080860I, November 17, 1995.

51. Stephane Lacroix, "Al-Albani's Revolutionary Approach to Hadith," *ISIM Review* 21 (Spring 2008): 6–7.

52. Pall, "Kuwaiti Salafism," 9–10; Tadros, "Mapping Egyptian Islamism," 6.

53. Meijer, "Politicising *al-jarh wa-l-ta'dīl*," 387–90.

54. Sheikh Madkhali's reputation for refuting deviant and heretical beliefs was such that his disciples gave him the title of "bearer of the flag of critique and fair evaluation in our time." See Lacroix, *Awakening Islam*, 216.

55. Tariq Nelson, interview with the author.

56. Shadee Elmasry, "The Salafis in America: The Rise, Decline, and Prospects for a Sunni Muslim Movement among African-Americans," *Journal of Muslim Minority Affairs* 30, no. 2 (2010): 234.

57. Chris Heffelfinger, *Radical Islam in America: Salafism's Journey from Arabia to the West* (Washington, DC: Potomac Books, 2011), 86–87.

58. Vidino describes CAIR as one of a number of Western Islamist groups that have "historical, financial, personal, organisational and ideological ties to the Muslim Brotherhood and other Islamic revivalist movements world-wide." Lorenzo Vidino, "The Muslim Brotherhood in the West: Evolution and Western Policies," International Center for the Study of Radicalisation, King's College London, February 2011, 8.

59. Yasir Qadhi, interview with the author.

60. Heffelfinger, *Radical Islam in America*, 87. See also Paul M. Barratt, *American Islam: The Struggle for the Soul of a Religion* (London: Picador, 2007).

61. Among al-Timimi's most influential works is a 1996 lecture called "New World Order," which is a commentary on Hawali's work *Jerusalem between the True Promise and the Bogus Promise*. On his connections to Hawali, see Milton Viorst, "The Education of Ali al-Timimi," *Atlantic*, June 2006; Michael A. Sells, "Armageddon in Christian, Sunni, and Shia Traditions," in *The Oxford Handbook of Religion and Violence*, ed. Mark Juergensmeyer, Margo Kitts, and Michael Jerryson (Oxford, U.K.: Oxford University Press, 2013), 481.

62. United States v. Ali al-Timimi, No. 1:04cr, Indictment, 5 (United States District Court for the Eastern District of Virginia, September 2004).

63. Ismail Royer, interview with the author, Washington, D.C., April 1, 2017.

64. Ismail Royer, email correspondence with the author, July 24, 2017.

65. *Ali al-Timimi*, No. 1:04cr.

66. The FBI investigated IANA because it believed that the group's mission was to "spread Islamic fundamentalism and Salafist doctrine throughout the United States. . . . The IANA solicits funds from wealthy Saudi benefactors, extremist Islamic Shaykhs, and suspect non-governmental organizations." See "Report of the Joint Inquiry," 431.

67. Shane, *Objective Troy*, 64.

68. Anwar al-Awlaki's lecture series "Stories from the *Hadith*" (c. 2000), "Quest for Truth" (2002), "Lessons from the Companions Living as a Minority" (2002), "Young Ayesha & Mothers of The Believers" (date unknown), and "Understanding the Quran" (c. 2001–2002), were produced on CD and audio cassette by the Center for Islamic Information and Education (CIIE), which was the English name of al-Timimi's Dar al-Arqam. More informa-tion on Dar al-Arqam and CIIE can be found in archived versions of its official website, available at https://web.archive.org/web/20010225115750 /http://www.ciie.org:80/. Awlaki is listed as a "lecturer" for CIIE here: https://web.archive.org/web/20020609184133/http://www.ciie.org:80 /shoponline.htm.

69. Opposition to Motion to Compel, U.S.A. vs Ali al-Timimi, United States
    District Court for the Eastern District of Virginia, November 5, 2015, 4.
    Also see Susan Schmidt, "Imam From Va. Mosque Now Thought to Have
    Aided al-Qaeda," *Washington Post,* February 27, 2008.

70. "Lawyers Question Use of U.S. Spy Program," *Los Angeles Times,* De-
    cember 29, 2005.

71. Transcript of meeting between Ali al-Timimi and FBI special agent Wade
    Ammerman, Alexandria, Virginia, June 25, 2004, 9.

72. Transcript of meeting between Ali al-Timimi and Wade Ammerman, 9.

73. Anwar al-Awlaki, "Stories from the *Hadith,*" CIIE, c. 2000.

74. Anwar al-Awlaki, "The Life of Muhammad: The Makkan Period,"
    Awakening Media, c. 2003. While the lectures were published on CD in 2003,
    they were initially delivered and recorded by Awlaki while he was still in
    the United States, with the rights sold afterwards.

75. Anwar al-Awlaki, "The Life of Muhammad: The Makkan Period."

76. Yasir Qadhi, interview with the author.

77. Awlaki, "The Life of Muhammad: The Makkan Period." The Thomas
    Friedman article Awlaki quotes from is "A Manifesto for the Fast World,"
    The New York Times, March 28, 1999.

78. Elmasry, "The Salafis in America."

79. Awlaki, "The Life of Muhammad: The Makkan Period."

80. On SAAR, see Douglas Farah, *Blood from Stones: The Secret Financial Network
    of Terror* (New York: Broadway Books, 2004), 153.

81. Anwar al-Awlaki, Friday sermon (a), unconfirmed location but probably the
    Dar al-Hijrah Mosque in Virginia, March 2002.

82. Awlaki, Friday sermon (a).

83. Awlaki, Friday sermon (a).

84. In 2009 Babar Ahmed was awarded £60,000 in compensation by the British
    state. "Terror Suspect Wins £60,000 Damages from Met Police over
    Assault," *Daily Telegraph,* March 19, 2009.

85. "Stop police terror: about us," December 2003, available at http://web
    .archive.org/web/20040203003438/http://www.stoppoliceterror.com
    /aboutus.htm.

86. "Stop police terror: about us." Emphasis in original.

87. "ELM Trust Statement on Anwar Al-Awlaki," November 6, 2010, available
    at http://archive.eastlondonmosque.org.uk/uploadedImage/pdf/2010_11
    _07_15_44_46_Awlaki%20Statement%206%20Nov10%20-%20Full%20
    Statement.pdf.

88. Anwar al-Awlaki, Friday Sermon (b), December 26, 2003, East London
    Mosque, London.

89. See "Terrorism Pre-Charge Detention: Comparative Law Study," *Liberty,* July 2010; "Extending Detention Without Charge," Human Rights Watch, available at www.hrw.org/legacy/backgrounder/eca/uk1007/3.htm; "Neither Just nor Effective: Indefinite Detention Without Trial in the United Kingdom Under Part 4 of the Anti-Terrorism, Crime and Security Act 2001," Human Rights Watch, Briefing Paper, June 24, 2004.

90. Awlaki, Friday sermon (b).

91. Usama Hasan, interview with the author.

92. Anwar al-Awlaki, "Tolerance: A Hallmark of Muslim Character," Awlaki speech given at annual convention, Islamic Society of North America, September 2001.

93. The purist sheikh al-Albani's most famous and controversial *fatwa,* for example, called on Muslims living in Palestine to leave rather than fight, because the priority was their ability to practice Islam correctly and preserve their *aqidah,* not to keep hold of sacred land.

94. Awlaki, Friday sermon (a).

95. Awlaki, "The Life of Muhammad: The Makkan Period."

96. Awlaki, "Tolerance."

97. On the Western Muslim identity crisis and its role in radicalization, see Wiktorowicz, *Radical Islam Rising,* 91–92; Tufyal Choudhury, "The Role of Muslim Identity Politics in Radicalisation," U.K. Department for Communities and Local Government, Preventing Extremism Unit, March 2007, 20–23.

98. Awlaki, Friday sermon (b).

99. Awlaki, Friday sermon (b). Awlaki is here referring to *Sahih al-Bukhari* 3.622.

100. I could find no other instance of the *hadith* being translated into English in this way.

101. Awlaki, Friday sermon (b).

102. "ELM Trust Statement on Anwar Al-Awlaki."

103. Anwar al-Awlaki, "The Life and Times of Umar bin Khattab," al-Basheer publications c. 2003. This series relied mainly on the work of ninth-century Islamic historian Abu Jafar Muhammad ibn Jarir al-Tabari as well as *Umar ibn al-Khattab: His Life and Times,* a modern collection and analysis of the primary Islamic sources by the Libyan cleric and scholar Ali Muhammad al-Sallabi.

104. The Meccan period was a time in the history of Islam when Muhammad and his followers were persecuted by the Quraysh tribe and not allowed to propagate their religion.

105. Wiktorowicz, "Anatomy of the Salafi Movement," 215; Pall, "Kuwaiti Salafism," 6.

106. Awlaki, "The Life and Times of Umar bin Khattab."
107. Awlaki, "The Life and Times of Umar bin Khattab."
108. Awlaki, "The Life and Times of Umar bin Khattab."
109. Wiktorowicz, "New Global Threat," 21–22.
110. Meijer, "Re-Reading al-Qaeda," 17. A comprehensive Salafi-jihadist treatment of *al-taifa al-mansura* was written by the Jordanian Abu Qatada al-Filistini, one of the most influential living Salafi-jihadi scholars. Like other Salafi-jihadis, he argues that only they are worthy of the *taifa al-mansura* because, unlike other Salafis, jihadis engage in armed conflict. See Abu Qatada al-Filistini, "Characteristics of the Victorious Party in the Foundation of the State of the Believers," at-Tibyan Publications, undated.
111. Awlaki, "Stories from the *Hadith*."
112. Awlaki, "Stories from the *Hadith*."
113. *Constants on the Path of Jihad* is undated, but Uyayree was killed in 2003 and was writing tomes in support of jihad before 9/11. Meijer, "Yusuf al-Uyairi and the Making of a Revolutionary Salafi Praxis."
114. See Hannah Stuart and Rashad Ali, "Refuting Jihadism, Can Jihad Be Reclaimed?" Hudson Institute, August 1, 2014.
115. Yusuf al-Uyayree, "The Islamic Ruling on the Permissibility of Self-Sacrifice Operations: Suicide or Martyrdom?" at-Tibyan Publications, c. 2001, 37.
116. Awlaki, "The Life of Muhammad: The Makkan Period."
117. Anwar al-Awlaki, "Companions of the Ditch," al-Noor Publications, c. 2003–2004.
118. This helps to explain and corroborate the comments of Abu Muntasir and others from chapter 1 that related to Awlaki's efforts to introduce and justify the doctrine of suicide bombing and present jihad as *ibadah* to Western Muslim audiences.
119. Anwar al-Awlaki, "Understanding the Quran," CIIE, c. 2001–2002.
120. Awlaki, "Understanding the Quran."
121. Awlaki, "The Life of Muhammad: The Makkan Period."
122. Euben and Zaman, *Princeton Readings,* 131. For a thorough examination of Qutb's interpretation of *jahiliyyah,* see Sayed Khatab, *The Political Thought of Sayyid Qutb: The Theory of Jahiliyyah* (Abingdon, U.K.: Routledge, 2006).
123. Sayyid Qutb, *Milestones* (Birmingham, U.K.: Maktabah, 2006), 26–27.
124. Jamal Zarabozo, interview with the author, Sacramento, California, April 20, 2017.
125. Vidino, "Muslim Brotherhood in the West."
126. Ismail Royer, interview with the author, Washington, D.C., March 15, 2017.

127. Anwar al-Awlaki, "The Islamic Education of Shaikh Anwar al Awlaki," www.anwar-alawlaki.com, August 12, 2008.

128. Awlaki, "Islamic Education of Shaikh Anwar al Awlaki."

129. Awlaki, "Islamic Education of Shaikh Anwar al Awlaki."

130. Al-Islah has various factions within it, including ones influenced by the Muslim Brotherhood and Salafism. However, it has also been described as having an "ideological hard core of party leaders with clear Muslim Brotherhood ties." Similarly, al-Iman University has often acted as the base for Salafis who pursue "heavily politicized dawa." See Stacey Philbrick Yadav, "Yemen's Muslim Brotherhood and the Perils of Powersharing," Brookings Project on U.S. Relations with the Islamic World, August 2015, 1–4; Bonnefoy, *Salafism in Yemen*, 76.

131. Yadav, "Yemen's Muslim Brotherhood," 2.

132. Obituary: "The death of Dr Hassan Maqbool al-Ahdal, one of the most famous scholars of Islamic jurisprudence in the world", July 31, 2005, available at www.hunaradaa.com/news.php?action=view&id=282.

133. Laurent Bonnefoy, "How Transnational is Salafism in Yemen?" in *Global Salafism*, ed. Meijer, 325.

134. Laurent Bonnefoy, "Deconstructing Salafism in Yemen," *CTC Sentinel*, Special Yemen Issue, January 2010; Bonnefoy, "How Transnational is Salafism in Yemen?" 329.

135. Herbert Berg, *The Development of Exegesis in Early Islam: The Authenticity of Muslim Literature from the Formative Period* (Abingdon, U.K.: Routledge, 2000), 106–7.

136. This chain of transmission is known as *isnad*.

137. For a scholarly Salafi analysis of the problems surrounding *sira* and its exploitation by activists, see Moosa Richardson, "Connecting Seerah to Your Life," 2016, available at www.spreaker.com/user/radio1mm /connecting-seerah-to-your-life-part-1.

138. Wiktorowicz, "Anatomy of the Salafi Movement," 217.

139. Abdullah Pocius, telephone interview with the author, Washington, D.C., April 4, 2017.

140. Johari Abdul Malik, interview with the author.

141. Elmasry, "The Salafis in America."

142. Yasir Qadhi, interview with the author.

143. Tweet from @Al_FirdausiA, March 10, 2013, available at https://twitter .com/Al_firdausiA/status/311005838959595520. At his trial it was confirmed that this was one of at least two Twitter accounts run by Dzokhar Tsarnaev.

144. Donald Holbrook, "The Spread of its Message: Studying the Prominence of al-Qaida Materials in UK Terrorism Investigations," *Perspectives on Terrorism* 11, no. 6 (2017).

145. On these preachers, see Raffaello Pantucci, *We Love Death as You Love Life: Britain's Suburban Terrorists* (London: Hurst, 2015).

146. Awlaki, "Understanding the Quran."

3. Awlaki and Salafi-Jihadism

1. On how and why this thinking evolved, see Sara Silvestri, "Public Policies Towards Muslims and the Institutionalization of 'Moderate Islam' in Europe," in *Muslims in 21st Century Europe: Structural and Cultural Perspectives*, ed. Anna Triandafyllidou (Abingdon, U.K.: Routledge, 2010); Yvonne Yazbeck Haddad and Tyler Golson, "Overhauling Islam: Representation, Construction, and Cooption of Moderate Islam in Western Europe," *Journal of Church and State* 49 (2007); M. A. Muqtedar Khan, *Debating Moderate Islam: The Geopolitics of Islam and the West* (Salt Lake City: University of Utah Press, 2007).

2. Recent polling suggests that, since 9/11, Muslims in the West perceive themselves to be the targets of increasing levels of various forms of discrimination due to their religion. See European Union Agency for Fundamental Rights, "Experience of Discrimination, Social Marginalisation and Violence among Muslim and Non-Muslim Youth," 2010; European Union Agency for Fundamental Rights, "Second European Union Minorities and Discrimination Survey Muslims—Selected Findings," 2017; Sarah Wilkins-Laflamme, "Islamophobia in Canada: Measuring the Realities of Negative Attitudes Toward Muslims and Religious Discrimination," *Canadian Journal of Sociology* 55, no. 1 (2017); Gallup, "Islamophobia: Understanding Anti-Muslim Sentiment in the West," 2011; Pew Research Center, "Muslim Americans: No Signs of Growth in Alienation or Support for Extremism," 2011.

3. These are also in line with objectives pursued by social movements and social movement entrepreneurs, as identified in Bert Klandermans and Dirk Oegema, "Potentials, Networks, Motivations, and Barriers: Steps Towards Participation in Social Movements," *American Sociological Review* 52, no. 4 (1987).

4. On mobilization potential, see Klandermans and Oegema, "Potentials, Networks, Motivations, and Barriers," 518; Kraig Beyerlein and John Hipp, "A Two-Stage Model for a Two-Stage Process: How Biographical Avail-

ability Matters for Social Movement Mobilization," *Mobilization* 11, no. 3 (2006); Hanspeter Kriesi, Willem Saris, and Anchrit Wille, "Mobilization Potential for Environmental Protest," *European Sociological Review* 9, no. 2 (1993).

5. Klandermans and Oegema, "Potentials, Networks, Motivations, and Barriers," 520. See also Anthony Oberschall, *Social Conflict and Social Movements* (Englewood Cliffs, NJ: Prentice-Hall, 1973); Anthony Oberschall, "Loosely Structured Collective Conflicts: A Theory and an Application," in *Research in Social Movements, Conflict, and Change,* vol. 3, ed. Louis Kreisberg (Greenwich, CT: JAI Press, 1980), 45–68.

6. Anwar al-Awlaki, "44 Ways to Support Jihad," Victorious Media, 2009.

7. This roughly translates to "The correct path for those who seek the battlefield." The book is more commonly known as *Kitab al-Jihad* [*Book of Jihad*].

8. Jarret Brachman and Will McCants characterize Ibn Nuhaas's work as "extremely popular among modern jihadis." Jarret Brachman and Will McCants, "The Militant Ideology Atlas," Combating Terrorism Center, November 2009, 321. Similarly, Wiktorowicz notes that "jihadists drew extensively from the work of Ibn Nuhaas." Quintan Wiktorowicz, "A Geneology of Radical Islam," *Studies in Conflict and Terrorism* 28, no. 2 (2006): 84. See also Donald Holbrook, "Using the Qur'an to Justify Terrorist Violence: Analysing Selective Application of the Qur'an in English-Language Militant Islamist Discourse," *Perspectives on Terrorism* 4, no. 3 (2010): 1–3.

9. Scott Shane, "The Enduring Influence of Anwar al-Awlaki in the Age of the Islamic State," *CTC Sentinel* 9, no. 7 (2016): 18.

10. This approach is particularly popular among Sufi sheikhs. See Sheikh Muhammad Hisham Kabbani and Sheikh Seraj Hendricks, "Jihad: A Misunderstood Concept from Islam," Islamic Supreme Council of America.

11. The eradication of barriers to movement participation is among the most important roles of a social movement leader. See Klandermans and Oegema, "Potentials, Networks, Motivations, and Barriers."

12. Anwar al-Awlaki, "The Story of Ibn al-Akwa: Shaykh Noor al-Din Shahaada," Dar Ibn al-Mubarak, 2003. A transcript of Awlaki's translation was also published by Maktabah Booksellers and Publishers, Birmingham, England.

13. Anwar al-Awlaki, "Story of Ibn al-Akwa."

14. Awlaki used a number of Koranic verses to back this up, including: 9:41—"March forth whether you are light or heavy and strive hard with your wealth and your lives in the cause of Allah"; and 9:86—"And when a

Surah [chapter from the Koran] is revealed, enjoining them to believe in Allah and to strive hard and fight along with His Messenger, the wealthy among them ask your leave to exempt them [from *Jihad*] and say, 'Leave us [behind], we would be with those who sit [at home].'"

15. Anwar al-Awlaki, "Story of Ibn al-Akwa."
16. The four categories of *hadith* authenticity and reliability are: *sahih* (sound), *hasan* (good), *daif* (weak), and *maudu* (fabricated).
17. Roel Meijer, "Re-Reading al-Qaeda: Writings of Yusuf al-Ayiri," *ISIM Review* 18 (Autumn 2006): 16.
18. AQAP was formed in January 2009 as a result of a merger between al-Qaeda's Saudi and Yemeni branches. See Gregory Johnsen, *The Last Refuge: Yemen, al-Qaeda, and America's War in Arabia* (New York: Norton, 2012).
19. Anwar al-Awlaki, "Constants on the Path of Jihad," 2005.
20. J. M. Berger, "The Enduring Appeal of Al-`Awlaqi's 'Constants on the Path of Jihad,'" *CTC Sentinel* 4, no. 10 (2011).
21. U.S. Department of Homeland Security, "Countering Radicalization: Popular Lecture Encourages Violence in the Homeland," Unclassified / For Official Use Only, September 15, 2008. The Extremism and Radicalization Branch, part of the Homeland Environment Threat Analysis Division, was mainly responsible for tracking and analyzing media and other propaganda efforts by al-Qaeda and its affiliates that were specifically directed at radicalizing Western Muslims.
22. U.S. Department of Homeland Security, "Countering Radicalization."
23. Awlaki, "Constants on the Path of Jihad."
24. Yusuf al-Uyayree, *Constants on the Path of Jihad*, undated.
25. These are recognized by all Muslims as fasting during the month of Ramadan; charitable giving; prayer; making the Hajj pilgrimage; and the declaration of faith that there is only one God and that Muhammad is his final messenger.
26. Awlaki, "Constants on the Path of Jihad."
27. Awlaki, "Constants on the Path of Jihad."
28. Awlaki, "Constants on the Path of Jihad."
29. al-Uyayree, *Constants on the Path of Jihad*.
30. Awlaki, "Constants on the Path of Jihad."
31. Awlaki, "Constants on the Path of Jihad."
32. Awlaki, "Message to the American People," Global Islamic Media Front, 2010.
33. One of the most influential texts about the *tarbiyah* methodology was written by a former student of al-Albani's named Ali Hasan al-Halabee. In *Tarbiyah: The Key to Victory*, he writes: "So if the Muslims desire good, unity

and establishment upon the earth, then they should make their manners
and behaviour like that of the Salaf of this Ummah and begin by changing
themselves. However, he who is unable to change even himself, will not be
able to change his family, not to mention changing the Ummah. . . . So
take heed—O people of understanding and hearts—and beware of the
punishment and the power of Allah! And know that change begins with
the soul and is not achieved through having many helpers, nor strength of
information, nor the clamour of those who clap and shout, nor by the
arenas and streets being filled with huge crowds." *Tarbiyah,* however, is not
only part of the quietist Salafi approach. Islamist groups such as the
Muslim Brotherhood have also developed a version that is based on
preparing society for the establishment of an Islamic state. See Ehud Rosen,
"The Muslim Brotherhood's Concept of Education," *Current Trends in
Islamist Ideology,* November 2008.

34. Awlaki, "Constants on the Path of Jihad."
35. The 2008 Department of Homeland Security assessment of the lecture
recognized this as one of the main features of the work, noting that "to
strengthen the impact of his message, al-Awlaki orders readers to ignore
prominent counter-violence messages such as those from mainstream U.S.
religious leaders, foreign government clerics, and reformed former violent
extremist leaders." U.S. Department of Homeland Security, "Countering
Radicalization."
36. Awlaki, "Constants on the Path of Jihad."
37. Awlaki, "Constants on the Path of Jihad."
38. Awlaki, "Constants on the Path of Jihad."
39. Awlaki, "Constants on the Path of Jihad."
40. Known as "Rumsfeld's war on terror memo," this internal document was
leaked to the press in October 2003 and is publicly available.
41. Awlaki, "Constants on the Path of Jihad."
42. al-Uyayree, *Constants on the Path of Jihad.*
43. al-Uyayree, *Constants on the Path of Jihad.*
44. al-Uyayree, *Constants on the Path of Jihad.*
45. A similar point is made in Berger, "The Enduring Appeal of Al-`Awlaqi's
'Constants on the Path of Jihad,'" 13–14.
46. Awlaki, "Constants on the Path of Jihad."
47. Some claims made in the article were later retracted. See Howard Kurtz,
"*Newsweek* Apologizes: Inaccurate Report on Koran Led to Riots,"
Washington Post, May 16, 2005.
48. John Mintz, "Pentagon Probes Detainee Reports of Koran Dumping,"
Washington Post, May 14, 2005.

49. Carsten Andersen, "Dyb angst for kritik af islam" [Profound anxiety about criticism of Islam], *Politiken*, September 17, 2005.
50. Awlaki, "Constants on the Path of Jihad."
51. Awlaki, "Constants on the Path of Jihad."
52. It is unlikely that there was a connection between his release of *Constants on the Path of Jihad* and his imprisonment.
53. Moazzam Begg of Cageprisoners makes this suggestion in "Cageprisoners and the Great Underpants Conspiracy," January 14, 2010, available at https://web.archive.org/web/20101110080009/http://old.cageprisoners.com/articles.php?id=30886.
54. The articles he wrote about his time in prison were reviews of books he had read and the food he had eaten. See for example Anwar al-Awlaki, "Book Reviews from Behind Bars," www.anwar-alwalaki.com, August 21, 2008. The impact of Awlaki's time in prison should not necessarily be dismissed entirely. It is certainly possible that it was one of a number of external push factors which, combined with his preexisting ideology, may have motivated him to join al-Qaeda.
55. Awlaki's website, www.anwar-alawlaki.com, operated between May 2008 and November 2009.
56. The Islamic Forum of Europe is an influential subsidiary of the East London Mosque.
57. In the article, Ali also notes that he disagrees with Awlaki on his stance that Muslims should not participate in democracy. Azad Ali, "Iman, the New President and You!" *Between the Lines Blog*, November 5, 2008, available at http://web.archive.org/web/20140824072053/http://blog.islamicforumeurope.com/2008/11/05/iman-the-new-president-and-you.
58. Howard Clark, interview with the author, London, U.K., December 5, 2010.
59. Isa al-Awshan (also known as Muhammad bin Ahmed as-Salim), "39 Ways to Serve and Participate in Jihad," *Sawt al-Jihad*, c. 2003. Hegghammer describes him as an AQAP "media mogul." Thomas Hegghammer, *Jihad in Saudi Arabia: Violence and Pan-Islamism Since 1979* (Cambridge, U.K.: Cambridge University Press, 2010), 126.
60. Awlaki, "A Question." It should be noted here that Awlaki misreads Clausewitzian theory, which has no concept of "total war." Rather this derives, depending on the sources, from the Napoleonic Wars and World War I and was later developed in the 1930s. In *On War*, Clausewitz writes about the theory of "absolute war," an entirely different philosophical concept of a war that is unaffected by common constraints such as politics and geographical location. See Carl von Clausewitz, *On War*, trans. Michael Eliott Howard and Peter Paret (Princeton, NJ: Princeton University Press, 1989).

61. As McAdam explains, "It is precisely these tentative forays into new roles that paves the way for more thoroughgoing identity changes." Doug McAdam, "Recruitment to High-Risk Activism: The Case of Freedom Summer," *American Journal of Sociology* 92, no. 1 (1986): 69.

62. Brachman and Levine suggest that, through encouraging more online participation, Awlaki was attempting to create a larger pool from which to recruit fighters by narrowing "the distance between non-violent propagandist and violent al-Qaeda activist." Jarret Brachman and Alix Levine, "You Too Can Be Awlaki!" *Fletcher Forum of World Affairs* 35, no. 1 (2011): 43.

63. Awlaki, "44 Ways to Support Jihad."

64. Awlaki, "44 Ways to Support Jihad."

65. The term is also used by non-jihadi Salafis to describe the process of leaving a certain area for the purposes of ensuring that a believer is able to properly practice their faith. It does not have to entail leaving a country and can even refer to moving to another neighborhood that is deemed as having a detrimental impact on one's ability to practice Islam.

66. Muhammad Khalid Masud, "The Obligation to Migrate: The Doctrine of *Hijra* in Islamic Law," in *Muslim Travellers: Pilgrimage, Migration, and the Religious Imagination,* ed. Dale F. Eickelman and James Piscatori (Berkeley: University of California Press, 1990), 29–31.

67. It is estimated that over forty thousand people from 120 different countries traveled to join IS in Syria and Iraq between 2011 and 2016, including around five thousand from Western Europe. "Responses to Returnees: Foreign Terrorist Fighters and Their Families," Radicalisation Awareness Network, July 2017, 6; Richard Barrett, "Beyond the Caliphate: Foreign Fighters and the Threat of Returnees," Soufan Group, October 2017, 9–14.

68. Anwar al-Awlaki, "The Ruling on Dispossessing the Disbelievers Wealth in Dar al-Harb," *Inspire* no. 2, October 2010.

69. On Feiz Mohammad and his role in the Australian jihadist scene, see Sam Mullins, "Islamist Terrorism and Australia: An Empirical Examination of the 'Home-Grown' Threat," *Terrorism and Political Violence* 23, no. 2 (2011): 272–73.

70. Anwar al-Awlaki, "Hijrah," ASWJ Media, 2009.

71. Awlaki, "Hijrah."

72. Anwar al-Awlaki, "State of the Ummah," March 2009.

73. Awlaki, "44 Ways to Support Jihad."

74. Anwar al-Awlaki, "Tawfique Chowdhury's Alliance With the West," www .anwar-alawlaki.com, February 12, 2009.

75. Fathali Moghaddam, "The Staircase to Terrorism: A Psychological Exploration," *American Psychologist* 60, no. 2 (2005): 165–66.

76. The verse reads: "O you who have believed, do not take My enemies and your enemies as allies, extending to them affection while they have disbelieved in what came to you of the truth, having driven out the Prophet and yourselves [only] because you believe in Allah, your Lord. If you have come out for jihad in My cause and seeking means to My approval, [take them not as friends]. You confide to them affection, but I am most knowing of what you have concealed and what you have declared. And whoever does it among you has certainly strayed from the soundness of the way."

77. Awlaki, "State of the Ummah."

78. Anwar al-Awlaki, "Voting for the American President: Part 1," www.anwar -alawlaki.com, October 31, 2008.

79. Awlaki, "Voting."

80. The Mahdi refers to a member of Muhammad's family who it is believed will descend from heaven with Jesus to fight the Antichrist before the Day of Judgment.

81. Anwar al-Awlaki, "Now That the Elections Are Over," www.anwar -alawlaki.com, November 2008.

82. Anwar Awlaki, "The Life of Muhammad: The Makkan Period," *Awakening Media*, c. 2003.

83. Awlaki, "Now That the Elections Are Over."

84. Anwar al-Awlaki, "Battle of Hearts and Minds," May 2008. The RAND reports are Angel Rabasa, Cheryl Bernard, Lowell H. Schwartz, and Peter Sickle, "Building Moderate Muslim Networks," RAND, 2007; Cheryl Bernard, "Civil Democratic Islam," RAND, 2003.

85. Awlaki, "Battle of Hearts and Minds."

86. Awlaki, "Tawfique Chowdhury's Alliance With the West."

87. Awlaki, "Battle of Hearts and Minds."

88. "Terror Plot BA Man Rajib Karim Gets 30 Years," BBC News, March 18, 2011, available at www.bbc.co.uk/news/uk-12788224.

89. The transcripts of the emails between Awlaki and the Karim brothers were released by the Metropolitan Police in February 2011. They have since been removed from the internet but remain in the author's possession.

90. Rajib Karim, email message to Awlaki, January 29, 2010.

91. Karim, email message to Awlaki, January 29, 2010.

92. Karim, email message to Awlaki, January 29, 2010.

93. Anwar al-Awlaki, email message to Rajib Karim, January 25, 2010.

94. Awlaki, "A Question."

95. Anwar al-Awlaki, "Salutations to al-Shabaab in Somalia," www.anwar -alawlaki.com, December 21, 2008.

96. Osama bin Laden, "May Our Mothers Be Bereaved of Us If We Fail to Help Our Prophet," *as-Sahab,* March 19, 2008.

97. Transcripts of the lecture can be found in Arabic, Bengali, Urdu, Russian, Georgian, German, and French, among others.

98. This promotion of Awlaki's live online lecture appeared, among other places, on Sunni Forum, available at www.sunniforum.com/forum /showthread.php?34423-Live-lecture-by-Imam-Anwar-al-Awlaki-on -PalTalk.

99. Anwar al-Awlaki, "Dust Will Never Settle Down," 2008.

100. Awlaki's presentation of this *hadith* has been challenged by a variety of scholars and experts. While few deny that al-Ashraf was killed, it is often pointed out that he was targeted not simply because of his poetry but also because he was a spy and was conspiring against Muhammad with the Meccan tribes he was fighting. According to Badr ul-Din al-Ayni in his commentary on al-Bukhari: "he [Kaab ibn al-Ashraf] was not killed merely for insulting the [prophet], but rather it was surely for the fact that he was an aide / spy against him, and conspired with those who fought wars against him, and supported them." See Badr ul-Din al-Ayni, *Umdat ul-Qari Shar'h Sahih al-Bukhari,* vol. 24 (Dr. Ihya Turath al-Arabi Beirut, Lebanon, 2003) 121; Rashad Ali, "Blasphemy, *Charlie Hebdo,* and the Freedom of Belief and Expression: The Paris Attacks and the Reactions," Institute for Strategic Dialogue, 9–11.

101. Awlaki, "Dust Will Never Settle Down."

102. Awlaki, "Dust Will Never Settle Down." This appears to be one of the only English translations of any part of Ibn Taymiyya's *As-Saram Al-Maslool 'Ala Shatim Ar-Rasul.* The only other one appears to be a two-page summary of the work, provided by the now-defunct Salafi-jihadi website www .IslamicEmirate.com: "Shaykhul Islam Ibn Taymiyyah on the necessity of killing whoever curses the Prophet, Peace and Blessings be upon Him," June 2010.

103. "Paris Killer Cherif Kouachi Gave Interview to TV Channel Before He Died," NBC News, January 9, 2015, available at www.nbcnews.com /storyline/paris-magazine-attack/paris-killer-cherif-kouachi-gave -interview-tv-channel-he-died-n283206.

104. Jason Burke and Monica Mark, "Al-Qaida in Yemen Uses Video to Claim Responsibility for Charlie Hebdo Attack," *The Guardian,* January 14, 2015.

105. United States v. Lawal Babafemi, No. 13-109, Letter by Loretta Lynch submitted in connection with the defendant's sentencing (United States District Court of the Eastern District of New York, August 11, 2015).

4. "And Inspire the Believers . . ."

1. "Natural History Museum Crash 'Not Terror-Related,'" BBC News, October 8, 2017, available at www.bbc.co.uk/news/uk-41538762.
2. Tweet from @metpoliceuk, October 7, 2017, available at https://twitter .com/metpoliceuk/status/916709921080659968; "Natural History Museum Crash 'Not Terror-Related'"; Patrick Sawyer and Nicola Harley, "Natural History Museum Incident: Several Injured After Car Mounts Pavement and Hits Pedestrians, But Police Rule Out Terror," *Daily Telegraph*, October 7, 2017, available at www.telegraph.co.uk/news/2017/10/07/car-mounts -pavement-outside-london-museum-according-reports1/.
3. See Elisabeth Kendall, "Contemporary Jihadi Militancy in Yemen," Middle East Institute, July 2018.
4. See Ron Eyerman and Andrew Jamison, *Social Movements: A Cognitive Approach* (London: Polity Press, 1991); Lauren Kessler, *The Dissident Press: Alternative Journalism in American History* (New York: Sage, 1984), 42.
5. Mohammed Atef (Abu Hafs al-Masri), "Jihad Media Document Regarding Means of Communication with the Population and the Importance of Slogans and Truthfulness," c. 1990, AQ-SHPD-D-001-157, Conflict Records Research Center, Washington, D.C.; Abu Hudaifa, "Letter from Abu Hudaifa to Osama bin Laden Regarding Request to Publicize al-Qaeda's Goals and Accomplishments in the Media to Rally Public Support and Invigorate al-Qaeda's Mission in Saudi Arabia," June 20, 2000, AQ-SHBD-D-000-035, Conflict Records Research Center, Washington, D.C.
6. Abu Hafs, "Jihad Media Document."
7. Peter Bergen, *Holy War, Inc.: Inside the Secret World of Osama bin Laden* (New York: Free Press, 2001), 85–86.
8. Abu Hudaifa, "Letter."
9. For a comprehensive analysis of his life and work, see Brynjar Lia, *Architect of Global Jihad: The Life of Al-Qaeda Strategist Abu Mus'ab Al-Suri* (London: Hurst, 2009). At the time of writing, whether or not al-Suri is still alive is unknown.
10. Al-Suri devoted a section in his work to praise Abu Hafs, along with Osama bin Laden, for their strategic vision. Abu Musab al-Suri, *The Call of Global Islamic Resistance*, 2004, translation provided by CIA Office of Terrorism Analysis, October 2006, 53.
11. Al-Suri, *Call of Global Islamic Resistance*, 62.
12. Al-Suri, *Call of Global Islamic Resistance*, 13.
13. Al-Suri, *Call of Global Islamic Resistance*, 1020–1021.

14. The fourth edition, for example, quotes a section from al-Suri's book devoted specifically to the school of individual jihad and small cells. "The Jihadi Experiences: The Schools of Jihad," *Inspire*, no. 1, June 2010.
15. Jesse Morton was released from prison in March 2015 after serving a three-year sentence (reduced from eleven and a half years after cooperating with the FBI) for conspiracy to solicit murder after his distribution of *Inspire* and his direct involvement with Samir Khan.
16. Jesse Morton, interview with the author, Washington, D.C., December 14, 2016.
17. Jesse Morton, interview with the author.
18. On the roots of Islamic Thinkers Society and its links to al-Muhajiroun and Revolution Muslim, see Charles Kurzman, David Schanzer, and Ebrahim Moosa, "Muslim American Terrorism Since 9/11: Why So Rare?" *The Muslim World* 101, no. 3 (2011): 474; Evan F. Kohlmann, "'Homegrown' Terrorists: Theory and Cases in the War on Terror's Newest Front," *Annals of the American Academy of Political and Social Science* 618, no. 1 (2008): 96.
19. Jesse Morton, interview with the author.
20. *Jihad Recollections*, no. 1, April 2009.
21. Jesse Morton, interview with the author.
22. United States v. Minh Quang Pham, No. 12Cr.423, Indictment, 4 (United States District Court for the Southern District of New York).
23. United States v. Minh Quang Pham, Document 111-1: Handwritten Statement to Judge.
24. Minh Quang Pham, Statement to Judge.
25. United States v. Minh Quang Pham, Document 113-4: Government Sentencing Memorandum, 15.
26. "Member of Al Qaeda in the Arabian Peninsula Pleads Guilty to Terrorism Charges," United States Department of Justice Press Release, January 8, 2016.
27. United States v. Lawal Babafemi, letter by Loretta Lynch submitted in connection with the defendant's sentencing.
28. See, for example, Peter Bergen, "Al Qaeda the Loser in Arab Revolutions," CNN, February 23, 2011, available at www.cnn.com/2011/OPINION/02/23/bergen.revolt.binladen/index.html; Fareed Zakaria, "Al-Qaeda Is Over," CNN, May 2, 2011, available at http://globalpublicsquare.blogs.cnn.com/2011/05/02/al-qaeda-is-dead/; Scott Shane, "As Regimes Fall in Arab World, Al Qaeda Sees History Fly By," *New York Times*, February 27, 2011.
29. Anwar al-Awlaki, "The Tsunami of Change," *Inspire*, no. 5, March 2011.
30. "The Dust Will Never Settle Down Campaign," *Inspire*, no. 1, June 2010.

31. Anwar al-Awlaki, "May Our Souls be Sacrificed for You," *Inspire*, issue 1, June 2010.
32. Awlaki, "May Our Souls be Sacrificed for You."
33. Bruce Hoffman, *Inside Terrorism* (New York: Columbia University Press, 2006), 5.
34. See Arthur H. Garrison, "Defining Terrorism: Philosophy of the Bomb, Propaganda by Deed, and Change Through Fear and Violence," *Criminal Justice Studies* 17, no. 3 (2004).
35. Carlo Pisacane quoted in Hoffman, *Inside Terrorism*, 5.
36. "Open Source Jihad," *Inspire*, no. 1, June 2010.
37. Yahya Ibrahim, "The Ultimate Mowing Machine," *Inspire*, no. 2, October 2010.
38. "The Operation of Umar Farouk al-Nigiri," *Inspire*, no. 1, June 2010.
39. "The Operation of Umar Farouk al-Nigiri."
40. Choudhry told the police shortly after her attack that Awlaki's work had helped her to understand that "as Muslims we're all brothers and sisters and we should all look out for each other and we shouldn't sit back and do nothing while others suffer. We shouldn't allow the people who oppress us to get away with it and to think that they can do whatever they want to us and we're just gonna lie down and take it." Vikram Dodd, "Roshonara Choudhry: Police Interview Extracts," *The Guardian*, November 3, 2010.
41. "Roshonara and Taimour: Followers of the Borderless Loyalty," *Inspire*, no. 4, January 2011.
42. See Robert. F. Worth, "Yemen Emerges as Base for Qaeda Attacks on U.S.," *New York Times*, October 29, 2010.
43. Yahya Ibrahim, "$4,200," *Inspire*, special edition, November 2010.
44. *Inspire*, special edition, November 2010.
45. Anwar al-Awlaki, "Message to the American People," March 2010.
46. Sheryl Gay Stolberg, "Obama Offers Sympathy and Urges No 'Jump to Conclusions,'" *New York Times*, November 7, 2009.
47. Republican congressman Peter Hoekstra was particularly vocal in his claims that the Obama administration was trying to downplay the significance of the attack and, as part of this effort, was withholding the email correspondence between Awlaki and Hasan from the public. Marc Ambinder, "Did Hoekstra Compromise a Sensitive Intelligence Program?" *Atlantic*, November 12, 2009.
48. Awlaki, "Message to the American People."
49. Awlaki, "Message to the American People."
50. Awlaki, "Message to the American People."
51. Anwar al-Awlaki, "Western Jihad Is Here to Stay," 2010.

52. Jon Hurdle, "10 Years for Plot to Murder Cartoonist," *New York Times*, January 6, 2014.

53. On female involvement in jihadism, see Anita Peresin and Alberto Cervone, "The Western *Muhajirat* of ISIS," *Studies in Conflict and Terrorism* 38, no. 7 (2015); Elizabeth Pearson, "The Case of Roshonara Choudhry: Implications for Theory on Online Radicalization, ISIS Women, and the Gendered Jihad," *Policy and Internet* 8, no. 1 (2015); Audrey Alexander, "Cruel Intentions: Female Jihadists in America," George Washington University Program on Extremism, November 2016.

54. See "Cartoon Trial: Kurt Westergaard's Attacker Convicted," BBC News, February 3, 2011, available at www.bbc.co.uk/news/world-europe-12353863.

55. Awlaki, "Western Jihad."

56. This sentiment is expressed in Osama bin Laden's letters written in 2010 to senior al-Qaeda member Attiya al-Libi. They are categorized in the archive of the recovered documents as SOCOM-2012-0000015 and SOCOM-2012-0000019. For further analysis, see Nelly Lahoud, "Letters from Abbottabad: Bin Ladin Sidelined?" Combating Terrorism Center, May 3, 2012.

57. On *aqd al-aman* and how it is viewed by jihadists, see Petter Nesser, "Ideologies of Jihad in Europe," *Terrorism and Political Violence* 23, no. 2 (2011): 175, 187.

58. Anwar al-Awlaki, "The Ruling on Dispossessing the Disbelievers Wealth in Dar al-Harb," *Inspire* no. 2, October 2010.

59. Scott Shane and Mark Mazzetti, "Times Sq. Bomb Suspect Is Linked to Militant Cleric," *New York Times*, May 6, 2010.

60. Osama bin Laden letter to Attiya al-Libi, SOCOM-2012-0000015, 7.

61. "Thou Art Responsible only for Thyself," *as-Sahab*, June 2011.

62. "Thou Art Responsible only for Thyself."

63. "Thou Art Responsible only for Thyself."

64. Sherry Towers, Andres Gomez-Lievano, Maryam Khan, Anuj Mubayi, and Carlos Castillo-Chavez, "Contagion in Mass Killings and School Shootings," *PLoS ONE* 10, no. 7 (2015).

65. As Nesser and colleagues remind us, however, "jihadi terrorism in Europe cannot be reduced to either-or dichotomies," and there are a variety of methods and strategies being employed today. However, single-actor terrorism was found to comprise 55 percent of all terrorist plots in Europe between 2001 and 2016 and is on the rise. Petter Nesser, Anne Stenersen, and Emilie Oftedal, "Jihadi Terrorism in Europe: The IS Effect," *Perspectives on Terrorism* 10, no. 6 (2016).

66. Quintan Wiktorowicz, *Radical Islam Rising* (Lanham, MD: Rowman and Littlefield, 2005), 5, 85–128.

5. Umar Farouk Abdulmutallab

1. For an example of how young British Muslims were feeling at the time, see Tahir Abbas, "After 9/11: British South Asian Muslims, Islamophobia, Multiculturalism, and the State," *American Journal of Islamic Social Sciences* 23, no. 1 (2004): 26–38. Polling from the time also reflects British Muslims' feelings of persecution. In a July 2005 poll of five hundred British Muslims, 20 percent of respondents claimed that they or members of their family had directly experienced discrimination due to their faith, while 63 percent said they were considering whether or not to leave the country, and 30 percent were pessimistic about the future of young Muslims in the U.K. ICM-Guardian Poll, July 26, 2005, available at http://image.guardian.co.uk/sys-files/Politics/documents/2005/07/26/Muslim-Poll.pdf.

2. FBI interview with Umar Farouk Abdulmutallab at Milan Federal Correctional Institution, May 12, 2010.

3. As noted in Chapter 1, it is unclear if those promoting Awlaki in Britain were aware of his more extreme pronouncements, even though they received wide coverage at the time.

4. See Noah Shachtman, "Analyze This: The Mind of the Underpants Bomber," *Wired*, December 29, 2009; Alexander Meleagrou-Hitchens and Jacob Amis, "The Making of the Christmas Day Bomber," *Current Trends in Islamist Ideology*, July 23, 2010.

5. Farouk1986 comment on "I think I feel lonely," February 20, 2005, available at www.gawaher.com/topic/7544-i-think-i-feel-lonely/page-2.

6. Farouk1986 comment on "Islam in Nigeria," March 25, 2005, available at www.gawaher.com/topic/10728-islam-in-nigeria/.

7. Farouk1986 comment on "Marital problems," January 31, 2005, available at www.gawaher.com/topic/7738-marital-problems/; Farouk1986 comment on "Light out . . . or . . . ," March 24, 2005, available at www.gawaher.com/topic/10651-lights-outor/.

8. Farouk1986 comment on "Forgive me?" March 24, 2005, available at www.gawaher.com/topic/10601-forgive-me/.

9. Farouk1986 comment on "I think I feel lonely," January 28, 2005, available at www.gawaher.com/topic/7544-i-think-i-feel-lonely/.

10. Farouk1986 comment on "I think I feel lonely," January 28, 2005.

11. Farouk1986 comment on "Ball/prom," May 7, 2005, available at www.gawaher.com/topic/13054-ballprom.

12. Farouk1986 comment on "Marriage proposals," February 1, 2005, available at www.gawaher.com/topic/7855-hmm-marriage-proposalsconfused.

13. Farouk1986 comment on "Getting married," January 31, 2005, available at www.gawaher.com/topic/6623-getting-married/page-2.

14. Farouk1986 comment on "I don't even know what to put the title as," January 30, 2005, available at www.gawaher.com/topic/7105-i-dont-even -know-what-to-put-as-the-title.

15. Farouk1986 comment on "Remembering what you have memorised," February 17, 2005, available at www.gawaher.com/topic/9041-remembering -what-you-have-memorised.

16. Farouk1986 comment in "Imams of the Haramain," March 23, 2005.

17. Farouk1986 comment on "Do you ever . . . ," February 19, 2005, available at www.gawaher.com/topic/8982-do-you-ever/page-2.

18. Farouk1986 comment on "Football," February 16, 2005, available at www .gawaher.com/topic/686-football/.

19. Farouk1986 comment on "Football."

20. Farouk1986 comment on "Ambiguous words on clothing," February 17, 2005, available at www.gawaher.com/topic/9053-ambiguous-words-on -clothing/.

21. Farouk1986 comment on "The Muslim type of sport," November 15, 2005, available at www.gawaher.com/topic/21780-the-muslim-type-of-sport.

22. Farouk1986 comment on "Qawalis?" November 15, 2005, available at www .gawaher.com/topic/21781-qawalis-islamic-songs-in-urdu-with-instruments.

23. Farouk1986 comment on "Halal meat," December 6, 2005, available at www.gawaher.com/topic/22754-halal-meat.

24. Farouk1986 comment on "So, who went to the London march today?" February 14, 2006, available at www.gawaher.com/topic/25665-so-who -went-to-the-london-march-today.

25. Yvonne Ridley, "Operation Moshtarak," *Counterpunch*, February 15, 2010, available at www.counterpunch.org/ridley02152010.html. See also her speech at a 2009 Gaza demonstration in London, available at www.youtube .com/watch?v=ruF3h_hZSE8&feature=player_embedded.

26. Farouk1986 comment on "The Road to Guantanamo," March 11, 2006, available at www.gawaher.com/topic/27175-the-road-to-guantanamo/ page-2.

27. Farouk1986 comment on "War on terror week in UCL," January 26, 2007, available at www.gawaher.com/topic/37634-war-on-terror-week-in-ucl.

28. On Islamist activism in Britain, see Sarah Khan, *The Battle for British Islam: Reclaiming Muslim Identity from Extremism* (London: Saqi Books, 2018); Innes Bowen, *Medina in Birmingham, Najaf in Brent: Inside British Islam* (London: Hurst, 2014).

29. The campaign was later renamed "Stop Political Terror."

30. This website is no longer online; archived versions are in the author's possession.

31. Farouk1986 comment on "I need a quick answer please Inshallah," January 29, 2005, available at www.gawaher.com/topic/7318-i-need-a-quick -answer-please-inshallah/.

32. Vicki Barker, "Few Clues to Student's Evolution into Terror Suspect," National Public Radio, December 29, 2009, available at www.npr.org /templates/story/story.php?storyId=122010560.

33. "About FOSIS," available at www.fosis.org.uk/about.

34. Ziauddin Sardar, *Desperately Seeking Paradise: Journeys of a Sceptical Muslim* (London: Granta, 2005), 24–29. As recently as 2007, FOSIS distributed free copies of Maududi's *Towards Understanding the Quran* to university Islamic societies, see for example https://web.archive.org/web/20090410002145 /http://oldsite.fosis.org.uk:80/resources/index.php.

35. It is worth noting that today FOSIS is a rather different organization than it was during and before Abdulmutallab's time in the United Kingdom. It is no longer overtly Islamist and has adopted mainstream positions.

36. UCL and FOSIS organized a series of charity events between October 22– 28, 2007. Promotional materials are in the author's possession.

37. Sarah Netter, "Close Friend of 'Underwear Bomber' Saw No Hint of Militancy," ABC News, December 30, 2009, available at http://abcnews.go .com/WN/experts-terrorists-abdulmutallab-drawn-cult-radicalism/story ?id=9441562.

38. Promotional material for the event in the author's possession.

39. Promotional material for the event in the author's possession. This was also reported in David Barrett, Patrick Sawer, and Sean Rayment, "Revealed: The True Extent of Islamic Radical Influence at UCL," *Daily Telegraph*, January 3, 2010.

40. "Dispatches: Undercover Mosque," Channel 4 (U.K.), January 15, 2007. Khan also stated: "This whole delusion about the equality of women is a bunch of foolishness, there's no such thing," and described the AIDS virus as a "conspiracy" orchestrated by the World Health Organization and "Christian groups."

41. FBI interview with Umar Farouk Abdulmutallab at Milan Federal Correctional Institution, February 2, 2010.

42. FBI interview with Umar Farouk Abdulmutallab at Milan Federal Correctional Institution, February 8, 2010. In its official U.K. Charity

Commission documents, HHUGS lists Cageprisoners member Fahad Ansari as a trustee.

43. Adam Nossiter, "Lonely Trek to Radicalism for Terror Suspect," *New York Times,* January 17, 2010.

44. Fahad Ansari, "Beyond Guantanamo—Review of Cageprisoners Fund-raising Dinner," October 2, 2009, available at https://web.archive.org/web /20160402141228/http://old.cageprisoners.com/articles.php?id=30493.

45. Asim Qureshi, "Jihad—The Solution?" January 15, 2010, available at www .cageprisoners.com/articles.php?id=30900.

46. Qureshi, "Jihad—The Solution?"

47. Asim Qureshi public speech at Hizb ut-Tahrir rally, London, August 2006, available at www.youtube.com/watch?v=5wpGn3VgNMA.

48. Moazzam Begg, "Jihad and Terrorism: A War of Words," *Arches Quarterly* 2, no. 1 (2008): 21, 23, 26.

49. On the use of jihad as an offensive means to spread Islam, Azzam wrote: "In Islam, fighting is legitimate when its aim is to spread God's word, save humanity from unbelief, and lead humanity from the darkness of this world to its light and the light of the next life. This is why, in our holy religion, combat was established to transcend political, economic, and social obstacles to preaching the Muslim faith. It may even be said that the function of jihad is to bring down the barriers preventing this religion from spreading across the face of the earth." Abdullah Azzam, *Morals and Jurisprudence of Jihad,* translated by Thomas Hegghammer in *Al-Qaeda in its Own Words,* ed. Gilles Kepel and Jean-Pierre Milelli (Cambridge, MA: Harvard University Press, 2008), 127.

50. United States v. Umar Farouk Abdulmutallab, No. 2:10-cr-20005, Document 130–1: Simon Perry, "Memorandum for the Court: The Level of Danger Posed by Umar Farouk Abdulmutallab," 5–9 (United States District Court for the Eastern District of Michigan Southern Division, January 2012), 5–10.

51. FBI interview with Umar Farouk Abdulmutallab at Milan Federal Correctional Institution, January 2010.

52. "Memorandum," 15.

53. FBI interview with Umar Farouk Abdulmutallab at Milan Federal Correctional Institution, January 2010.

54. "Memorandum," 14.

55. FBI interview with Umar Farouk Abdulmutallab at Milan Federal Correctional Institution, January 2010.

56. "Memorandum," 11. Awlaki's article, "Suicide or Martyrdom," was published on his blog on January 22, 2009.

57. FBI interview with Umar Farouk Abdulmutallab at Milan Federal Correctional Institution, January 2010.
58. "Memorandum," 18.
59. FBI interview with Umar Farouk Abdulmutallab at Milan Federal Correctional Institution, January 2010.
60. FBI interview with Umar Farouk Abdulmutallab at Milan Federal Correctional Institution, January 2010.
61. Quoted in "Memorandum," 11.
62. United States v. Umar Farouk Abdulmutallab, No. 2:10-cr-20005, Government Sentencing Memorandum, 12–14 (United States District Court for the Eastern District of Michigan Southern Division, February 10, 2012).
63. FBI interview with Umar Farouk Abdulmutallab at Milan Federal Correctional Institution, January 2010.
64. Government Sentencing Memorandum, 13.
65. "Memorandum," 14.
66. FBI interview with Umar Farouk Abdulmutallab at Milan Federal Correctional Institution, January 2010.
67. Michael Crowley, "Trump Confirms 2017 Killing of Feared Bomb Maker for Al Qaeda," *New York Times*, October 10, 2019.
68. Video in author's possession. The two Koran verses cited are 5:51 and 9:39.
69. FBI interview with Umar Farouk Abdulmutallab at Milan Federal Correctional Institution, January 2010.
70. Anwar al-Awlaki, *al-Malahim* interview, May 2010.
71. FBI interview with Umar Farouk Abdulmutallab at Milan Federal Correctional Institution, January 2010.
72. Chris McGreal, "Ibrahim Hassan al-Asiri: The Prime Bombmaking Suspect," *The Guardian*, October 31, 2010.
73. FBI interview with Umar Farouk Abdulmutallab at Milan Federal Correctional Institution, January 2010.
74. Government Sentencing Memorandum, 14.

6. Nidal Hasan

1. Katharine Poppe, "Nidal Hasan: A Case Study in Lone-Actor Terrorism," George Washington University Program on Extremism, October 2018, 6–7.
2. Nidal Hasan's comments recorded in "Full Report of Sanity Board, United States v. MAJ Nidal Hasan," January 13, 2011, 13.
3. Anas Hasan's comments recorded in "Full Report of Sanity Board, United States v. MAJ Nidal Hasan," 13.

4. Poppe, "Nidal Hasan," 6–7.

5. Unpublished extract of May 23, 2017 correspondence between Nidal Hasan and researcher Katharine Poppe shared with the author. The two lectures that so impressed Hasan are "The Life of Muhammad: The Makkan Period" and "The Life of Muhammed: The Medina Period," *Awakening Media,* c. 2004.

6. Kitty Bennett and Sarah Wheaton, "The Life and Career of Major Hasan," *New York Times,* November 6, 2009, available at https://archive.nytimes .com/www.nytimes.com/interactive/2009/11/07/us/20091107-HASAN -TIMELINE.html.

7. Mary Pat Flaherty, William Wan, Derek Kravitz, and Christian Davenport, "Suspect, Devout Muslim from Va., Wanted Army Discharge, Aunt Said," *Washington Post,* November 6, 2009.

8. "Nidal Hasan's June 2007 'Grand Rounds' Presentation," Fox News, available at http://video.foxnews.com/v/2663135028001/nidal-hasans-june -2007-grand-rounds-presentation-part-1/?#sp=show-clips.

9. Nidal Hasan's comments recorded in "Full Report of Sanity Board, U.S.A. v MAJ Nidal Hasan," 34.

10. Manuel Roig-Franzia, "Army Soldier Is Convicted in Attack on Fellow Troops," *Washington Post,* April 22, 2005.

11. "Nidal Hasan's June 2007 'Grand Rounds' Presentation."

12. "Nidal Hasan's June 2007 'Grand Rounds' Presentation."

13. "Nidal Hasan's June 2007 'Grand Rounds' Presentation."

14. "Nidal Hasan's June 2007 'Grand Rounds' Presentation."

15. Anita Belles Porterfield and John Porterfield, *Death on Base* (Denton: University of North Texas Press, 2015), 121, 124.

16. "Nidal Hasan's June 2007 'Grand Rounds' Presentation."

17. "Nidal Hasan's June 2007 'Grand Rounds' Presentation."

18. "Nidal Hasan's June 2007 'Grand Rounds' Presentation."

19. "Nidal Hasan's June 2007 'Grand Rounds' Presentation."

20. William H. Webster et al., "Final Report of the William H. Webster Commission on the Federal Bureau of Investigation, Counterterrorism Intelligence, at the Events at Fort Hood, Texas, on November 5, 2009," Washington, D.C., August 1, 2012, 66.

21. Lt. Col. Kris Poppe (Ret.), telephone interview with the author, Washington, D.C., March 1, 2017.

22. Unpublished extract of May 23, 2017, correspondence between Nidal Hasan and researcher Katharine Poppe shared with the author.

23. Poppe, "Nidal Hasan," 7.

24. Webster et al., "Final Report of the William H. Webster Commission," 40.

25. Nidal Hasan, email message to Awlaki, December 17, 2009, in Webster et al., "Final Report of the William H. Webster Commission," 41.

26. Hasan, email message to Awlaki, December 17, 2009.

27. Nidal Hasan, email message to Awlaki, January 1, 2009, in Webster et al., "Final Report of the William H. Webster Commission," 43.

28. Nidal Hasan, email message to Awlaki, January 16, 2009, in Webster et al., "Final Report of the William H. Webster Commission," 47.

29. Nidal Hasan, email message to Awlaki, January 18, 2009, in Webster et al., "Final Report of the William H. Webster Commission," 47–48.

30. Hasan, email message to Awlaki, January 18, 2009.

31. Hasan, email message to Awlaki, January 18, 2009.

32. Hasan, email message to Awlaki, January 18, 2009.

33. Nidal Hasan, email message to Awlaki, February 16, 2009, in Webster et al., "Final Report of the William H. Webster Commission," 50.

34. Nidal Hasan, email message to Awlaki, February 19, 2009, in Webster et al., "Final Report of the William H. Webster Commission," 51.

35. Nidal Hasan, email message to Awlaki, February 22, 2009, in Webster et al., "Final Report of the William H. Webster Commission," 52.

36. Nidal Hasan, email message to Awlaki, February 19, 2009.

37. Nidal Hasan, email message to Awlaki, May 31, 2009, in Webster et al., "Final Report of the William H. Webster Commission," 58.

38. Nidal Hasan, email message to Awlaki, June 16, 2009, in Webster et al., "Final Report of the William H. Webster Commission," 61.

39. Richard Esposito, Mary Rose Abraham, and Rhonda Schwartz, "Major Hasan: Soldier of Allah; Many Ties to Jihad Web Sites," ABC News, November 12, 2009, available at http://abcnews.go.com/Blotter/hasan-multiple-mail-accounts-officials/story?id=9065692.

40. Nidal Hasan's comments recorded in "Full Report of Sanity Board, U.S.A. v MAJ Nidal Hasan," 40.

41. Nick Allen, "'I am the Shooter': US Army Major Nidal Hasan Declares as He Faces Court Martial over Fort Hood Massacre," *Daily Telegraph*, August 6, 2013.

42. Lt. Col. Kris Poppe (Ret.), telephone interview with the author.

43. "Handwritten Statement by Maj. Nidal Hasan," October 18, 2012, available at www.foxnews.com/politics/interactive/2013/08/01/statement-by-nidal-hasan/.

44. Webster et al., "Final Report of the William H. Webster Commission," 54.

45. Anwar al-Awlaki, "Nidal Hassan Did the Right Thing," www.anwar-alawlaki.com, November 9, 2009.

46. Anwar al-Awlaki, interview with al-Jazeera (Arabic), December 23, 2009.

7. Zachary Adam Chesser

1. United States v. Zachary Adam Chesser, No. 1:10-cr-00395-LO, Document 44: Government's Sentencing Memorandum, 6 (United States Court for the Eastern District of Virginia, February 18, 2011).

2. United States Senate Committee on Homeland Security, "Zachary Chesser: A Case Study in Online Islamist Radicalization and Its Meaning for the Threat of Homegrown Terrorism," February 2012, 9. This was also confirmed by terrorism analyst Jarret Brachman, who had engaged in a correspondence with Chesser in mid-2010, about which he would later admit he was at his most extreme. Brachman refers to Awlaki as Chesser's "hero." See Jarret Brachman, "My Pen Pal the Jihadist," *Foreign Policy,* July 29, 2010.

3. This was revealed in his written letters to the senate staff authoring "Zachary Chesser: A Case Study," which are provided in full in Appendix B of that report.

4. United States Senate Committee on Homeland Security, "Zachary Chesser: A Case Study," 8.

5. *Chesser,* Document 44-2: Megan Chesser's character reference for Zachary Adam Chesser, 2.

6. United States Senate Committee on Homeland Security, "Zachary Chesser: A Case Study," 7.

7. Zachary Chesser, written letters.

8. United States Senate Committee on Homeland Security, "Zachary Chesser: A Case Study," 12–13.

9. Zachary Chesser, written letters.

10. A number of studies have warned against focusing on the internet as a cause of radicalization. These include Cristina Archetti, "Terrorism, Communication, and New Media: Explaining Radicalization in the Digital Age," *Perspectives on Terrorism* 9, no. 5 (2015): 49–59; Paul Gill, Maura Conway, Emily Corner, and Alex Thornton, "What Are the Roles of the Internet in Terrorism? Measuring Online Behaviours of Convicted UK Terrorists," VOX-Pol Network of Excellence, 2015; David C. Benson, "Why the Internet Is Not Increasing Terrorism," *Security Studies* 23, no. 2 (2014).

11. *Chesser,* Affidavit, 4.

12. *Chesser,* Affidavit, 4–10.

13. United States Senate Committee on Homeland Security, "Zachary Chesser: A Case Study," 3.

14. Zakariya comment on Awlaki, "Voting for the American President 1," November 1, 2008.

15. United States Senate Committee on Homeland Security, "Zachary Chesser: A Case Study," 8.

16. Zakariya comment on Awlaki, "Voting for the American President 1."

17. Zakariya comment on Awlaki, "Voting for the American President 1."

18. Zakariya comment on Awlaki, "Now that the elections are over," November 6, 2008.

19. Zakariya comment on Awlaki, "Now that the elections are over."

20. Zakariya comment on Awlaki, "Now that the elections are over," November 17, 2008.

21. Zakariya comment on Awlaki, "Meaning of Gaza," December 31, 2008.

22. Zakariya comment on Awlaki, "Meaning of Gaza," December 29, 2008.

23. Brother al-Khurasani comment on Awlaki, "Meaning of Gaza," December 31, 2008.

24. Zakariya comment on Awlaki, "Meaning of Gaza," January 1, 2009.

25. Zakariya comment on Awlaki, "Meaning of Gaza," December 30, 2008.

26. Zakariya comment on Anwar al-Awlaki, "Finding a balance," December 2, 2008.

27. Zakariya comment on Awlaki, "Finding a balance."

28. Zakariya comment on Awlaki, "Meaning of Gaza," December 30, 2008.

29. Zakariya comment on Awlaki, "44 Ways to Support Jihad," January 7, 2009.

30. Zakariya comment on Anwar al-Awlaki, "New Year: Reality and aspirations," January 4, 2009.

31. Ibn Adam comment on Awlaki, "New Year," January 4, 2009.

32. Zakariya comment on Awlaki, "New Year," January 4, 2009.

33. Zakariya comment on Awlaki, "44 Ways to Support Jihad."

34. Zakariya comment on Awlaki, "44 Ways to Support Jihad."

35. Anwar al-Awlaki, "Suicide or Martyrdom?," www.anwar-alawlaki.com, January 22, 2009.

36. Zakariya comment on Awlaki, "Suicide or Martyrdom?" January 23, 2009.

37. Zakariya comment on Awlaki, "Suicide or Martyrdom?"

38. Zakariya comment on Awlaki, "Suicide or Martyrdom?"

39. Zakariya comment on Awlaki, "Two Muslim Women," January 31, 2009.

40. United States Federal Bureau of Investigation, "Leader of Revolution Muslim Websites Sentenced for Using Internet to Threaten Jewish Organizations," April 25, 2014, available at www.fbi.gov/washingtondc /press-releases/2014/leader-of-revolution-muslim-websites-sentenced-for -using-internet-to-threaten-jewish-organizations.

41. Jesse Morton, interview with the author, Washington, D.C., December 14, 2016.

42. Anti-Defamation League, "Abu Talhah al-Amrikee: An Extensive Online Footprint," 2011, available at www.adl.org/assets/pdf/combating-hate/Abu -Talhah-Al-Amrikee-An-Extensive-Online-Footprint-2013-1-11-v1.pdf.

43. Zachary Chesser email message to Jesse Morton, January 27, 2010.

44. Abu-Talhah al-Amrikee, "How to Propagate a Call to Jihad," www .revolutionmuslim.com, February 17, 2010.

45. Abu-Talhah al-Amrikee, "Open Source Jihad," www.revolutionmuslim .com, March 8, 2010.

46. Abu-Talhah al-Amrikee, "Open Source Jihad."

47. Zachary Chesser, personal letters.

48. See Laura Yuen, "Minnesota Men Who Joined 'Jihad' in Somalia," Minnesota Public Radio, November 2011, available at http://minnesota .publicradio.org/projects/ongoing/somali_timeline/missing_men2.

49. Abu-Talhah al-Amrikee, "An Overview of Jihad in Somalia," www .themujahidblog.com, April 1, 2010.

50. @mujahidblog tweet, April 15, 2010.

51. Abu Talhah al-Amrikee, "South Park aired episode showing cartoon of the Prophet Muhammad," www.themujahidblog.com, April 15, 2010.

52. Video in author's possession.

53. Abu Talhah al-Amrikee, "Revolution Muslim Official Press Release on the South Park Issue," www.themujahidblog.com, April 21, 2010.

54. Abu Talhah al-Amrikee, "Revolution Muslim Official Press Release."

55. Chesser, Affidavit, 2.

56. Chesser, Affidavit, 3.

57. "Virginia Jihadist Zachary Chesser Arrested," SITE Intelligence, January 15, 2014, available at https://news.siteintelgroup.com/Featured-Article /chesserarrest.html.

58. Chesser, Affidavit, 8, 11.

59. Chesser, Affidavit, 4.

60. The details of these replies have not been publicized.

61. Chesser, Affidavit, 5.

62. Chesser, Affidavit, 5, 6.

63. Chesser, Affidavit, 9.

64. See John Simpson, "Three Generations of One Family Died After Travelling to Isis-Held Syria," The Times, June 29, 2019; Rukmini Callimachi and Catherine Porter, "2 American Wives of ISIS Militants Want to Return Home," New York Times, February 19, 2019; "UK Mum Who Took Her Children to the 'Islamic State' Speaks," Channel 4 (UK), October 14, 2015, available at www.channel4.com/news/uk-mum-who-took-her-children-to -the-islamic-state-speaks.

65. *Chesser,* Affidavit, 7–8.
66. Zachary Chesser, personal letters.
67. Zachary Chesser, personal letters.
68. Zachary Chesser, personal letters.
69. Zachary Chesser, personal letters.
70. Zakariya comment on Awlaki, "Two Muslim Women," February 12, 2009.
71. Jarret Brachman and Alix Levine, "You Too Can Be Awlaki!" *Fletcher Forum of World Affairs* 35, no. 1 (2011): 35.

8. Awlaki and the Islamic State in the West

1. Two studies have revealed the influence of new online preachers, including the Michigan-based Ahmad Musa Jibril: Joseph A. Carter, Shiraz Maher, and Peter Neumann, "Greenbirds: Measuring Importance and Influence in Syrian Foreign Fighter Networks," International Centre for the Study of Radicalisation, King's College London, 2014; and Jytte Klausen, "Tweeting the Jihad: Social Media Networks of Western Foreign Fighters in Syria and Iraq," *Studies in Conflict and Terrorism* 38, no. 1 (2015).
2. In Nesser, Stenersen, and Oftedal's empirical analysis of jihadist plots and attacks in Europe, for example, it was shown that since the start of the Syrian Civil War and the rise of IS in 2014 until the end of 2016, more people were killed by jihadists in Western Europe than in all previous years combined. Petter Nesser, Anne Stenersen, and Emilie Oftedal, "Jihadi Terrorism in Europe: The IS Effect," *Perspectives on Terrorism* 10, no. 6 (2016): 1. Meanwhile, according to the Program on Extremism at George Washington University, in the United States between March 2014 and May 2019, 182 Americans have been either charged or convicted for IS-related terrorism offenses. Forty percent of those had attempted or successfully traveled to join the group, while 33 percent were involved in plotting or conducting a domestic terrorist attack. For more, see "GW Extremism Tracker: The Islamic State in America," Program on Extremism, George Washington University, 2017, available at https://extremism.gwu.edu/sites/g/files/zaxdzs2191/f/May19%20Update.pdf.
3. On the organizational roots of IS, see Cole Bunzel, *From Paper State to Caliphate* (Washington: Brookings Institute, March 2015); Joby Warrick, *Black Flags: The Rise of ISIS* (London: Corgi, 2016); Brian Fishman, *The Master Plan: ISIS, al-Qaeda, and the Jihadi Strategy for Final Victory* (New Haven, CT: Yale University Press, 2017).

4. "U.S. Cites Big Gains Against Al-Qaeda," *Washington Post,* May 30, 2008.

5. For the most comprehensive overview and chronology of jihadist attacks in Western Europe, see Petter Nesser, "Toward an Increasingly Heterogeneous Threat: A Chronology of Jihadist Terrorism in Europe, 2008–2013," *Studies in Conflict and Terrorism* 37, no. 5 (2014). Nesser finds that, since 9/11, the period during which there were the fewest annual plots and attacks in the West was between 2005 and 2010.

6. "Establishment of the Islamic State Series," vol. 1, *al-Hayat.*

7. On the rivalry between al-Qaeda and the Islamic State, see Tore Hamming, "The Al Qaeda–Islamic State Rivalry: Competition Yes, but No Competitive Escalation," *Terrorism and Political Violence* (2017).

8. Shiraz Maher, *Salafi-Jihadism: The History of an Idea* (London: Hurst, 2016), 105.

9. Muhammad al-Ubaydi, Nelly Lahoud, Daniel Milton, and Bryan Price, "The Group That Calls Itself a State: Understanding the Evolution and Challenges of the Islamic State," Combatting Terrorism Center, December 2014; Cole Bunzel, "From Paper State to Caliphate," Brookings Institute, March 2015. The importance of the end times prophecy was initially embraced by Jabhat al-Nusra when the group was still part of ISI in 2012. See Charles Lister, *The Syrian Jihad: Al-Qaeda, the Islamic State and the Evolution of an Insurgency* (Oxford, U.K.: Oxford University Press, 2015), 65–67.

10. This is mentioned in Sahih Muslim Hadith 41, chapter 9, hadith 6924: "The Last Hour would not come until the Romans land at al-A'maq or in Dabiq. An army consisting of the best (soldiers) of the people of the earth at that time will come from Medina [to fight them]."

11. "Introduction," *Dabiq,* no. 1, July 2014, 3.

12. Will McCants, *The ISIS Apocalypse* (London: Picador, 2016).

13. McCants, *ISIS Apocalypse,* 28.

14. Anwar al-Awlaki, "Allah is preparing us for victory," 2006.

15. "Establishment of the Islamic State Series," vol. 6, *al-Hayat.*

16. Awlaki, "Allah is preparing us for victory."

17. Awlaki, "Allah is preparing us for victory."

18. "Sham is the Land of al Malahim," *Dabiq,* no. 3, July/August 2014, 9.

19. "Hijrah to Sham is from the Millat of Ibrahim," *Dabiq,* no. 3, July/August 2014, 10.

20. Awlaki, "Allah is preparing us for victory."

21. "The Extinction of the Grayzone," *Dabiq,* no. 7, February 2015, 66.

22. "The Extinction of the Grayzone," 62.

23. Tweet from @VVAoVV, November 9, 2016. The term *coconuts* is a crude and racially derogatory term often found in IS propaganda that is used to describe Western Muslims who refuse to join the global jihad movement. The idea is that, like a coconut, they are brown (Muslim) on the outside but white (supporters of the West) on the inside.

24. Tweet from @CreedOfAbraham, November 9, 2016.

25. Awlaki, "Allah is preparing us for victory."

26. "Foreign Fighters: An Updated Assessment of the Flow of Foreign Fighters into Syria and Iraq," Soufan Group, 2015.

27. On the varied motivations of Westerners who joined IS, see Seran de Leede, "Western Women Supporting IS / Daesh in Syria and Iraq—An Exploration of their Motivations," *International Annals of Criminology* 56 (2018); Lorne L. Dawson and Amarnath Amarasingam, "Talking to Foreign Fighters: Insights into the Motivations for Hijrah to Syria and Iraq," *Studies in Conflict and Terrorism* 40, no. 3 (2017); Anita Perešin, "Fatal Attraction: Western Muslimas and ISIS," *Perspectives on Terrorism* 9, no. 3 (2015); Alice Ross, Mark Townsend, and Martin Chulov, "British Students Killed in Iraq after Joining Isis," *Guardian,* March 1, 2017.

28. "Indeed Your Lord Is Ever Watchful," speech by Abu Muhammad Al-Adnani Ash-Shami, *al-Hayat,* September 22, 2014.

29. "Foreword," *Dabiq,* no. 12, November 2015, 3.

30. "Just Terror Tactics," *Rumiyah,* no. 2, October 2016, 12.

31. "Foreword," 3. For more on IS and propaganda of the deed, see Charlie Winter, "ISIS Is Using the Media Against Itself," *Atlantic,* March 23, 2016.

32. "Just Terror Tactics," *Rumiyah,* no. 5, January 2017, 8.

33. Out of fifty-one IS-related attacks in Europe and North America between 2014 and 2017, 92 percent were either "carried out by individuals who had some form of connection to the Islamic State or other jihadist groups but acted independently" or by "individuals with no connections whatsoever to the Islamic State or other jihadist groups, but were inspired by its message." Lorenzo Vidino, "Fear Thy Neighbor: Radicalization and Jihadist Attacks in the West," International Centre for Counter-Terrorism / Program on Extremism / Italian Institute for International Political Studies, 2017, 16–17.

34. The most notorious of these is the Abaaoud Network, which planned and conducted the attacks in Paris in November 2015. See Jean-Charles Brisard, "The Paris Attacks and the Evolving Islamic State Threat to France," *CTC Sentinel* 8, no. 11 (2015).

35. According to Nesser, Stenersen, and Oftedal, between 2014 and 2016, nineteen plots in France, Germany, the United Kingdom, Spain, and Austria involved online instruction from "'members of IS' networks."

Nesser, Stenersen, and Oftedal, "Jihadi Terrorism in Europe." In the only study on this phenomenon in the United States, Seamus Hughes and I found that eight terrorist attacks or plots involved a "virtual entrepreneur." Alexander Meleagrou-Hitchens and Seamus Hughes, "The Threat to the United States from the Islamic State's Virtual Entrepreneurs," *CTC Sentinel* 10, no. 3 (2017).

36. Meleagrou-Hitchens and Hughes, "Threat to the United States"; Daveed Gartenstein-Ross and Madeleine Blackman, "Isil's Virtual Planners: A Critical Terrorist Innovation," *War on the Rocks,* January 4, 2017, available at https://warontherocks.com/2017/01/isils-virtual-planners-a-critical -terrorist-innovation.

37. Stacy Meichtry and Sam Schechner, "How Islamic State Weaponized the Chat App to Direct Attacks on the West," *Wall Street Journal,* October 20, 2016.

38. These cases are: *United States. v. Munir Abdulkader; United States v. Usaamah Abdullah Rahim; United States v. Justin Nolan Sullivan;* and *United States v. David Daoud Wright and Nicholas Alexander Rovinski.*

39. Spencer Ackerman and Alice Ross, "Airstrike Targeting British Hacker Working for Isis Killed Three Civilians Instead, US Admits," *The Guardian,* January 29, 2016.

40. Mark Berman, "Ohio College Student Who Plotted to Kill Military Employee, Police Officers for ISIS Is Sentenced to 20 Years in Prison," *Washington Post,* November 23, 2016.

41. United States v. Munir Abdulkader, No. 1:16-CR-019, Government Sentencing Memorandum, 3–10 (United States District Court for the Southern District of Ohio Western Division, November 10, 2016).

42. "Exclusive Q & A with Junaid Hussain—British ISIS fighter and hacker," *5Pillars,* September 24, 2014, available at http://5pillarsuk.com/2014/09/24 /exclusive-q-and-a-with-junaid-hussain-british-isis-fighter-and-hacker. In the interview, Junaid Hussain quotes Awlaki's "Message to the American People," a video message distributed online in 2010.

43. The Twitter handles he used included: @AbuHussain101, @AbuHussain102, and @_AbuHu55ain.

44. As of May 2018. This figure is based on original research of court documents and media sources carried out by the author. While this number may not seem very significant at first glance, it is also likely to be higher than this. Not only do many other cases show an indirect influence of Awlaki's work, which has permeated all aspects of Western jihadism, but many court documents do not include detailed discussions about the sources referred to by the defendants.

45. One database is run by the International Centre for the Study of Radicalisation, King's College London, while the other is run by the Program on Extremism, George Washington University.

46. Based on original research by the author, with thanks to Audrey Alexander.

47. Based on original research by the author, with thanks to Shiraz Maher, Joseph Carter, and Nick Kaderbhai.

48. "Briton Ifthekar Jaman 'Killed Fighting in Syria', Family Says," BBC News, December 17, 2013, available at www.bbc.co.uk/news/uk-england-25415113.

49. These quotes are taken from an archive of now-defunct British pro-IS accounts, which is maintained by Shiraz Maher, director of the International Centre for the Study of Radicalisation, King's College London.

50. "Anwar al-Awlaki," Telegram channel now defunct.

51. United States v. Abdul Malik Abdul Kareem, No. 2:15-CR-00707-SRB, Document 441-1: Prosecution Exhibit 7—Elton Simpson's online discussions with Muhammad Abdullahi Hussain (United States District Court for the District of Arizona, November 30, 2016). Kareem was a friend of Simpson's and was involved in the planning of and preparation for the attack, including helping to fund it. Simpson and Soofi were not the only IS supporters to have targeted people associated with the event in Garland. In mid-May 2015, after the event, David Daoud Wright, Nicholas Alexander Rovinski, and Usaamah Abdullah Rahim identified its organizer, anti-Muslim activist Pamela Geller, and plotted to behead her. Unlike the Simpson and Soofi case, it has been confirmed that Rahim was in direct contact with Junaid Hussain, who suggested Geller as a target. While Awlaki is not mentioned as an inspiration in this case, his influence on this sort of target selection is undeniable.

52. Rukmini Callimachi, "Clues on Twitter Show Ties Between Texas Gunman and ISIS Network," New York Times, May 11, 2015. It has not, however, been confirmed that Junaid Hussain had any hand, direct or indirect, in this plot.

53. Dan Frosch and Ana Campoy, "Mother of Texas Gunman Sought to Keep Son from Extremism," Wall Street Journal, May 6, 2015.

54. United States v. Elton Simpson, No. CR10-055-PHX-MHM, Judge's Order, 3 (United States District Court for the District of Arizona).

55. Kellan Howell, "Suspected American Islamic State Recruiter Turns Himself In," Washington Times, December 8, 2015; Abby Simons and Libor Jany, "Ex-Minneapolis Student 'Mujahid Miski' Denies Ties to Islamic State," Star Tribune, December 8, 2015.

56. Kareem, Exhibit 7.

57. United States v. Enrique Marquez Junior, No. 5:15MJ498, Criminal Complaint, 7–9 (United States District Court for the Central District of California, December 17, 2015).

58. *Marquez Junior*, Criminal Complaint, 8.

59. United States v. Mohamed Bailor Jalloh, No. 1:16-MJ296, Affidavit, 6 (United States District Court for the Eastern District of Virginia, July 3, 2016).

60. *Jalloh*, Affidavit, 7, 9–10.

61. This point has been made in: Nesser, Stenersen, and Oftedal, "Jihadi Terrorism in Europe"; Sarah Gilkes, "Not Just the Caliphate: Non–Islamic State–Related Jihadist Terrorism in America," Program on Extremism, George Washington University, 2016.

62. Rukmini Callimachi and Andrew Higgins, "Video Shows a Paris Gunman Declaring His Loyalty to the Islamic State," *New York Times*, January 11, 2015.

63. Thomas Joscelyn, "Nine Pages from Ahmad Rahami's Journal," *The Long War Journal*, September 21, 2016.

64. Katie Mettler, "Ohio State Attacker Complained Bitterly in Facebook Post of Treatment of Muslims 'Everywhere,' Reports Say," *Washington Post*, November 29, 2016.

65. *Rumiyah*, no. 4, December 2016, 37.

66. Michael Horton, "Why Islamic State Has Failed to Expand in Yemen," *Jamestown Terrorism Monitor* 15, no. 6 (2015); Elisabeth Kendall, "Al-Qaeda and the Islamic State in Yemen," in *Jihadism Transformed: Al-Qaeda and Islamic State's Global Battle of Ideas*, ed. Akil Awan and Simon Staffell (Oxford, U.K.: Oxford University Press, 2016).

67. Nadwa Al-Dawsari, "Foe Not Friend: Yemeni Tribes and Al-Qaeda in the Arabian Peninsula," Project on Middle East Democracy, February 2018, 23.

68. While the Awalik have accommodated AQAP in the past, their relationship is not one of clear support and backing for the goals of al-Qaeda. According to Al-Dawsari, "AQAP has a presence in some tribal areas, and some tribal members (along with other Yemenis, and some foreigners) have joined the group. But in doing so, they have acted independently, against the wishes of their tribes. Yemeni tribes as collective entities—as opposed to individual tribesmen—have not allied with AQAP or agreed to give its fighters sanctuary. Tribes reject the group's radical and violent ideology and tend to see AQAP as a serious challenge to their authority." Al-Dawsari, "Foe Not Friend," 2.

69. Elisabeth Kendall, "The Failing Islamic State Within the Failed State of Yemen," *Perspectives on Terrorism* 13, no. 1 (2019): 83.

Conclusion

1. It appears that during November 2017 YouTube undertook a final crack-down on Awlaki's presence on their platform, removing (as far as this author can tell) all of his remaining audio and video lectures, of which "The Dust Will Never Settle" appeared to be the most prevalent. See Scott Shane, "In 'Watershed Moment,' YouTube Blocks Extremist Cleric's Message," *New York Times,* November 12, 2017.

2. This term was first used in John Lofland and Rodney Stark, "Becoming a World-Saver: A Theory of Conversion to a Deviant Perspective," *American Sociological Review* 30, no. 6 (1965). It was first applied to jihadist radicalization in Quintan Wiktorowicz, *Radical Islam Rising* (Lanham, MD: Rowman and Littlefield, 2005).

3. David Snow and Scott Byrd, "Ideology, Framing Processes, and Islamic Terrorist Movements," *Mobilization* 12, no. 2 (2007), 129.

Acknowledgments

This book began with research I undertook at King's College London with my mentor, John Bew, who was also a friend. John's patience and commitment ensured that I stayed on track even during times when publishing this book felt like little more than a pipe dream. I consider myself very fortunate to have been able to work alongside one of the leading scholars of his generation, and I gained insights and knowledge from him that I hope are reflected in the following pages.

Much of the research I conducted for the book was undertaken while I was working for the International Centre for the Study of Radicalisation (ICSR) at King's College London. The quality of my research was improved immeasurably by two colleagues and friends at ICSR, Shiraz Maher and Peter Neumann. A host of ICSR researchers were involved in helping me gather and analyze primary sources. While I cannot list them all here, special mention must go to Joana Cook, Nick Kaderbhai, and Joseph Carter.

As I drew nearer to completing my manuscript, I moved to Washington, D.C., to work as the research director for the Program on Extremism at George Washington University. I benefited greatly from working with the program's director, Lorenzo Vidino, and its deputy director, Seamus Hughes. Their generosity in sharing primary sources and offering comments on early drafts will never be forgotten. Alongside them, a team of committed and brilliant researchers, including Audrey Alexander and Bennett Clifford, assisted me with a verve and commitment that I can only hope to one day reciprocate.

There are many others to whom I owe thanks, including old friends who gave up their time to help me whenever I had questions related to my research. In particular, I would like to express my sincere gratitude to Martyn Frampton, Ryan Evans, Inshaf Mann, Shafaqat Qadri, Mumtaz Kalil, and Shuaib Mohammed.

Funding for the early stages of this book was generously provided by the University of Maryland's National Consortium for the Study of Terrorism and Responses to Terrorism (START) through the Department of Homeland Security Science and Technology Directorate's Office of University Programs, Award No. 2012-ST-061-CS0001. However, the views and conclusions expressed in the book belong to me alone and do not reflect those of the DHS or START in any way.

Finally, such an undertaking would not have been remotely possible were it not for the support and patience of my family: my mother, Eleni; my aunt, Mando; and my sisters, Sophia and Antonia. Such career landmarks often also bring to mind those loved ones who, while they had a significant impact on one's intellectual development, are no longer here to share the experience. With this in mind, I particularly want to mention the influence of my father, Christopher, my grandfather, Yannis, and my grandmother, Evie. By far the biggest debt I owe, however, is to my wife, Lee-Anne, who inspires me every day with her strength and work ethic. Thank you, Lee-Anne, for everything. This book is dedicated to you and our two sons, Leonidas and Aristos.

Index

Organization names beginning with the Arabic article *al-* are alphabetized on *al-*. Personal names are alphabetized on the part of the name following *al-*.

Charitable Society for Social Welfare
(CSSW), 22
Chechnya, 233
Chen, Pang Ching Bobby, 11–12
Chesser, Zachary Adam: analysis, 232–235;
attempts to join al-Shabaab, 228–231;
and Awlaki's blog, *hijrah* and jihad, 216,
221–222; and Awlaki's blog, ideological
war on Islam, 217–220; and Awlaki's
blog, suicide bombing, 220–221; and
Awlaki's blog, voting and *al-wala
wal-bara*, 212–216; contact with Awlaki,
42–44; online activism, assassination,
226–228; online activism, open source
jihad, 224–225, 232; online activism,
Revolution Muslim, 222–224; overview,
16, 209–212, 273
Choudhry, Roshonara, 148–149
Clapper, James, 42
Clark, Howard, 116
collective identity. *See* identity
Colorado State University (CSU), 19–20
Constants on the Path of Jihad (al-Uyayree):
Awlaki's reframing of, 100–103, 104; as
Awlaki's source, 79–80, 119, 129, 262;
jihad's transcendence of groups and
personalities, 110–111; *al-taifa al-mansura*,
106, 109; victory of the idea, 111–113. *See
also* jihad recruitment strategy;
al-Uyayree, Yusuf

Dabiq (IS online magazine), 238–239, 243,
244, 248
Dar al-Arqam, 61, 62–63
Dar al-Hijrah Mosque: Awlaki as imam, 19,
23–24, 62; Islamist influence in, 84; Saudi
funding of, 23–24; war on Islam sermon,
29, 68–69
Dean, Aimen, 34
Della Porta, Daniela, 8
democracy: and Arab 2011 uprisings,
143–144; rejection of, 33, 104, 124–126, 130,
205, 213–215
Denver Islamic Society, 21
al-Dhahabi, Abu Usama, 174
Diani, Mario, 7
The Drawn Sword (Ibn Taymiyya), 132

East London Mosque (ELM), 33, 39, 70–71
Elmasry, Shadee, 60

Farook, Syed Rizwan, 254–256
FBI: and Awlaki–al-Timimi relationship,
63–64; counterterrorism concerns of, 38;
as external factor in Awlaki's ideology,
94; interrogations claimed by Awlaki, 37;
investigations by, 22–23, 30, 264–265;
monitoring of communications by, 198
Federation of Student Islamic Societies
(FOSIS), 32, 172–174
framing. *See* framing theory; identity;
jihad; jihad recruitment strategy; *sira*
(narrative histories); storytelling and
narrative creation
—, diagnostic: infighting among Muslims,
72–73; overview, 268–269; war on Islam,
26–29, 68–72, 96; war on Islam,
ideological, 3–4, 66–68, 103–104
—, motivational: Arab uprisings (2011),
143–144; cost-benefit arguments for
jihad, 96, 112, 113, 271–272; disrespect to
Islam and Muslims, 113–115, 130–133,
144–146; propaganda value of jihad,
147–152, 158–159, 272, 274; triumph of
jihad, 129–130
—, prognostic: change in, 93–94, 96–97,
156–158; gray area, 158, 245–246; *hijrah* or
jihad, 104–105, 127–129, 158, 205–207;
Islamic education (*tarbiyah*), 73, 93,
105–106; low-risk activism, 117–119;
overview, 269–270; in translation of
Constants, 101–103, 112–113; use of *sira* in,
75–77; *al-wala wal-bara*, 74–75, 92,
124–127, 157–158, 243–246
framing theory, 9–10, 12. *See also* framing;
identity; *sira* (narrative histories);
storytelling and narrative creation
Francesca Polletta, 11–12

Ganz, Marshall, 11
George Washington University, 23
global jihad movement. *See* jihad; jihad
recruitment strategy
glossary, 277–280